Driver & Vehicle
Standards
Agency

The **Official DVSA**
Theory Test
for Motorcyclists

London: TSO

Written and compiled by the Learning Materials section of the Driver and Vehicle Standards Agency (DVSA).

Questions and answers are compiled by DVSA.

Published with the permission of the Driver and Vehicle Standards Agency on behalf of the Keeper of the Public Record.

First published 2000
Fifteenth edition 2020

ISBN 978 0 11 553695 3

A CIP catalogue record for this book is available from the British Library.

Other titles in the Driving Skills series

The Official DVSA Guide to Riding – the essential skills
The Official DVSA Theory Test for Motorcyclists (DVD-ROM)
The Official DVSA Guide to Learning to Ride
Better Biking – the Official DVSA Training Aid (DVD)

The Official DVSA Theory Test Kit iPhone/Android App
The Official DVSA Highway Code iPhone/Android App
The Official DVSA Hazard Perception Practice iPhone/Android App

The Official DVSA Guide to Driving – the essential skills
The Official DVSA Theory Test for Car Drivers
The Official DVSA Theory Test for Car Drivers (DVD-ROM)
The Official DVSA Guide to Learning to Drive
The Official DVSA Guide to Better Driving
The Official DVSA Guide to Hazard Perception (DVD-ROM)

The Official DVSA Guide to Driving Buses and Coaches
The Official DVSA Guide to Driving Goods Vehicles
The Official DVSA Theory Test for Drivers of Large Vehicles
The Official DVSA Theory Test for Drivers of Large Vehicles (DVD-ROM)
Driver CPC – the official DVSA guide for professional bus and coach drivers
Driver CPC – the official DVSA guide for professional goods vehicle drivers

The Official DVSA Guide to Tractor and Specialist Vehicle Driving Tests (eBook)
The Official DVSA Theory Test for Approved Driving Instructors (DVD-ROM)

We're turning over a new leaf.

100% recycled
This book is printed
on 100% recycled paper

RECYCLED
Paper made from
recycled material
FSC® C002151
FSC
www.fsc.org

Find us online

GOV.UK – Simpler, clearer, faster

GOV.UK is the best place to find government services and information for

- car drivers
- motorcyclists
- driving licences
- driving and riding tests
- towing a caravan or trailer
- medical rules
- driving and riding for a living
- online services.

Visit **www.gov.uk** and try it out.

You can also find contact details for DVSA and other motoring agencies like DVLA at **www.gov.uk**

You'll notice that links to **GOV.UK**, the UK's central government site, don't always take you to a specific page. This is because this kind of site constantly adapts to what people really search for and so such static links would quickly go out of date. Try it out. Simply search what you need from your preferred search site or from **www.gov.uk** and you should find what you're looking for. You can give feedback to the Government Digital Service from the website.

Message from Mark Winn, the Chief Driving Examiner

Learning to ride is an exciting experience. As with getting to grips with any new skill, you may be nervous and it may be challenging at first. Before long, though, you'll be ready to take the step towards getting your full motorcycle licence and enjoying the freedom that comes with it.

A sound understanding of riding theory will help you to reach that stage. So, my advice is to take some practical lessons with an approved training body while you're studying for your theory test. Learning the theory and practical skills at the same time is the best approach; combining the two means you are more likely to understand and remember what you have learnt, something you'll be glad of on the day of your theory test!

I wish you a lifetime of safe riding.

Mark Winn

Mark Winn
Chief Driving Examiner

Contents

Introduction

 # About the theory test

In this section, you'll learn about

- how to use this book
- getting started
- the theory test
- after the theory test
- using the questions and answers sections
- using this book to learn and revise.

How to use this book

To prove that you have the right knowledge, understanding and attitude to be a safe and responsible rider, you'll need to pass the theory test.

It includes

- a multiple choice test, to assess your knowledge of riding theory
- a hazard perception test, to assess your hazard recognition skills.

This book contains hundreds of questions, which are very similar to the questions you'll be asked in the test and cover the same topics. It's easy to read, and explains why the answers are correct. References to the source material also appear with each question.

Everyone learns in different ways, so this book has features to help you understand riding theory whatever kind of learner you are, including

- bite-size chunks of information, which are easier to understand at your own pace
- lots of photographs and images to illustrate what you're learning
- fourteen topic-specific case studies and six mixed-topic ones, just like those you'll get in the test
- things to discuss and practise with your trainer, to put your learning about each topic into practice
- meeting the standards, to help you understand how each topic relates to the National Standard for Riding.

This book is designed to help you learn about the theory of riding and to practise for the test. To prepare thoroughly, you should also study the source materials that the questions are taken from. These are

The Official Highway Code
Know Your Traffic Signs
The Official DVSA Guide to Riding – the essential skills

There's always more you can learn, so keep your knowledge up to date throughout your riding career.

Getting started

Applying for your licence

You must have a valid provisional driving licence before you can ride on the road.

Licences are issued by the Driver and Vehicle Licensing Agency (DVLA). You can apply online at **www.gov.uk**. Alternatively, you can apply by post. When applying by post, you'll need to fill in application form D1, which you can **download from www.gov.uk** or collect from certain post office branches. Send your form to the appropriate office, as shown on the form. You must enclose the required passport-type photographs, as all provisional licences are now photocard licences.

In Northern Ireland, the issuing authority is the Driver and Vehicle Agency (DVA; online at **nidirect.gov.uk/motoring**) and the form is a DL1. For more information, see **nidirect.gov.uk/information-and-services/motoring/learners-and-new-drivers**.

When you receive your provisional licence, check that all the details are correct before you ride on the road. If you need to contact DVLA, the telephone number is 0300 790 6801. (DVA's telephone number is 0300 200 7861.)

Residency requirements

You can't take a test or get a full licence unless you're normally resident in the United Kingdom. Normal residence means the place where you live because of personal or occupational (work) ties. However, if you moved to the United Kingdom having recently been permanently resident in another state of the EC/EEA (European Economic Area), you must have been normally resident in the UK for 185 days in the 12 months before your application for a driving test or full driving licence.

Compulsory basic training

Before you take your practical motorcycle tests, you must hold a valid compulsory basic training (CBT) course certificate of completion (DL196). This doesn't apply to riders upgrading from one A category to another; for example, upgrading from category A1 to category A. CBT courses can only be given by training bodies approved by DVSA. These are checked regularly to make sure that there's a high standard of instruction.

The course will include classroom training and practical skills training. You can find out about CBT courses from

- DVSA (visit **www.gov.uk** or call 0115 936 6547)
- the Safe Driving for Life website (**safedrivingforlife.info**)
- your motorcycle dealer
- your local road safety officer, by contacting your local council.

DVSA also produces *The Official DVSA Guide to Learning to Ride* (see pages 11 and 22 for further details), which will give you details about the course.

> About the theory test

You'll take the theory test on-screen in two parts. It's designed to test your knowledge of riding theory – in particular, the rules of the road and best riding practice.

The first part is a series of multiple choice questions. Some multiple choice questions will be presented as a case study. More information about this part of the test is given on pages 17–19. The revision questions are given in the main part of the book, beginning on page 30.

Each question has references to the learning materials; for example

RES s8, HC r162–163, KYTS p32

RES s indicates the section within *The Official DVSA Guide to Riding – the essential skills*.

HC r/HC p indicates the rule or page in *The Official Highway Code*.

KYTS p indicates the page in *Know Your Traffic Signs*.

The second part of the theory test is the hazard perception part. More information about this is given on pages 19–20.

Can I take the practical test first?

No. You must pass your theory test before you can book a practical test.

Does everyone have to take the theory test?

All motorcycle test candidates have to pass the theory test before a booking for a practical test will be accepted. However, you won't have to take a theory test if you want to take an A1 small motorcycle test and hold a full moped licence obtained by passing both a theory and practical moped test or if you're upgrading your motorcycle licence from an A1 to A2 or A2 to category A under the progressive access rules.

If you want to take a practical motorcycle test under the direct access rules then you do need a valid motorcycle theory test pass certificate.

If you have any questions about whether you need to take a theory test, write to DVSA theory test enquiries, PO Box 381, Manchester M50 3UW. Tel 0300 200 1122 or email **customercare@pearson.com**

For Northern Ireland, contact the Driver Licensing Division, County Hall, Castlerock Road, Coleraine, BT51 3TB. Tel 0300 200 7861.

Foreign licence holders: if you hold a foreign licence issued outside the EC/EEA, first check with DVLA (Tel 0300 790 6801; for Northern Ireland call 0300 200 7861), to see whether you can exchange your licence. If you can't, you'll need to apply for a provisional licence, then take a theory test and a practical test.

Preparing for your theory test

Although you must pass your theory test before you can take your practical tests, it's best to start studying for your theory test as soon as possible – but don't actually take it until you have some practical experience of riding.

To prepare for the multiple choice part of the theory test, DVSA strongly recommends that you study the books from which the theory test questions are taken, as well as the questions you'll find in this book.

It's important that you study, not just to pass the test but to become a safer driver.

10

The Official Highway Code This is essential reading for all road users. It contains the very latest rules of the road and up-to-date legislation, as well as advice on road safety and best practice.

Know Your Traffic Signs This contains most of the signs and road markings that you're likely to see.

The Official DVSA Guide to Riding – the essential skills This is the official reference book, giving practical advice and best practice for all riders.

The Official DVSA Guide to Learning to Ride This gives full details of basic machine handling for compulsory basic training and the full practical test syllabus.

These books will help you to answer the questions correctly and will also help you when studying for your practical tests. The information in them will be relevant throughout your riding life, so make sure you always have an up-to-date copy.

Other study aids

The Official DVSA Theory Test for Motorcyclists (DVD-ROM) This is an alternative way of preparing for the multiple choice part of the theory test. It contains all the revision questions and answers, and also allows you to take mock tests.

The Official DVSA Guide to Hazard Perception (DVD-ROM) We strongly recommend that you use this, preferably with your riding trainer, to prepare for the hazard perception part of the test. The DVD-ROM is packed with useful tips, quizzes and expert advice. It also includes more than 100 interactive hazard perception clips, which you can use to test yourself and see if you're ready to take the real test.

Better Biking – the Official DVSA Training Aid (DVD) This DVD gives expert advice on improving your skills. It covers all the key skills, including negotiating bends, junctions and roundabouts. An ideal solo ride is demonstrated to show the standard of riding for which you should be aiming.

The Official DVSA Highway Code iPhone/Android App All the latest rules of the road and traffic signs at your fingertips.

The Official DVSA Hazard Perception Practice iPhone/Android App A simple and convenient way to prepare for your hazard perception test on the go. The app is compatible with Android, iPhone and iPad, and contains 14 official interactive DVSA practice clips.

You can buy official DVSA learning materials online at **safedrivingforlife.info/ shop** or by calling our expert publications team on **0333 200 2401**. The team can give you advice about learning materials and how to prepare for the tests and beyond. They can also help you select a suitable learning material if you have a special need; for example, if you have a learning disability or English isn't your first language.

DVSA publications are also available from book shops and online retailers. DVSA apps can be downloaded from the iOS App Store, Google Play store and Amazon Appstore, and eBooks are available from your device's eBook store.

Why do the questions change?

To make sure that all candidates are being tested fairly, questions and video clips are under continuous review. Some questions may be changed as a result of customer feedback. They may also be altered because of changes to legislation, and DVSA publications are updated so that the revision questions reflect these changes.

Can I take a mock test?

You can take mock tests for the multiple choice part of the theory test online at **safedrivingforlife.info/practicetheorytest**

The theory test

Booking your theory test

Visit **www.gov.uk** to book your theory test online (for Northern Ireland, use **nidirect.gov.uk/motoring**).

If you have any special needs for the theory test, call 0300 200 1122 (0845 600 6700 for Northern Ireland). If you're a Welsh speaker, call 0300 200 1133.

If you have hearing or speech difficulties and use a minicom machine, call 0300 200 1166.

You'll need your

- DVLA or DVA driving licence number
- credit or debit card details (if you do this over the phone, the card holder must book the test). We accept Mastercard, Visa, Delta and Visa Electron.

You'll be given a booking number and you'll receive an appointment email on the same day if you book online.

If you book over the phone and don't provide an email address, you'll receive an appointment letter within 10 days.

Where can I take the test?

There are over 150 theory test centres throughout England, Scotland and Wales, and six in Northern Ireland. Most people have a test centre within 20 miles of their home, but this will depend on the density of population in your area. To find your nearest test centre, please visit **www.gov.uk**

What should I do if I don't receive an acknowledgement?

If you don't receive an acknowledgement within the time specified, please visit **www.gov.uk** or telephone the booking office to check that an appointment has been made. We can't take responsibility for postal delays. If you miss your test appointment, you'll lose your fee.

When are test centres open?

Test centres are usually open on weekdays, some evenings and some Saturdays.

How do I cancel or postpone my test?

You can cancel or postpone your test online by visiting **www.gov.uk** or by telephone. You should contact the booking office at least **three clear working days** before your test date, otherwise you'll lose your fee.

Short-notice cancellation and rebooking (not refund) is permitted in the following circumstances:

- if you're ill or injured and have a supporting medical certificate
- if you've been affected by a bereavement
- if you're sitting school examinations.

Booking by post If you prefer to book by post, you'll need to fill in an application form. The form can be downloaded from **www.gov.uk**, or your riding trainer may have one.

You should normally receive confirmation of your appointment within 10 days of posting your application form. This will be by email if you've provided an email address or by post if not.

If you need support for special needs, please turn to page 16.

Taking your theory test

Arriving at the test centre You must make sure that when you arrive at the test centre you have all the relevant documents with you. If you don't have them, you won't be able to take your test and you'll lose your fee.

You'll need

- your signed photocard licence, or
- your signed driving licence and valid passport (your passport doesn't have to be British).

No other form of identification is acceptable in England, Wales or Scotland.

Other forms of identification may be acceptable in Northern Ireland; please check **nidirect.gov.uk/motoring** or your appointment letter.

All documents must be original. We can't accept photocopies.

The test centre staff will check your documents and make sure that you take the right category of test.

Remember, if you don't bring your documents your test will be cancelled and you'll lose your fee.

Make sure you arrive in plenty of time so that you aren't rushed. If you arrive after the session has started, you may not be allowed to take the test.

 Watch the 'Theory test 2020: official DVSA guide' video on DVSA's YouTube channel. This explains how to prepare for the theory test, what to expect on the day and what you need to do to pass.

youtube.com/dvsagovuk

Languages other than English

In Wales, and at theory test centres on the Welsh borders, you can take your theory test with Welsh text on-screen. A voiceover can also be provided in Welsh.

All Great Britain driving test candidates must take their theory test in either English or Welsh. Unless you're taking the test in Northern Ireland

- no voiceovers will be provided in any other language
- translators cannot attend the test with you to translate it from English into any other language.

Provision for special needs

Every effort is made to ensure that the theory test can be taken by all candidates.

It's important that you state your needs when you book your test so that the necessary arrangements can be made.

Reading difficulties There's an English-language voiceover on a headset to help you if you have reading difficulties or dyslexia.

You can ask for up to twice the normal time to take the multiple choice part of the test.

You'll be asked to provide a letter from a suitable independent person who knows about your reading ability, such as a teacher or employer. Please check with the Special Needs section (call on the normal booking number; see page 13) if you're unsure who to ask.

We can't guarantee to return any original documents, so please send copies only.

Hearing difficulties If you're deaf or have other hearing difficulties, the multiple choice part and the introduction to the hazard perception part of the test can be delivered in British Sign Language (BSL) by an on-screen signer.

A BSL interpreter, signer or lip speaker can be provided if requested at the time of booking. If you have any other requirements, please call the Special Needs section on the normal booking number (see page 13).

Physical disabilities If you have a physical disability that would make it difficult for you to use a mouse button in the theory test, we may be able to make special arrangements for you to use a different method if you let us know when you book your test.

Multiple choice questions

The first part of the theory test consists of 50 multiple choice questions. Some of these will be in the form of a case study. You select your answers for this part of the test by using the mouse.

Before you start, you'll be given the chance to work through a practice session for up to 15 minutes to get used to the system. Staff at the test centre will be available to help you if you have any difficulties.

The questions will cover a variety of topics relating to road safety, the environment and documents. Only one question will appear on the screen at a time, and you'll be asked to mark one correct answer.

shows the category of the test and your name

shows the time remaining: a warning will pop up when you have five minutes left

shows how many answers are required

shows the question

click the answer that you think is correct

shows the question number

click this if you're not sure of the answer and want to come back to it again

click this to move on to the next question

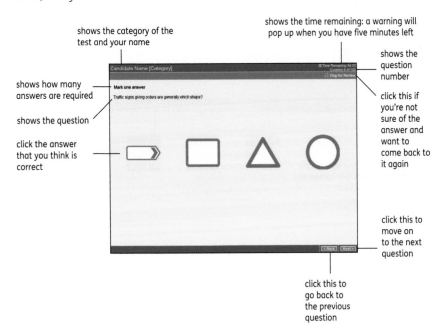

click this to go back to the previous question

To answer, you need to click the box beside the answer you think is correct. If you change your mind and don't want that answer to be selected, click it again. You can then choose another answer.

Take your time and read the questions carefully. You're given 57 minutes for this part of the test, so relax and don't rush. Some questions will take longer to answer than others, but there are no trick questions. The time remaining is displayed on the screen.

You may be allowed extra time to complete the test if you have special needs and you let us know when you book your test.

You'll be able to move backwards and forwards through the questions and you can also 'flag' questions you'd like to look at again. It's easy to change your answer if you want to.

complete question

question you haven't yet looked at

question you haven't yet answered

click this to go back to all the questions you've marked with a flag. You can then work through all the flagged questions

if you click this during the practice session, it will take you to the start of the test. **During the actual test this button will end the test session**

click this to go back to the beginning of the test; you can look at all the questions again and change your answers if you want

click this to see the questions that you haven't yet answered

Try to answer all the questions. If you're well prepared, you shouldn't find them difficult.

At the end of this part of the test, you can use the 'review' feature to check your answers. If you click the 'review' button and then the 'end' button on the review screen, it will end your test. When you click the review button, you'll see the following screen.

Case studies

Some of the multiple choice questions will be presented as part of a case study. Case studies are designed to test

- knowledge (recall of facts)
- comprehension (understanding)
- application (practical use of knowledge and understanding).

This is done by creating a set of circumstances that you may encounter in a real-life situation. You'll then be asked some questions relating to the scenario, and you'll have to decide how you would react or behave in each case. For an example of a case study, see page 452.

The case studies at the end of each section in this book set out scenarios and then ask you relevant questions. This is to help you test your knowledge in a format similar to the case studies in the theory test. However, the layout isn't the same as the theory test screens.

Hazard perception

After you've finished the multiple choice part, there's a break of up to three minutes before you start the hazard perception part of the test. You can't leave your seat during this break. This part of the test is a series of computer-generated image (CGI) video clips, shown from a rider's point of view. You'll be using a mouse for this part of the theory test.

Before you start this part of the test, you'll be shown a short CGI video that explains how the test works and gives you a chance to see a sample clip. This will help you to understand what you need to do. You can play this video again if you wish.

During the hazard perception part of the test, you'll be shown 14 CGI video clips. Each clip contains one or more developing hazards. You should press the mouse button **as soon as you see** a hazard developing that may need you, the rider, to take some action, such as changing speed or direction.

The earlier you notice a developing hazard and make a response, the higher your score. There are 15 hazards for which you can score points.

Your response won't change what happens in the scene in any way. However, a red flag will appear on the bottom of the screen to show that your response has been noted.

Before each clip starts, there'll be a 10-second pause to allow you to see the new road situation.

The hazard perception part of the test lasts about 20 minutes. For this part of the test no extra time is available, and you can't repeat any of the clips – you don't get a second chance to see a hazard when you're riding on the road.

Trial questions

We're constantly checking the questions and clips to help us decide whether to use them in future tests. After the hazard perception part of the test, you may be asked to try a few trial questions and clips. You don't have to do these if you don't want to, and if you answer them they won't count towards your final score.

Customer satisfaction survey

We want to make sure our customers are completely satisfied with the service they receive. At the end of your test you'll be shown some questions designed to give us information about you and how happy you are with the service you received from us.

Your answers will be treated in the strictest confidence. They aren't part of the test and they won't affect your final score or be used for marketing purposes. You'll be asked if you want to complete the survey, but you don't have to.

The result

You should receive your result at the test centre within 10 minutes of completing the test.

You'll be given a score for each part of the test (the multiple choice part and the hazard perception part). You'll need to pass both parts to pass the theory test. If you fail one of the parts, you'll have to take the whole test again.

Why do I have to retake both parts of the test if I only fail one?

It's really only one test. The theory test has always included questions relating to hazard awareness – the second part simply tests the same skills in a more effective way. The two parts are only presented separately in the theory test because different scoring methods are used.

What's the pass mark?

To pass the multiple choice part of the theory test, you must answer at least 43 out of 50 questions correctly. For learner car drivers and motorcyclists, the pass mark for the hazard perception part is 44 out of 75.

If I don't pass, when can I take the test again?

If you fail your test, you've shown that you're not fully prepared. You'll have to wait at least three clear working days before you can take the theory test again.

Good preparation will save you both time and money.

After the theory test

When you pass your theory test, you'll be given a certificate. Keep this safe, as you'll need it when you go for your practical test.

The certificate is valid for two years from the date of your test. This means that you have to take and pass the practical test within this two-year period. If you don't, you'll have to take and pass the theory test again before you can book your practical test.

Your practical tests

To help you, *The Official DVSA Guide to Learning to Ride* has details of the Module 1 off-road and Module 2 on-road practical tests. As well as giving the full test syllabus, it explains the skills that you should show and the faults that you should avoid when taking your tests.

Please refer to the back of this book for information about other publications that will help you prepare for your practical tests.

 Remember: getting a licence takes a lot of hard work and dedication, but losing it only takes one bad decision.

New Drivers Act

When you pass your practical motorcycle test, if it's your first full licence and you get six penalty points in the first two years of riding, your licence will be revoked and you'll have to go right back to the beginning and retake your theory test (see page 393). **Don't risk it; ride safely.**

Using the questions and answers sections

Sections 1 to 14 contain the revision questions for the multiple choice part of the theory test. These are very similar to the questions you'll be asked in the test and cover the same topics.

Section five

◉ Hazard awareness

For easy reference, the questions are divided into topics. Although this isn't how you'll find them in your test, it's helpful if you want to look at particular subjects.

At the start of each topic, before the questions, there are a few pages of useful information to help you learn more about each topic.

The questions are in the left-hand column with a choice of answers below.

On the right-hand side of the page there's a brief explanation to help you understand the question. There'll also be some advice on correct riding procedures and some short references to the relevant source materials. These refer to the books listed on pages 10–11.

14. Motorcycle loading

The correct answers are at the back of the book, in section 16.

Case study practice – 1
Alertness

The morning is clear and fine, but very cold.
You're riding your motorcycle and using dipped headlights.
There's an unmarked junction. You look over your
right shoulder before turning right. Ahead, there's a dip
in the road.
Later, a school crossing patrol signals you to stop while
children are crossing.

1.1 Why would you be using your headlights?
Mark one answer
☐ To help you see the road ahead
☐ To help you to be seen by others
☐ To help you see other road users
☐ To help others see the road ahead

YES in UK GB

1.2 Why did you look over your right shoulder?
Mark one answer

Don't just learn the answers; it's important that you know why they're correct. To help you do this, there's a short scenario at the end of each question section, with five questions to answer. This will give you an idea of how the case study part of the theory test will assess your understanding of the subject covered. This knowledge will help you with your practical skills and prepare you to become a safe and confident rider.

Taking exams or tests is rarely a pleasant experience, but you can make your test less stressful by being confident that you have the knowledge to answer the questions correctly.

Make studying more enjoyable by involving friends and relations. Take part in a question-and-answer game. Test those 'experienced' riders who've had their licence a while: they might learn something too!

Some of the questions in this book won't be relevant to Northern Ireland theory tests. These questions are marked as follows: **NI EXEMPT**

Best wishes for your theory test. Once you're on the road, remember what you've learnt and be prepared to keep learning.

Using this book to learn and revise

We're all different. We like different foods, listen to different music and learn in different ways.

This book is designed to help you learn the important information that you'll need for the theory test in a variety of different formats, so you can find a way of learning that works best for you.

Features

A summary, at the start of each section, of what you'll learn.

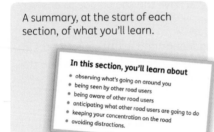

All the key information presented in bite-size chunks with clear headings.

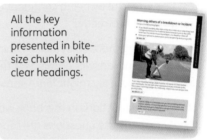

Images to help you relate the information to the real world.

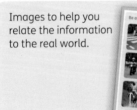

Diagrams and tables to help make information clear and summarise key points.

Self-reflection points to help you think about the way you drive.

Links and QR codes to online videos and interactive activities, to further increase your knowledge and skills. Scan the QR code on your smartphone (you'll need a QR code reader app) to access the online content.

Links to other relevant publications, like *The Official Highway Code* and *The Official DVSA Guide to Riding – the essential skills.*

Tips containing useful extra information about riding safely.

A summary, at the end of each section, of what you'll need to know and be able to do to meet the National Standard for Riding.

Pages for your own notes, with suggested things to think about.

Ideas to discuss with your motorcycle trainer and practise when riding.

Self-assessment – revision questions like the ones you'll get in the test.

Case studies showing how the information might work in practice, and related questions.

The theory test is just one part of the process of learning to ride. You need to learn the facts, but it's important to understand how they relate to real riding.

The combination of knowing rider theory and having good practical riding skills won't only help you pass your test; it will also make you a safer rider for life.

What kind of learner are YOU?

Ask yourself these questions

- Why are you doing this? What's motivating you?
- How have you learned best in the past? What helped you to remember what you needed to know?
- What are your strengths and weaknesses as a learner?

Think about the way that you learn best. You could try any combination of the following ideas.

I remember what I see or read

- Create flashcards with important facts or statistics
- Make diagrams and charts
- Use mind maps
- Use colour coding
- Watch the DVSA short films
- Make your own notes
- Cross-reference information using a variety of books, eg *The Official Highway Code*
- Draw your own diagrams to show key information.

I remember best when I physically do something

- Short study sessions
- Do things – create models or diagrams; make lists
- Use props
- Try the interactive activities
- Watch and copy what your riding trainer does
- Mime or act out different riding moves.

I remember what I hear

- Repeat rules out loud
- Use a voice recorder to make recordings of key information
- Work with others and discuss things
- Watch and listen to the DVSA video content.

Top tips

Remember your motivation

Think about the reason you're learning to ride. Is it for independence? For work? To ride a dream motorcycle? Remind yourself, from time to time, of your motivation for learning. Don't give up!

Relate to your personal experience

Information is more memorable when it's linked to what you already know. Try to picture yourself in the position of the rider. The case studies throughout the book can help you think about how the ideas would work in real life.

Use mnemonics

Mnemonics are little sayings, stories or techniques that help you remember something. A classic example is '**R**ichard **O**f **Y**ork **G**ave **B**attle **I**n **V**ain', which you can use to remember the colours of the rainbow (**r**ed, **o**range, **y**ellow, **g**reen, **b**lue, **i**ndigo, **v**iolet). You can use similar techniques to memorise statistics, facts or information to help you ride safely.

Question format

However you choose to learn the content, make certain you're familiar with the format of the test and how the questions will be presented. Go through the self-assessment questions in each chapter and see if you can answer them. Mark any you struggle with and try them again at a later date.

Plan your study

Set yourself timelines and targets. Try to set aside dedicated time for study, when you're feeling awake and are unlikely to be interrupted. The environment in which you study is important – try to find an area where you can concentrate.

Getting help

Think about the people you can speak with to ask questions, get advice or share experiences about riding – such as your riding trainer, parents, friends or colleagues at work.

Taking your test

Don't rush into the theory test before you're ready. You need to be confident with the information, and have enough practical experience to give you a deep understanding of the information too.

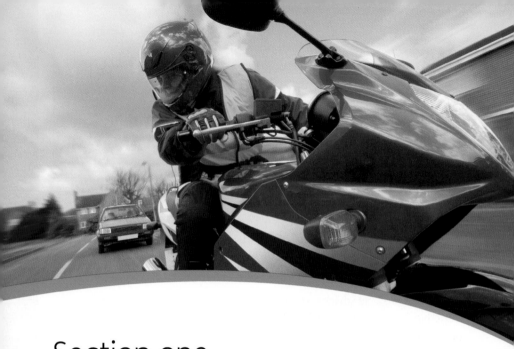

Section one

❗ Alertness

In this section, you'll learn about

- observing what's going on around you
- being seen by other road users
- being aware of other road users
- anticipating what other road users are going to do
- keeping your concentration on the road
- avoiding distractions.

Alertness

Being alert to what's going on around you is vital to riding safely and will help you to avoid dangerous situations.

Observation and awareness

It's important to be aware of what's happening around you while you're riding, including

- other road users
- pedestrians
- signs and road markings
- weather conditions
- the area you're riding through.

Keep scanning the road ahead and to the sides, and assess the changing situations as you ride.

Before you move off, you should

use your mirrors or look around to check how your actions will affect traffic behind you

signal, if necessary

take a final look behind to check your blind spots.

HC r159–161 RES s6

blind spot

the area behind you that you're unable to see in the mirrors

'lifesaver' check

the 'lifesaver' is a last check over the shoulder into the blind spot to make sure nothing unexpected is happening before committing yourself to a manoeuvre

Getting a clear view

If your elbows obstruct your view in the mirrors, you may be able to fit mirrors with longer stems to get an unobstructed view. Having mirrors fitted to both sides of your motorcycle will give you the best view of the road behind.

Looking over your shoulder before manoeuvring may also warn other drivers that you may be about to change lane, direction or speed. Don't forget your **'lifesaver' check**.

If your view is blocked by parked cars when you're coming out of a junction, move forward slowly and carefully until you have a clear view.

 Watch the 'Test your awareness' TFL video.

youtube.com/watch?v=Ahg6qcgoay4

Overtaking

Observation is particularly important when you're overtaking another vehicle. Make sure you can see the road ahead clearly, looking out for

- vehicles coming towards you
- whether you're near a junction – vehicles could come out of the junction while you're overtaking
- whether the road gets narrower – there may not be enough space for you to overtake
- bends or dips in the road, which will make it difficult for you to see traffic coming towards you
- road signs that mean you **MUST NOT** overtake.

Before you overtake, check that

- it's safe, legal and necessary
- you have enough time to complete the overtaking manoeuvre.

HC r162–163, 165 RES s8 KYTS p64

Being seen by others

Other road users can find it difficult to see motorcyclists, so it's important to make sure you can be seen as clearly as possible.

- Wear a light or brightly coloured helmet and fluorescent clothing or strips.
- Use dipped headlights, even in good daylight, to make yourself easy to see.
- At night, reflective clothing or strips make you more visible.
- Where you can't be seen, such as at a hump bridge, you may need to use your horn.

HC r86–87, r115

If you're following a large vehicle, stay well back. This will help the driver to see you in their mirrors. Staying back will also help you see the road ahead much more clearly. This is especially important if you're planning to overtake the vehicle.

HC r164

Tip
Remember, if you can't see a large vehicle's mirrors, the driver may not be able to see you.

Watch this DVSA video to see how difficult it can be for a car driver at a junction to see a motorcyclist approaching.

youtube.com/watch?v=tcNT83m4VGU

As a motorcyclist, you're particularly vulnerable at junctions. Car drivers may not 'expect' to see you, which could mean they pull out without warning. Make sure you're wearing hi-visibility clothing, slow down on your approach and scan ahead for hazards.

Anticipation

Anticipation can help you to avoid problems and incidents so that you can ride more safely. For example, a 'give way' sign warns you that a junction is ahead, so you can slow down in good time.

Look at the road signs and markings: these give you information about hazards.

You should

- follow their advice
- slow down if necessary.

RES s7 **KYTS p10, 62**

Circles

give orders

Triangles

give warnings

Rectangles

give information

When turning right onto a **dual carriageway**, check that the **central reservation** is wide enough for your vehicle to stop in. Do this in case you have to wait before joining the traffic. If there's not enough space for your vehicle, only emerge when it's clear both to the right and left.

 dual carriageway

a road that has a central reservation to separate the carriageways

central reservation

an area of land that separates opposing lanes of traffic

If you're approaching traffic lights that have been green for some time, be prepared to stop because they may change.

Road conditions will affect how easy it is to anticipate what might happen. It's more difficult when you're not familiar with the route, and when your view ahead is reduced; for example, when

- the weather is very wet or windy
- the light is poor
- the traffic volume is heavy.

In these conditions, you need to slow down and be particularly aware of what's happening around you.

RES s8

Anticipating what other road users might do

Watch other road users. Try to anticipate their actions so that you're ready if you need to slow down or change direction.

Be aware of more vulnerable road users. Watch out for

 pedestrians approaching a crossing, especially young, older or disabled people who may need more time to cross the road

 cyclists – always pass them slowly and leave plenty of room, especially if the cyclist is young and may have little experience of dealing with traffic

 horses, which may be startled by the noise of your vehicle – pass them slowly and leave plenty of room.

HC r204–218 RES s10

35

Always be ready to stop

However well prepared you are, you may still have to stop quickly in an emergency. Keep both hands on the handlebars as you brake to keep control of your motorcycle.

RES s6, 10

Staying focused

Riding safely takes a lot of concentration – as well as controlling the motorcycle, you need to be aware of what's happening on the road and what could happen next. Stay focused on riding and try not to get distracted.

Always plan your journey so that you

- know which route you need to take
- have regular rest stops.

Avoiding tiredness

You won't be able to concentrate properly if you're tired. It can also be difficult to concentrate if you're riding on a motorway where boredom and tiredness could make you feel sleepy, especially at night, so

- don't ride continuously for more than two hours
- if you start to feel drowsy, leave at the next exit. Find a safe and legal place to stop and take a break.

 Tip
Stop in a safe place and have a cup of coffee or another caffeinated drink. Remember that this is only a short-term solution: it isn't a substitute for proper rest. If possible, take a short nap.

HC r91, 262 RES s1, 11

Sometimes it's tempting to keep riding, no matter how tired you are. Plan rest breaks along your route; this will help you stay alert and arrive safely. Remember: when you're tired you're more likely to be involved in an incident. If you start to feel drowsy, find a safe place to stop and rest.

 See the Think! road safety website for more information about riding when tired.

think.gov.uk/road-safety-laws/#fatigue

Keeping warm

It's just as easy to lose concentration if you're cold. Proper motorcycle clothing will help to keep you warm and will also help to protect you if you're involved in a road traffic incident.

Distraction

It's easy to be distracted by devices such as hands-free phones, intercom systems or music players because your concentration is divided between the road ahead and what you're hearing.

Losing your concentration, or just taking your eyes off the road for a second, could be disastrous. At 60 mph, your motorcycle will travel 27 metres in one second.

HC r149–150 RES s1

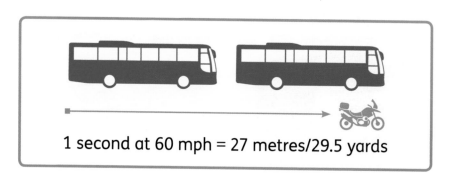

1 second at 60 mph = 27 metres/29.5 yards

Watch DVSA's 'Out of time' video to find out more about the risks of distraction.

youtube.com/safedrivingforlifeinfo

Don't listen to music through an earpiece while you're riding, and make sure you switch off your phone and any hands-free kits. Wait until you're parked in a safe place before you

- retrieve any messages
- make any calls
- send or receive texts
- go online.

If you're riding on a motorway, you should leave the motorway and stop in a safe place before using your phone or programming a navigation system.

RES s1, 16, 18

You could also be distracted by something that has happened on the road, such as an incident on the other side of a motorway. Don't slow down or try to see what's happening; continue with your journey and keep your concentration on your riding.

Meeting the standards

The National Standard for Riding sets out the skills, knowledge and understanding that DVSA believes are required to be a safe and responsible rider. If you know, understand and are able to do the things described in the standard, then you'll not only be in a great position to pass your test but will also be well on your way to becoming a safe rider for life.

You can view the National Standard for Riding at **www.gov.uk**

You must be able to

decide if you're fit to ride. You shouldn't be
- too tired
- too ill
- too emotional
- under the influence of drugs or alcohol

keep concentrating and avoid being distracted

be aware of what's around you (nearby and far away) at all times

ride at such a speed that you can always stop in the clear space ahead of you.

You must know and understand

how these can make you tired
- a poor seating position
- bad posture
- too much noise
- lack of protective clothing

what can distract you. For example
- talking to pillion passengers
- using a sat-nav system

and how to manage these distractions

how helmets and visors may affect your field of vision and how to allow for this

how to read the road ahead and be prepared for the unexpected.

Notes

You can use this page to make your own notes or diagrams about the key points you need to remember.

Think about

- Which clues can you use to help you anticipate what other road users might do? For example, a filling station at the side of the road could mean traffic slowing down to pull in, or vehicles pulling out.
- Why is it important to keep well back from large vehicles?
- What might you use to plan a long journey, and how would you make sure you took breaks at suitable points?
- Can you find a way to remind yourself to switch off your phone or put it to voicemail before you begin riding?

Your notes

_____

_____

_____

_____

_____

_____

_____

 ## Things to discuss and practise with your trainer

These are just a few examples of what you could discuss and practise with your trainer. Read more about alertness to come up with your own ideas.

Discuss with your trainer

- the 'lifesaver' check. What is it and when should you make it?
- what you need to take into account before overtaking, such as road markings, bends, etc
- what could distract you while riding; for example, music via an earpiece, etc.

Practise with your trainer

- seeing and being seen when emerging from junctions, especially when your view is obstructed by parked cars
- turning right onto dual carriageways with different widths of central reservation
- riding at night, to get used to
  - using your dipped and main-beam headlights
  - coping with the lights from approaching vehicles
  - wearing the appropriate clothing to be seen.

You're about to turn right. What should you do just before you turn?

☐ Give the correct signal

☐ Take a lifesaver glance over your shoulder

☐ Select the correct gear

☐ Get in position ready for the turn

When you're turning right, plan your approach to the junction. Signal and select the correct gear in good time. Just before you turn, take a lifesaver glance for a final check behind and to the side of you.

What's the 'lifesaver' when riding a motorcycle?

☐ A certificate every motorcyclist must have

☐ A final rearward glance before changing direction

☐ A part of the motorcycle tool kit

☐ A mirror fitted to check blind spots

This action makes you aware of what's happening behind and alongside you. The lifesaver glance should be timed so that you still have time to react if it isn't safe to perform the manoeuvre.

What should you do when you see this road sign ahead?

☐ Continue at the same speed

☐ Slow down as you go around the bend

☐ Slow down as you come out of the bend

☐ Slow down before the bend

Always look for any advance warning of hazards, such as road signs and hazard warning lines. Use this information to plan ahead and to help you avoid the need for late, harsh braking. Your motorcycle should be upright and moving in a straight line when you brake. This will help you keep maximum control when dealing with the hazard.

What should you do if you're riding at night and are dazzled by the headlights of an oncoming car?

☐ Slow down or stop

☐ Close your eyes

☐ Flash your headlights

☐ Turn your head away

If you're dazzled by the headlights of an approaching vehicle, slow down or stop until your eyes have adjusted. A dirty or scratched visor could make the dazzle worse and further impair your vision.

1.5 · Mark one answer · RES s5

When riding some motorcycles, your shoulders and arms can obstruct your view in the mirrors. What can you do to overcome this difficulty?

☐ Indicate earlier than normal
☐ Fit smaller mirrors
☐ Extend the mirror arms
☐ Brake earlier than normal

It's essential that you have a clear view all around. Adjust your mirrors to give you the best view of the road behind. If your body obscures the view, try fitting mirrors with longer stems.

1.6 · Mark one answer · RES s1, HC r149

You're riding a motorcycle on the road. What should you do before using your mobile phone?

☐ Turn on the speaker phone function
☐ Stop in a safe place
☐ Slow down to 20 mph
☐ Increase the separation distance to 4 seconds

It's important that you're in full control at all times. Even using a hands-free phone kit can distract your attention from the road. If you need to use a mobile phone, stop in a safe place before making the call.

1.7 · Mark one answer · RES s13, HC r115

You're riding at night. You have your headlights on main beam. When should you dip your headlights if another vehicle overtakes you?

☐ When the other vehicle signals to overtake
☐ As soon as the other vehicle moves out to overtake
☐ As soon as the other vehicle passes you
☐ After the other vehicle pulls in front of you

At night, you should dip your headlights to avoid dazzling oncoming drivers or those ahead of you. If you're being overtaken, dip your headlights as the other vehicle comes past. When you switch to dipped beam, your view of the road ahead will be reduced, so look ahead for hazards on your side of the road before you do so.

Mark one answer **RES s6, HC r159**

What should you do to move off safely from a parked position?

☐ Signal if other drivers will need to slow down

☐ Leave your motorcycle on its stand until it's safe to move off

☐ Give an arm signal as well as using your indicators

☐ Look over your shoulder just before you move off

Just before you move off from the side of the road, you should take a look over your shoulder to check your blind spot. This will help you to see any road user who isn't visible in your mirrors.

1.9 **Mark one answer** **RES s4**

What will happen if you become very cold while you're riding your motorcycle?

☐ You'll be more alert

☐ You'll be more relaxed

☐ You'll react more quickly

☐ You'll lose concentration

It can be difficult to keep warm when riding a motorcycle. It's well worth buying good-quality motorcycle clothing, which will help to keep you warm and is essential for your safety. If you become very cold while riding, you'll find it difficult to concentrate on the road.

1.10 **Mark one answer** **RES s13, HC r115**

What should you do if you're riding at night and are dazzled by the headlights of an approaching vehicle?

☐ Switch off your headlights

☐ Switch to main beam

☐ Slow down and stop if necessary

☐ Flash your headlights

If your view of the road ahead is restricted because you're being dazzled by approaching headlights, slow down and, if you need to, find a safe place to stop until your vision is restored.

1.11 **Mark one answer** **RES s8, HC r133, 159**

When should check your blind spots?

☐ Before moving off

☐ Before slowing down

☐ Before changing gear

☐ Before giving a signal

Your blind spots are the areas behind and to either side of you that aren't covered by your mirrors. You should always check the relevant side when there's a risk of a hazard that isn't visible in your mirrors.

1.12 — Mark one answer — RES s8

Why can it be helpful to have mirrors on each side of your motorcycle?

☐ To judge the gap when filtering in traffic

☐ To give protection when riding in poor weather

☐ To make your motorcycle appear larger to other drivers

☐ To give you the best view of the road behind

When riding on the road, you need to know as much about following traffic as you can. A mirror fitted on each side of your motorcycle will help give you the best view of the road behind.

1.13 — Mark one answer — RES s8

What does the term 'lifesaver' mean?

☐ A rearward glance just before manoeuvring

☐ An approved safety helmet

☐ A reflective jacket

☐ The two-second rule

There are areas behind and to either side of you that aren't visible in your mirrors. These are known as blind spots. Just before turning or changing direction, you should look around to check that there's nothing hazardous in the blind spot. This check is known as a 'lifesaver'.

1.14 — Mark one answer — RES s14

You're about to emerge from a junction. Your pillion passenger tells you it's clear. When should you rely on their judgement?

☐ Never; you should always look for yourself

☐ When the roads are very busy

☐ When the roads are very quiet

☐ Only when they're a qualified rider

Your passenger may be inexperienced in judging traffic situations, may have a poor view or may not have seen a potential hazard. You're responsible for your own safety and that of your passenger. Always make your own checks to be sure it's safe to pull out.

1.15 — Mark one answer — RES s8, HC r161

You're riding your motorcycle on an urban road. What must you do before stopping on the left?

☐ Put both feet down

☐ Select first gear

☐ Use your mirrors

☐ Move into neutral

Check your mirrors before slowing down or stopping, as there could be vehicles close behind you. You should react to what you see, for example it may affect the timing of your signal or how quickly you stop.

Mark one answer

Why should you check over your shoulder before you change lanes in busy, slow-moving traffic?

☐ To avoid having to give a signal

☐ Mirrors don't cover blind spots

☐ So traffic ahead will make room for you

☐ So your balance won't be affected

Before changing lanes, make sure there's a safe gap to move into. Looking over your shoulder allows you to check the area not covered by your mirrors, where a vehicle could be hidden from view. It also warns following drivers that you want to change lanes.

Mark one answer

You've been waiting for some time to make a right turn into a side road. What should you do just before you start turning?

☐ Move close to the kerb

☐ Select a higher gear

☐ Make a lifesaver check

☐ Flash you headlights

Remember your lifesaver glance before you start to turn. If you've been waiting for some time and a queue has built up behind you, a vehicle further back may try to overtake. In this situation, it's especially important to look out for other motorcycles, which may be approaching at speed.

Mark one answer

You're riding a motorcycle that's towing a trailer. What should you do before turning right onto a dual carriageway?

☐ Stop, and then select a very low gear

☐ Position in the left gutter of the side road

☐ Assess the width of the central reservation

☐ Check that there's enough room for vehicles behind you

Before emerging right onto a dual carriageway, make sure that the central reservation is wide enough to protect both your motorcycle and its trailer. If it isn't, you should treat it as one road and check that it's clear in both directions before pulling out.

Mark one answer

What should you do before riding a motorcycle you've never ridden before?

☐ Ask someone to ride with you for the first time

☐ Push the bike around to get used to the brakes

☐ Wear thinner gloves so the switches can be operated more easily

☐ Make sure you know where all the controls and switches are

While control layouts are generally similar, different makes and models have subtle differences in the position and operation of the switches. Before you ride any motorcycle, make sure you're familiar with the layout of all the controls and switches.

1.20 — Mark one answer — RES s9, HC r184

You're turning right at a large roundabout. What should you do before you cross a lane to reach your exit?

- ☐ Take a lifesaver glance over your right shoulder
- ☐ Put on your right indicator
- ☐ Take a lifesaver glance over your left shoulder
- ☐ Cancel the left indicator

On busy roundabouts, traffic may be moving very quickly and changing lanes suddenly. You need to be aware of what's happening all around you. Before crossing lanes to the left, make sure you take a lifesaver glance to the left. This gives you time to react if it isn't safe to make the manoeuvre.

1.21 — Mark one answer — RES s9, HC r184

You're turning right on a multi-lane roundabout. When should you take a lifesaver glance over your left shoulder?

- ☐ After moving into the left-hand lane
- ☐ After leaving the roundabout
- ☐ Before signalling to the right
- ☐ Before moving into the left-hand lane

The 'lifesaver' is essential to motorcyclists and does exactly what it says: it could save your life. Its purpose is to check the blind spot that isn't covered by your mirrors. Learn and understand how and when you should use it.

1.22 — Mark one answer — RES s11, HC r282

What should you do if you see an incident on the other side of the motorway?

- ☐ Leave the motorway at the next exit
- ☐ Stop and cross the carriageway to help
- ☐ Concentrate on what's happening ahead
- ☐ Place a warning triangle in the road

Always concentrate on the road ahead. Try not to be distracted by an incident on the other side of the road. Many motorway collisions occur due to traffic slowing down because drivers are looking at something on the other side of the road.

1.23 — Mark one answer — RES s8, HC r159–161

What should you do before making a U-turn?

- ☐ Give an arm signal as well as using your indicators
- ☐ Check road markings to see that U-turns are permitted
- ☐ Look over your shoulder for a final check
- ☐ Select a higher gear than normal

If you have to make a U-turn, slow down and ensure that the road is clear in both directions. Make sure that the road is wide enough for you to carry out the manoeuvre safely. Use your mirrors and look round to check it's safe before turning across the road.

What should you do as you approach this bridge?

You should slow down and be cautious. Hump bridges are often narrow and there may not be enough room for you to pass an oncoming vehicle at this point. Also, there's no footpath, so be aware of pedestrians in the road.

- ☐ Move to the right
- ☐ Slow down
- ☐ Change gear
- ☐ Keep to 30 mph

Where should you avoid overtaking?

- ☐ Just after a bend
- ☐ In a one-way street
- ☐ On a 30 mph road
- ☐ Approaching a dip in the road

Oncoming vehicles or other hazards can be hidden from view by dips in the road. If you can't see into the dip, wait until you have a clear view and can see that it's safe before starting to overtake.

What does this curved arrow road marking mean?

In this picture, the road marking shows that overtaking drivers or riders need to return to the left. These markings show the direction drivers must pass hatch markings or solid double white lines. They're also used to show the route that high vehicles should take under a low arched bridge.

- ☐ Heavy vehicles should take the next road on the left to avoid a weight limit
- ☐ The road ahead bends to the left
- ☐ Overtaking traffic should move back to the left
- ☐ The road ahead has a camber to the left

1.27
Mark one answer RES s1, HC r149, 270

What should you do if your mobile phone rings while you're driving or riding?

☐ Stop immediately

☐ Answer it immediately

☐ Leave it until you have stopped in a safe place

☐ Pull up at the nearest kerb

It's illegal to use a hand-held mobile or similar device when driving or riding, except in a genuine emergency. The safest option is to switch off your mobile phone before you set off, and use a message service. If you've forgotten to switch your phone off and it rings, you should leave it. When you've stopped in a safe place, you can see who called and return the call if necessary.

1.28
Mark one answer RES s7, KYTS p68

Why are these yellow lines painted across the road?

These lines are often found on the approach to a roundabout or a dangerous junction. They give you extra warning to adjust your speed. Look well ahead and do this in good time.

☐ To help you choose the correct lane

☐ To help you keep the correct separation distance

☐ To make you aware of your speed

☐ To tell you the distance to the roundabout

1.29
Mark one answer RES s7, HC r175–176

What should you do when you're approaching traffic lights that have been green for some time?

☐ Accelerate hard

☐ Maintain your speed

☐ Be ready to stop

☐ Brake hard

The longer traffic lights have been green, the sooner they'll change. Allow for this as you approach traffic lights that you know have been green for a while. They're likely to change soon, so you should be prepared to stop.

What should you do before slowing down or stopping your vehicle?

☐ Sound the horn

☐ Use the mirrors

☐ Select a higher gear

☐ Flash the headlights

Before slowing down or stopping, check the mirrors to see what's happening behind you. Also assess what's ahead and make sure you give the correct signal if it will help other road users.

You're following a large vehicle. Why should you stay a safe distance behind it?

☐ You'll be able to corner more quickly

☐ You'll help the large vehicle to stop more easily

☐ You'll give the driver a chance to see you in their mirrors

☐ You'll keep out of the wind better

If you're following a large vehicle but are so close to it that you can't see its exterior mirrors, the driver won't be able to see you. Keeping well back will also allow you to see the road ahead by looking past the large vehicle.

1.32   Mark one answer   RES s10, HC r161

Why should you use your mirrors when you see a hazard ahead?

- ☐ Because you'll need to accelerate out of danger
- ☐ To assess how your actions will affect the traffic behind
- ☐ Because you'll need to brake sharply and stop
- ☐ To check what's happening on the road ahead

You should be constantly scanning the road for clues about what's going to happen next. Check your mirrors regularly, particularly as soon as you spot a hazard. What's happening behind may affect how you respond to hazards ahead.

1.33   Mark one answer   RES s9

You're waiting to turn right at the end of a road. What should you do if your view is obstructed by parked vehicles?

- ☐ Stop and then move forward slowly and carefully for a clear view
- ☐ Move quickly to where you can see so you only block traffic from one direction
- ☐ Wait for a pedestrian to let you know when it's safe for you to emerge
- ☐ Turn your vehicle around immediately and find another junction to use

At junctions, your view is often restricted by buildings, trees or parked cars. You need to be able to see in order to judge a safe gap. Edge forward slowly and keep looking all the time. Don't cause other road users to change speed or direction as you emerge.

Case study practice – 1
Alertness

The morning is clear and fine, but very cold.

You're riding your motorcycle and using dipped headlights.

There's an unmarked junction. You look over your right shoulder before turning right. Ahead, there's a dip in the road.

Later, a school crossing patrol signals you to stop while children are crossing.

1.1 Why would you be using your headlights?

Mark **one** answer

☐ To help you see the road ahead

☐ To help you to be seen by others

☐ To help you see other road users

☐ To help others see the road ahead

RES s4 **HC r86**

1.2 Why did you look over your right shoulder?

Mark **one** answer

☐ Because the junction is unmarked

☐ Because your mirrors are broken

☐ Because your mirrors have blind spots

☐ Because your indicators are flashing slowly

RES s8 **HC r180**

1.3 What should you guard against on this journey?

Mark **one** answer

☐ Losing your way after turning right

☐ Running out of fuel

☐ Rushing to keep an appointment

☐ Getting cold and losing concentration

RES s4

1.4 After you've turned right, how would the road feature affect you?

Mark **one** answer

☐ It would obstruct your view of the road

☐ It would increase your fuel consumption

☐ It would improve your brake function

☐ It would cause more wear on your tyres

RES s8

1.5 How must you react to the school crossing patrol?

Mark **one** answer

☐ Stop your motorcycle and wait patiently

☐ Stop the engine and get off your motorcycle

☐ Ride past, keeping within the speed limit

☐ Park on the left and switch on your hazard warning lights

RES s8 **HC r105, p105**

Section two

❗ Attitude

In this section, you'll learn about

- showing consideration and courtesy to other road users
- how to follow other road users safely
- giving priority to emergency vehicles, buses and pedestrians.

Attitude

Safe riding is all about developing the correct attitude and approach to road safety, together with a sound knowledge of riding techniques.

However modern, fast or expensive your motorcycle, it's you, the rider, who determines how safe it is.

Good manners on the road

Be considerate to other road users. Other types of vehicle, cyclists and horse riders have just as much right to use the road as you. If you ride in a competitive way, you'll make the road less safe for everyone using it.

> **RES s1**

It's also important to be patient with other road users. Unfortunately, not everyone obeys the rules. Try to be calm and tolerant, however difficult it seems. For instance, if someone pulls out in front of you at a junction, slow down and don't get annoyed with them.

> **HC r147 RES s1**

Can you think of a time when riding made you impatient and angry?

How did you react? Did you think about doing something dangerous? Ask yourself how your friends and family would feel if your riding created a serious incident. Is it worth taking the risk?

Helping other road users

You can help other road users know what you're planning to do by signalling correctly and moving to the correct position at junctions. For instance, if you want to turn right, get into the right-hand lane well before the junction. A badly positioned vehicle could obstruct traffic behind it.

> **HC r143 RES s8, 9**

55

If you're riding slowly, consider the other road users behind you. If there's a queue, pull over as soon as you can do so safely and let the traffic pass. Think how you would feel if you were one of the road users following behind you. They may not be as patient as you are.

HC r169 RES s10

Tip

If a large vehicle is trying to overtake you but is taking a long time, slow down and let it pass. It will need more time to pass you than a car would.

HC r168 RES s8

If you're travelling at the speed limit and a driver comes up behind flashing their headlights or trying to overtake, keep a steady course and allow them to overtake. Don't try to stop them – they could become more frustrated.

HC r168 RES s8, 11

Using your horn and lights

Only sound your horn if there's danger and you need to let others know you're there. Don't sound it through impatience.

HC r112 RES s5, 6, 10

At night, don't dazzle other road users. Dip your lights when you're

following another vehicle

meeting another vehicle coming towards you.

HC r114 RES s13

Tip
You should only flash your headlights to show other road users you're there. It's not a signal to show priority, impatience or to greet others.

HC r110–111 RES s6, 10

Animals on the road

Horses can be frightened easily and a rider could lose control of their horse. When passing horses

- keep your speed down
- give them plenty of room.

HC r214–215 RES s10

See the Think! road safety website for more information about horses on the road.

think.gov.uk/road-safety-laws/#horses

Take care if there are animals, such as sheep, on the road. If the road is blocked by animals, or if you're asked to, stop and switch off your engine until the road is clear.

HC r214

Following safely

Riding too closely behind another vehicle – known as tailgating – is

- intimidating and distracting for the road user in front
- very dangerous, as it could cause an incident if the vehicle stops suddenly.

RES s10

Travelling too closely to another vehicle also means that you can see less of the road ahead, so keep well back, especially from large vehicles. You'll be able to see further down the road and spot any hazards ahead more easily.

RES s8, 10

Keep a safe distance from the vehicle in front.

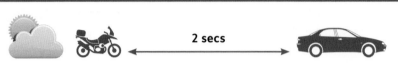

In good, dry conditions, leave a two-second gap.

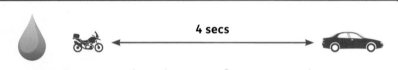

In wet weather, leave a four-second gap.

HC r126 RES s8, 10, 11

Tip
Use a fixed point, like a road sign, to help you measure the gap between you and the vehicle in front.

See section 4, Safety margins, for more information about the amount of space to leave between you and the vehicle in front.

Keeping well back also allows

- the road user in front to see you in their mirrors
- traffic emerging from junctions ahead to see you more easily.

RES s8, 10

When you're following large vehicles, you may see them move to the centre of the road before turning left – this is because they need more room to manoeuvre. Keep well back and don't try to pass on the left as the rear of the vehicle will cut in.

If the road user behind is following too closely, gradually slow down to increase the gap between you and the vehicle in front. This will give you a greater safety margin should traffic ahead slow down or stop suddenly. If another road user cuts in front of you, drop back until you've restored your safety margin.

HC r168

Giving priority to others

Who has priority on the road at any time can vary. Sometimes traffic going in one direction is given priority, and this is shown by a road sign. Having priority doesn't mean you can demand right of way. Be careful: the driver coming towards you may not have seen or understood the road sign.

Priority over oncoming vehicles

Emergency vehicles

Always give priority to emergency vehicles. It's important for them to move quickly through traffic because someone's life might depend on it. Pull over to let them through as soon as you can do so safely.

HC r219 RES s8

As well as fire, police and ambulance services, other emergency services (including those shown here) use a blue flashing light.

HM coastguard

Bomb disposal

Mountain rescue

Blood transfusion

Doctors' vehicles may use green flashing lights when answering an emergency call.

 Watch the Blue Light Aware video to find out more about how to help emergency vehicles get through traffic.

bluelightaware.org.uk

Priority for buses

Give priority to buses pulling out from bus stops, as long as you can do so safely.

In some areas, bus lanes allow buses to proceed quickly through traffic. Be aware of road signs and markings so that you don't use bus lanes while they're in operation, unless you're permitted to do so.

HC r223 RES s7, 8, 10

Unmarked crossroads

At unmarked crossroads, no-one has priority. Slow down, look both ways and only emerge into the junction when you can do so safely.

Pedestrian crossings

Be particularly careful around pedestrian crossings so that you're ready to stop if necessary.

Type of crossing	What you need to be aware of
Zebra crossing	Watch out for pedestrians at or approaching a zebra crossing. • Be ready to slow down and stop. • Be patient if they cross slowly. • Don't encourage them to cross by waving or flashing your headlights – there may be another vehicle coming. HC r195 RES s8
Pelican crossing	If you're approaching a pelican crossing and the amber light is flashing • give way to pedestrians on the crossing • don't move off until the crossing is clear. HC r196–198 RES s8

Type of crossing	What you need to be aware of
Puffin crossing	Puffin crossings are electronically controlled. Sensors ensure that the red light shows until the pedestrian has safely crossed the road. These crossings don't have a flashing amber light; they have a steady amber light, like normal traffic lights. **HC r199** RES s8
Toucan crossing	Toucan crossings, which work in a similar way to puffin crossings, allow cyclists to cross at the same time as pedestrians. **HC r199** RES s8

Meeting the standards

You must be able to

help other road users to understand what you intend to do by signalling correctly

support the signals that you make with the position of your machine. For example, if you're turning right, position the motorcycle in good time and use the right-turn lane if there is one

control your reaction to other road users. Try not to get annoyed or frustrated

give other road users enough time and space.

You must know and understand

what can happen if you wrongly use the headlights or the horn as a signal

what lane discipline is and why it's important

that it's an offence to ride
- without due care and attention
- without reasonable consideration for other road users.

Notes

You can use this page to make your own notes or diagrams about the key points you need to remember.

Think about

- To which vehicles do you need to give priority?
- What would you do if someone was tailgating you?
- In what conditions should you keep a four-second distance between you and the vehicle in front?
- What problems might you cause if you're impatient and inconsiderate while riding?

Your notes

_____

_____

_____

_____

_____

_____

_____

_____

 ## Things to discuss and practise with your trainer

These are just a few examples of what you could discuss and practise with your trainer. Read more about attitude to come up with your own ideas.

Discuss with your trainer

- the different crossings you may come across (puffin, toucan, etc) and who can use them
- which emergency vehicles you may see on the road (police, doctors, etc) and how to react to them
- how to behave when other road users don't obey the rules.

Practise with your trainer

- riding in an area with bus lanes, to
  - practise how to react when they're in operation
  - understand when motorcycles may or may not use them
- riding in heavy traffic, to get used to other vehicles that may be following you too closely
- riding in the countryside, or where you're likely to encounter horse riders.

You're riding towards a zebra crossing. What should you do if pedestrians are waiting to cross?

☐ Give way to the elderly and infirm only

☐ Slow down and prepare to stop

☐ Use your headlights to signal them to cross

☐ Wave at them to cross the road

As you approach a zebra crossing, look out for people waiting to cross and be ready to stop. Some pedestrians may be a little slow to understand that it's safe to cross, so give them time. Be patient and don't rev your engine or surge forward before the crossing is clear.

You're following a large vehicle that's travelling at 40 mph. Where should you position your motorcycle?

☐ Close behind the vehicle, to make it easier to overtake

☐ To the left of the road, to make it easier to be seen

☐ Close to the vehicle, to keep out of the wind

☐ Well back, so that you can see past the vehicle

You need to be able to see well down the road and be ready for any hazards. Staying too close to the vehicle will reduce your view of the road ahead and the driver of the vehicle in front may not be able to see you either. Without a safe separation gap, you don't have the time and space you need to react to any hazards.

What should you do when you're approaching these horse riders?

Animals are easily frightened by moving motor vehicles. If you're approaching horses, keep your speed down and watch to see if the rider has any difficulty keeping control. Always be ready to stop if necessary. When it's safe to pass, give them plenty of room.

☐ Continue at your normal speed

☐ Change down the gears quickly

☐ Slow down and be ready to stop

☐ Flash your headlights to warn them

2.4   Mark one answer   RES s10, HC r169

You're riding a motorcycle that has an engine of less than 50 cc. What should you do if you see a queue of traffic building up behind?

☐ Keep well out to stop vehicles overtaking dangerously

☐ Wave vehicles behind you to pass if you think they can overtake

☐ Pull in when you can to let faster vehicles behind you overtake

☐ Give a left signal when it's safe for vehicles to overtake you

Try not to hold up a queue of traffic. This might lead to other road users becoming impatient and attempting dangerous manoeuvres. If you're riding a slow-moving scooter or small motorcycle and a queue of traffic has built up behind you, look for a safe place to pull in so they can pass safely.

2.5   Mark one answer   RES s8, HC r146

You're riding a motorcycle on a single carriageway road. What should your road position allow?

☐ Other vehicles to pass easily on your left

☐ Pedestrians to hear you approaching

☐ Faster traffic to overtake you easily

☐ Drivers at junctions ahead to see you approaching

Aim to ride in the middle of your lane. Avoid riding in the gutter or in the centre of the road, where you might

• obstruct overtaking traffic
• put yourself in danger from oncoming traffic
• encourage other traffic to overtake you on the left.

2.6   Mark one answer   RES s1

Why are young motorcyclists more likely to be involved in crashes?

☐ Because they're too cautious at junctions

☐ Because they ride in the middle of lanes

☐ Because they're inexperienced

☐ Because they ride in groups

Overconfidence, lack of experience and poor judgement can cause a motorcyclist to make poor decisions, which can lead to a collision. It's just as important to make sure you have the right attitude and self-awareness as a rider as it is to develop skilful riding techniques.

Mark one answer RES s8, HC r196

What must you do when the amber light is flashing at a pelican crossing?

☐ Stop and wait for the green light

☐ Stop and wait for the red light

☐ Give way to pedestrians waiting to cross

☐ Give way to pedestrians already on the crossing

Pelican crossings are signal-controlled crossings operated by pedestrians. Push-button controls change the signals. Pelican crossings have no red-and-amber stage before green; instead, they have a flashing amber light. This means you must give way to pedestrians who are on the crossing but if the crossing is clear you can continue.

2.8 **Mark one answer** RES s8, HC r195

Why should you never wave people across at pedestrian crossings?

☐ Another vehicle may be coming

☐ They may not be looking

☐ It's safer for you to carry on

☐ They may not be ready to cross

If people are waiting to use a pedestrian crossing, slow down and be prepared to stop. Don't wave them across the road, because another driver may not have seen them, may not have seen your signal, and may not be able to stop safely.

2.9 **Mark one answer** RES s10, HC r126

Why is it dangerous to drive too close to the vehicle ahead?

☐ Your engine will overheat

☐ Your mirrors will need adjusting

☐ Your view of the road ahead will be restricted

☐ Your satnav will be confused

'Tailgating' is the term used when a driver or rider follows the vehicle in front too closely. It's dangerous because it restricts your view of the road ahead and leaves no safety margin if the vehicle in front needs to slow down or stop suddenly. Tailgating is often the underlying cause of rear-end collisions or multiple pile-ups.

2.10   Mark one answer   RES s10, HC r222

What will happen if you follow this vehicle too closely?

Staying back will increase your view of the road ahead. This will help you to see any hazards that might occur and give you more time to react.

☐ Your brakes will overheat

☐ Your fuel consumption will be increased

☐ Your engine will overheat

☐ Your view ahead will be reduced

2.11   Mark one answer   RES s8, 10, 11, HC r126

What's the minimum time gap you should leave when following a vehicle on a wet road?

Water will reduce your tyres' grip on the road. The safe separation gap of at least two seconds in dry conditions should be doubled, to at least four seconds, in wet weather.

☐ One second

☐ Two seconds

☐ Three seconds

☐ Four seconds

2.12   Mark one answer   RES s8, HC r168

You're being overtaken by a long, heavily laden lorry. What should you do if it's taking a long time for it to overtake?

A long lorry with a heavy load will need more time to pass you than a car, especially on an uphill stretch of road. Slow down and allow the lorry to pass.

☐ Speed up

☐ Slow down

☐ Hold your speed

☐ Change direction

2.13   Mark one answer   RES s8

Which vehicle will use a blue flashing beacon?

Emergency vehicles use blue flashing lights. If you see or hear one, move out of its way as soon as it's safe and legal to do so.

☐ Motorway maintenance

☐ Bomb disposal

☐ Snow plough

☐ Breakdown recovery

What should you do if you're being followed by an ambulance showing flashing blue lights?

☐ Pull over as soon as it's safe to do so

☐ Accelerate hard to get away from it

☐ Maintain your speed and course

☐ Brake harshly and stop well out into the road

Pull over in a place where the ambulance can pass safely. Check that there are no bollards or obstructions in the road that will prevent it from passing.

What type of emergency vehicle is fitted with a green flashing beacon?

☐ Fire engine

☐ Road gritter

☐ Ambulance

☐ Doctor's car

A green flashing beacon on a vehicle means the driver or passenger is a doctor on an emergency call. Give way to them if it's safe to do so. Be aware that the vehicle may be travelling quickly or may stop in a hurry.

Who should obey diamond-shaped traffic signs?

☐ Tram drivers

☐ Bus drivers

☐ Lorry drivers

☐ Taxi drivers

These signs apply only to tram drivers, but you should know their meaning so that you're aware of the priorities and are able to anticipate the actions of the driver.

2.17　　Mark one answer　　RES s7, HC r306

On a road where trams operate, which vehicles will be most at risk from the tram rails?

☐ Cars

☐ Cycles

☐ Buses

☐ Lorries

The narrow wheels of a bicycle can become stuck in the tram rails, causing the cyclist to stop suddenly, wobble or even lose balance altogether. The tramlines are also slippery, which could cause a cyclist to slide or fall off.

2.18　　Mark one answer　　RES s5, HC r112

When should you use your vehicle's horn?

☐ To alert others to your presence

☐ To allow you right of way

☐ To greet other road users

☐ To signal your annoyance

You mustn't use your vehicle's horn between 11.30 pm and 7 am in a built-up area or when you're stationary, unless a moving vehicle poses a danger. Its function is to alert other road users to your presence.

2.19　　Mark one answer　　RES s8, HC r143

You're in a one-way street and want to turn right. Where should you position your vehicle when there are two lanes?

☐ In the right-hand lane

☐ In the left-hand lane

☐ In either lane, depending on the traffic

☐ Just left of the centre line

When you're in a one-way street and want to turn right, you should take up a position in the right-hand lane. This will allow other road users, not wishing to turn, to pass on the left. Indicate your intention and take up the correct position in good time.

2.20　　Mark one answer　　RES s8, 9, HC r179

You wish to turn right ahead. Why should you take up the correct position in good time?

☐ To allow other drivers to pull out in front of you

☐ To give a better view into the road that you're joining

☐ To help other road users know what you intend to do

☐ To allow drivers to pass you on the right

If you wish to turn right into a side road, take up your position in good time. Move to the centre of the road when it's safe to do so. This will allow vehicles to pass you on the left. Early planning will show other traffic what you intend to do.

Which type of crossing allows cyclists to ride across while pedestrians are also crossing?

☐ Toucan

☐ Puffin

☐ Pelican

☐ Zebra

A toucan crossing is designed to allow pedestrians and cyclists to cross at the same time. Look out for cyclists approaching the crossing at speed.

You're travelling at the legal speed limit. What should you do if the vehicle behind approaches quickly, flashing its headlights?

☐ Accelerate to make a gap behind you

☐ Touch the brakes sharply to show your brake lights

☐ Maintain your speed to prevent the vehicle from overtaking

☐ Allow the vehicle to overtake

Don't enforce the speed limit by blocking another vehicle's progress. This will only cause frustration. Allow the other vehicle to pass when you can do so safely.

When should you flash your headlights at other road users?

☐ When showing that you're giving way

☐ When showing that you're about to turn

☐ When telling them that you have right of way

☐ When letting them know that you're there

You should only flash your headlights to warn others of your presence. Don't use them to greet others, show impatience or give priority to other road users, because they could misunderstand your signal.

You're approaching an unmarked crossroads. How should you deal with the junction?

☐ Accelerate and keep to the middle

☐ Slow down and keep to the right

☐ Accelerate and look to the left

☐ Slow down and look both ways

Be cautious, especially when your view is restricted by hedges, bushes, walls, large vehicles, etc. In the summer months, these junctions can become more difficult to deal with, because growing foliage may further obscure your view.

2.25   **Mark one answer**   **RES s8, 10, 11, HC r126**

The conditions are good and dry. When should you use the 'two-second rule'?

☐ Before restarting the engine after it has stalled

☐ When checking your gap from the vehicle in front

☐ Before using the 'Mirrors – Signal – Manoeuvre' routine

☐ When traffic lights change to green

In good conditions, the 'two-second rule' can be used to check the distance between your vehicle and the one in front. This technique works on roads carrying faster traffic. Choose a fixed object, such as a bridge, sign or tree. When the vehicle ahead passes this object, say to yourself 'Only a fool breaks the two-second rule.' If you reach the object before you finish saying this, you're too close.

2.26   **Mark one answer**   **RES s8, HC r199**

Which colour follows the green signal at a puffin crossing?

☐ Steady red

☐ Flashing amber

☐ Steady amber

☐ Flashing green

Puffin crossings have infra-red sensors that detect when pedestrians are crossing and hold the red traffic signal until the crossing is clear. The use of a sensor means there's no flashing amber phase as there is with a pelican crossing.

2.27   **Mark one answer**   **RES s8, 10, 11, HC r126**

You're in a line of traffic. What action should you take if the driver behind is following very closely?

☐ Ignore the driver behind and continue to travel within the speed limit

☐ Slow down, gradually increasing the gap between you and the vehicle in front

☐ Signal left and wave the driver behind to come past

☐ Move over to a position just left of the centre line of the road

If the driver behind is following too closely, there's a danger they'll collide with the back of your vehicle if you stop suddenly. You can reduce this risk by slowing down and increasing the safety margin in front of you. This reduces the chance that you'll have to stop suddenly and allows you to spread your braking over a greater distance. This is an example of defensive driving.

Case study practice – 2 Attitude

You ride your motorcycle to a motorcycle show on a single carriageway road.

The road surface is damp from overnight rain.

You come up behind two horse riders. Soon, you pass them.

Near the showground, the traffic volume increases. There's a large vehicle in front, so you drop back.

You see a vehicle with a green flashing light in your mirrors, so you make room for it to pass.

2.1 What's the national speed limit for motorcycles on this road?

Mark **one** answer

☐ 40 mph

☐ 50 mph

☐ 60 mph

☐ 70 mph

HC r124

2.2 How should you ride on this road surface?

Mark **one** answer

☐ Carefully, while increasing the distance from any vehicle in front

☐ Faster, as this will help warm the tyres and dry the road surface

☐ Very slowly, to help prevent surface water spraying over others

☐ As close as possible to the vehicle in front, for added protection

RES s8 HC r126

2.3 What's the safest way to pass the two riders?

Mark **one** answer

☐ Quickly, while flashing headlights

☐ Slowly, while sounding the horn

☐ Quickly, leaving a large gap

☐ Slowly, leaving plenty of room

RES s10 **HC r214–215**

2.4 Why did you drop back?

Mark **one** answer

☐ To avoid any buffeting from the wind

☐ To allow space for other road users to pull in

☐ To avoid any mud splashing up from the tyres

☐ To allow you to see past the large vehicle

RES s10 **HC r164**

2.5 What did you see in your mirrors?

Mark **one** answer

☐ A fire engine being driven to a fire

☐ A doctor driving to an emergency

☐ A police officer driving to a disturbance

☐ A traffic officer attending an incident

RES s8 **HC r219**

Section three

 # Safety and your motorcycle

In this section, you'll learn about

- carrying out basic maintenance on your motorcycle
- what to do if your motorcycle has a fault
- carrying passengers and loads safely
- being seen by, and making sure you can see, other road users
- making your motorcycle secure
- parking safely
- being aware of the environment
- avoiding congestion.

Safety and your motorcycle

Look after your motorcycle and it will look after you, not only by being less likely to break down, but also by being more economical and lasting longer. Remember that an efficient engine is kinder to the environment.

Looking after your motorcycle

Regular maintenance should ensure that your motorcycle is safe and fit to be on the road. It will also help to make sure that your motorcycle uses fuel as efficiently as possible and keep its exhaust emissions to a minimum.

Check the following items on a regular basis.

Controls: check hydraulic fluid levels and keep cables lubricated.

Electrical systems: battery, switches, lights, horn, indicators.

Lights and **number plates** should be kept clean at all times.

Engine/transmission: engine oil level, drive chain and sprockets or, for shaft-drive motorcycles, the transmission oil level; engine coolant (for liquid-cooled engines), air filter, exhaust system.

Suspension and steering: suspension, steering head bearings, wheels, tyres (for pressure, splits, tread depth and uneven wear).

HC p128 RES s6, 15

Helpful tips

The drive chain and sprockets: a loose drive chain and worn sprockets can cause the chain to jump off the rear sprocket and lock the rear wheel. When adjusting the chain tension, check the wheel alignment too as this can increase tyre wear and cause instability when cornering.

Tyre pressures: check them when the tyres are cold. Increase the pressure when you're carrying passengers or loads, or if riding at high speeds. Under-inflation can affect stopping and steering, as well as increase fuel consumption. Check your motorcycle handbook for correct pressures.

Tyre tread: the depth must be more than 1 mm to be legal. When replacing the tyres, replace the tubes as well if necessary. Check the wheel alignment after refitting the rear wheel. Ride carefully on your new tyres until the shiny surface wears off.

HC p129 RES s15

Also remember to check

- brake fluid levels regularly: low levels can affect braking efficiency
- oil and coolant levels and tyre pressures before a long journey
- battery fluid levels; if necessary, top up with distilled water to just above the cell plates.

HC p128 RES s6, 15

Dealing with faults

A basic understanding of how your motorcycle works will help you recognise when there's a problem with it. It's important that your motorcycle is checked regularly by a qualified mechanic, especially the brakes.

Warning lights on the instrument panel tell you about the performance of the engine and warn you of any faults.

- Check your motorcycle handbook to make sure that you know what all the warning lights mean.
- Don't ignore a warning: it could affect your safety.

HC p128 RES s5, 15

Motorcycles fitted with anti-lock braking systems (ABS) will have a warning light on the instrument panel, which should go out at a speed of 5–10 mph. If this doesn't happen, have the ABS checked by a qualified mechanic.

Remember to check oil seals for leakage. Leaks of damping oil from shock absorbers or front forks can

- make your shock absorbers stop working and make your motorcycle difficult to control
- get onto the brakes and increase your stopping distance
- get onto your tyres, causing loss of grip and increased risk of skidding.

Tip

Don't overfill your motorcycle's engine with oil as this could cause damage to engine seals resulting in oil leaks.

Visit a garage as soon as possible if

- the motorcycle vibrates – you may need to have the **wheels balanced**
- the motorcycle becomes difficult to control – the steering head bearings may be worn or need adjustment
- indicators flash too fast – they should flash between one and two times a second
- you notice uneven tyre wear – this can indicate faults with the brakes, suspension or wheel alignment.

RES s6, 15

wheel balancing
making sure that the wheels and tyres are balanced to prevent vibrations

	If this happens while you're riding ...	**here's what to do**
	The oil pressure light comes on.	Stop as quickly as possible and investigate.
	A tyre bursts.	Slow gently to a stop, holding the handlebars firmly.

HC p128 RES s6, 15

Carrying passengers and loads

Once you've passed your practical tests, you can carry a passenger if your motorcycle is designed to do so. You're responsible for ensuring that any passenger you carry is

- sitting properly
- facing forward
- on a proper seat with appropriate footrests
- wearing an approved safety helmet, which is correctly fastened.

Make sure that you secure any load or luggage so it doesn't fall off or affect your control of the motorcycle.

HC r83, 85 RES s14

Seeing and being seen

Many road traffic incidents are caused by one road user not seeing another. Motorcyclists are particularly vulnerable in this way, because they take up less space than cars and are more easily hidden by other vehicles.

Visibility

Before you start riding, adjust the mirrors so that you can see as clearly as possible all around. Convex mirrors give a wider view but can make vehicles look further away than they are.

If you're riding in conditions where visibility is seriously reduced, you **MUST** use dipped headlights. It's important for other road users to see you. If there's thick fog, use your fog lights (if fitted) but remember to switch them off again when visibility improves.

Hazard warning lights are fitted so that you can warn road users of a hazard ahead, such as

- when you've broken down
- queuing traffic on a dual carriageway or motorway.

Don't use them as an excuse to park illegally, even for a short time.

HC r116, 226, 274, 277–278 RES s5, 11

Clothing

You can make it easier for other road users to see you by wearing a light or brightly coloured helmet, brightly coloured clothing and a high-visibility or reflective jacket or vest. Reflective clothing is especially important at night.

Always wear proper protective clothing and footwear when riding. It can protect you in all types of weather and in the event of an incident. Having a fairing fitted to your motorcycle can protect your hands, legs and feet from bad weather and cold winds.

HC r83–88 RES s4

 Use this website to check the safety rating of your helmet.

sharp.dft.gov.uk

Helmet visors and goggles should be

- kept clean: check the manufacturer's guidelines for recommended cleaning materials
- undamaged: replace scratched visors or goggles as soon as possible.

If your visor or goggles become fogged up during a ride, stop as soon as possible to clear them.

HC r83–88 RES s4

Tip

Never use a second-hand helmet. Even if the helmet has no obvious damage, it could have damage that can't be seen. This could make it unreliable in a road traffic incident, so it's best not to take the risk.

RES s4

Security

It's impossible to make a motorcycle completely secure. However, the harder you make it for a potential thief to steal it, the less likely you are to be targeted.

Make it as difficult as you can for a thief to steal your motorcycle.

Use a steering lock.

Use an extra locking device; for example, a high-tension steel cable or chain with high-quality padlock, a U-lock or a disc lock.

Lock it to an immovable object or another motorcycle.

At night, park in a well-lit area.

HC p131 RES s8

To make it more difficult for an opportunist thief, you can

- fit an anti-theft alarm or immobiliser
- have the Vehicle Identification Number (VIN) security-marked onto the motorcycle.

RES s8

You **MUST NOT** leave your vehicle unattended with the engine running.

HC r123

Always switch off the engine and secure your motorcycle before leaving it. Use the steering lock and, if possible, chain the motorcycle to an immovable object for extra security.

Consider joining a Vehicle Watch scheme if there's one in your area. Contact the crime prevention officer at your local police station to find out more.

 Use this link to find out more about thefts from vehicles.

crimestoppers-uk.org/keeping-safe/vehicle-safety

Parking safely

Where you park your motorcycle can affect the safety of other road users. Avoid parking where your motorcycle would block access or visibility for others, such as

- in front of a property entrance
- at or near a bus stop
- near the brow of a hill, where the limited view of the road ahead makes it difficult to see whether it's safe to pass the obstruction
- at a dropped kerb, as this is a place for wheelchair and mobility scooter users to get onto the road or pavement.

HC r243

You **MUST NOT** stop or park on the zigzag lines at a pedestrian crossing. This would block the view of pedestrians and other road users, and endanger people trying to use the crossing.

HC r239–250, 291 RES s8

If you have to park on a hill or sloped area, make sure your motorcycle can't roll downhill by

- leaving it in a low gear
- blocking a wheel or wedging it against the kerb.

When leaving your motorcycle on a two-way road at night, park in the direction of the traffic. If the speed limit is more than 30 mph (46 km/h), switch on your parking lights.

Being aware of the environment

Motorcycle engines burn petrol, which is a fossil fuel. Burning fossil fuel causes air pollution and damages the environment, while using up natural resources that can't be replaced.

You can help the environment by riding in a fuel-efficient way. You'll help to

- improve road safety
- reduce exhaust emissions
- reduce your fuel consumption, which will save you money.

RES s17

Fuel-efficient riding

Follow these guidelines to make your riding fuel efficient.

Reduce your speed. Vehicles travelling at 70 mph (112 km/h) use about 15% more fuel than those travelling at 50 mph (80 km/h).

Plan well ahead so that you can ride smoothly. Avoiding rapid acceleration and heavy braking can cut your fuel bill by up to 15%.

Follow these guidelines to make your riding fuel efficient.

Have your motorcycle regularly serviced and tuned properly.

Make sure your tyres are correctly inflated.

RES s17

Avoid

- carrying unnecessary loads
- over-revving the engine in lower gears
- leaving the engine running unnecessarily – if your motorcycle is stationary and likely to remain so for some time, switch off the engine.

HC r123 RES s17

Try not to use your motorcycle to make lots of short journeys: consider walking or cycling instead. Using public transport or sharing a vehicle can reduce the volume of traffic and vehicle emissions.

RES s17

Keeping your motorcycle in good condition

Having your motorcycle serviced regularly will keep its fuel consumption and exhaust emissions down. If your motorcycle is over three years old (over four years old in Northern Ireland), it will have to pass an emissions test as part of the MOT test.

If you service your own motorcycle, dispose of old engine oil and batteries responsibly. Take them to a local-authority site or a garage. Don't pour oil down the drain.

>
> **Tip**
> Make sure your filler cap is securely fastened. If it's loose, it could spill fuel, which wastes both fuel and money. Spilt fuel makes the road slippery for other road users.
>
> **HC p130 RES s15**

If you notice a strong smell of petrol, check where it's coming from as soon as possible. Use the engine cut-out switch in an emergency.

RES s17

Noise pollution

Don't make excessive noise with your motorcycle. In built-up areas, you **MUST NOT** use your horn between 11.30 pm and 7.00 am, unless another vehicle poses a danger.

HC r112 RES s5

Avoiding congestion

Sometimes it's impossible to avoid road congestion, but if you can it will make riding less stressful for you.

Always try to

- plan your route before starting out
- avoid riding at times when roads will be busy, if possible
- allow plenty of time for your journey, especially if you have an appointment to keep or a connection to make.

RES s18

Plan your route by

- looking at a map
- using satellite navigation equipment
- checking for roadworks or major events with a motoring organisation
- using a route planner on the internet.

If you have any on-board technology, such as a satellite navigation (satnav) system, don't let it distract you from riding. Keep any interaction with the system to an absolute minimum and find a safe, legal place to stop before making any adjustments.

Tip

In some towns and cities, you may see red lines on the side of the road, which indicate 'Red Routes'. They help the traffic flow by restricting stopping on these routes.

HC p115 RES s7

If you're travelling on a new or unfamiliar route, it's a good idea to print out or write down the directions, and also to plan an alternative route in case your original route is blocked.

If you can avoid travelling at busy times, you'll

- be less likely to be delayed
- help to ease congestion for those who have to travel at these times.

Congestion charging has been introduced in London and is being considered in some other towns and cities. Motorcycles are currently exempt from paying this charge.

London also has a Low Emission Zone (LEZ) and an Ultra Low Emission Zone (ULEZ). Motorcycles are exempt from charges in the LEZ but in the ULEZ your motorcycle must meet Euro 3 emission standards for NOx or you'll have to pay the charge.

Generally speaking, engines meeting Euro 3 emission standards are those registered with DVLA after July 2007. Use the checker on Transport for London's website to see if your motorcycle meets the standard: **tfl.gov.uk/ modes/driving/ultra-low-emission-zone/motorcycles-mopeds-and-more**

Emission zone charging is also being considered by some other cities in an effort to improve their air quality.

RES s18

Find out more about congestion and emission zone charging in London using the Transport for London (TfL) website.

tfl.gov.uk/modes/driving/congestion-charge

tfl.gov.uk/modes/driving/low-emission-zone

tfl.gov.uk/modes/driving/ultra-low-emission-zone

Meeting the standards

You must be able to

check that all lights and reflectors are
- legal
- clean
- in good working order

make sure that your tyres
- are at the right pressure
- have enough tread depth

get to know the machine if it's the first time you've ridden it

carry out pre-start checks.

You must know and understand

that these must be kept clean at all times
- lights
- indicators
- reflectors
- number plates

how to check that tyres
- are correctly fitted
- are correctly inflated
- have enough tread depth
- are legal to use.

Notes

You can use this page to make your own notes or diagrams about the key points you need to remember.

Think about

- What maintenance does your motorcycle need each week, month and year?
- What should you do if a warning light appears on your instrument panel while you're riding?
- Which security features does your motorcycle have? How could you improve your machine's security?
- Are there more efficient alternative forms of transport available for your journey?
- How can you find out about local traffic congestion? (For example, local radio stations, websites and mobile phone apps.)

Your notes

_____
_____
_____
_____
_____
_____
_____
_____
_____

Things to discuss and practise with your trainer

These are just a few examples of what you could discuss and practise with your trainer. Read more about safety and your motorcycle to come up with your own ideas.

Discuss with your trainer

- the importance of the state of your tyres; for example, on safety, fuel consumption, vehicle handling, etc. Also, discuss how often you should check your tyres
- how you can ride in a fuel-efficient way, by using the gears, controlling your speed, etc
- what you think is suitable clothing for riding in different weather conditions.

Practise with your trainer

- riding through built-up areas to get used to different methods of traffic calming
- identifying the warning lights on your instrument panel
- planning your journey. Do this with a new lesson route and see how you can avoid busy times and places.

Mark one answer

What could happen if you ride your motorcycle when it has a very loose drive chain?

☐ The front wheel could wobble

☐ The ignition could cut out

☐ The brakes could fail

☐ The rear wheel could lock

Drive chains are subject to wear and need frequent adjustment to maintain the correct tension. Allowing the drive chain to run dry will greatly increase the rate of wear, so it's important to keep it lubricated. If the chain becomes very worn and loose, it can jump off the sprocket and lock the rear wheel.

Mark one answer

What's the most important reason to keep your motorcycle well maintained?

☐ To accelerate faster than other traffic

☐ So the motorcycle doesn't struggle when carrying panniers

☐ To keep the motorcycle roadworthy

☐ So the motorcycle can carry a passenger

Whenever you use any motorcycle on the road, it must be in a roadworthy condition. Regular maintenance should identify any faults at an early stage and help prevent more serious problems.

Mark one answer

How should you ride a motorcycle when new tyres have just been fitted?

☐ Slower-than-normal, until the shiny surface is worn off

☐ By braking hard, especially into bends

☐ Normally, but with higher tyre pressures

☐ By riding at faster-than-normal speeds

New tyres have a shiny finish, which needs to wear off before the tyre will give the best grip. Take extra care if the road surface is wet or slippery.

Mark one answer

How will wearing brightly coloured clothing improve your safety while you're riding a motorcycle?

☐ You'll blend into the background

☐ It will be easier for other road users to see you

☐ You'll distract other road users

☐ It will allow you to ride faster on unlit roads at night

For your own safety, you need other road users to see you easily. Wearing brightly coloured or fluorescent clothing will help you to achieve this during daylight. At night, wearing clothing that includes reflective material is the best way of helping others to see you.

3.5   Mark one answer   RES s4

What should you do when you're riding a motorcycle in very hot weather?

☐ Ride with your visor fully open

☐ Wear protective clothing

☐ Wear trainers instead of boots

☐ Slacken your helmet strap

Always wear your protective clothing, whatever the weather. In very hot weather it's tempting to ride in light summer clothes, but it isn't worth the risk. If you fall from your motorcycle, you'll have no protection from the hard road surface.

3.6   Mark one answer   RES s4, HC r86

Why should you wear fluorescent clothing when riding a motorcycle in daylight?

☐ It reduces wind resistance

☐ It prevents injury if you're involved in an incident

☐ It helps other road users to see you

☐ It keeps you cool in hot weather

Motorcycles are smaller and therefore harder to see than most other vehicles on the road. You need to make yourself as visible as possible to other road users. Fluorescent and reflective clothing will help achieve this.

3.7   Mark one answer   RES s4, HC r87

Why should motorcycle riders wear reflective clothing?

☐ To protect them from the cold

☐ To protect them from direct sunlight

☐ To be seen better in daylight

☐ To be seen better at night

Fluorescent clothing will help others to see you during the day. At night, however, you should wear clothing that reflects the light. This allows other road users to see you more easily in their headlights. Ask your local motorcycle dealer about fluorescent and reflective clothing.

3.8   Mark one answer   RES s4, HC r84

What should you do if your visor becomes very scratched?

☐ Polish it with a fine abrasive

☐ Replace it

☐ Wash it in soapy water

☐ Clean it with petrol

Your visor protects your eyes from wind, rain, insects and road dirt. It's important to keep it clean and in good repair. A scratched visor can obscure your view and cause dazzle from the lights of oncoming vehicles.

Mark one answer RES s15, HC p129

What's the legal minimum depth of tread for motorcycle tyres?

☐ 1 mm

☐ 1.6 mm

☐ 2.5 mm

☐ 4 mm

The law says that the entire original tread must be visible, with a depth of at least 1 mm in a continuous band across at least three-quarters of the breadth of the tread. However, your tyres are your only contact with the road, so it's recommended that you replace them before they get to this level.

Mark one answer RES s4, HC r86

What can you wear to make it easier for other road users to see you?

☐ A black leather jacket

☐ A helmet fitted with a tinted visor

☐ A brightly coloured helmet

☐ A silk balaclava

Many incidents and collisions involving motorcyclists occur because other road users don't see them. Be aware that you're vulnerable and make yourself as visible as possible by wearing fluorescent clothing and a light or brightly coloured helmet.

Mark one answer RES s5

What should you do if the oil-pressure warning light comes on while you're riding?

☐ Go to a dealer for an oil change

☐ Go to the nearest garage to ask their advice

☐ Ride slowly for a few miles to see if the light goes out

☐ Stop as soon as possible and try to find the cause

If the oil-pressure warning light comes on when the engine is running, pull over as soon as you can, stop the engine and investigate the cause; if you don't, you risk serious engine damage.

| 3.12 | Mark one answer | RES s15 |

What must you check on both the front and rear motorcycle tyres?

☐ That they're the same tread pattern

☐ That they're correctly inflated

☐ That they're the same size

☐ That they're the same make

Your safety and that of others depends on the condition of your tyres. Before every trip, make sure they

• are correctly inflated
• have at least the minimum legal depth of tread
• have no cuts or bulges.

Do these checks as part of a routine before every journey.

| 3.13 | Mark one answer | RES s15 |

What could happen if you ride your motorcycle with a slack or worn drive chain?

☐ The engine could misfire

☐ The tyres could wear more quickly

☐ The engine could produce more emissions

☐ The chain could lock the rear wheel

Check your drive chain regularly; adjust and lubricate it if necessary. It needs to be adjusted until the 'free play' is as it says in the vehicle handbook. If the chain is too loose, it can jump off its sprocket and lock your rear wheel while you're riding.

| 3.14 | Mark one answer | RES s15 |

What should you do if a tyre bursts while you're riding your motorcycle?

☐ Slow gently to a stop

☐ Brake firmly to a stop

☐ Change to a high gear

☐ Lower the side stand

If a tyre bursts, close the throttle smoothly and slow gently to a stop, holding the handlebars firmly to help you keep a steady course.

| 3.15 | Mark one answer | RES s15, 17 |

What will be the benefit of having your motorcycle engine properly maintained?

☐ It will have lower wind resistance

☐ It will have lower exhaust emissions

☐ It will reduce your insurance premiums

☐ It will reduce your journey times

A badly maintained engine will emit more exhaust fumes than one that's correctly serviced. This is damaging to the environment. The engine will also use more fuel.

What should you use to clean visors and goggles?

It's very important to keep your visor or goggles clean. Clean them using warm soapy water. Don't use solvents or petrol.

- ☐ Petrol
- ☐ White spirit
- ☐ Anti-freeze
- ☐ Soapy water

You're riding on a quiet road. What should you do if your visor fogs up?

- ☐ Continue at a reduced speed
- ☐ Stop as soon as it's safe and wipe it
- ☐ Build up speed to increase the air flow
- ☐ Close the helmet air vents

In cold and wet weather, your visor may fog up. If this happens when you're riding, choose somewhere safe to stop, and wipe it clean with a damp cloth. Special anti-fog products are available at motorcycle dealers.

You're riding in hot weather. What's the safest type of footwear?

- ☐ Sandals
- ☐ Trainers
- ☐ Shoes
- ☐ Boots

It's important to wear good boots when you ride a motorcycle. Boots protect your feet and shins from knocks, and give some protection in a crash. They also help keep you warm and dry in cold or wet weather.

3.19   Mark one answer   RES s4, HC r83

What's the purpose of the velcro tab fitted to some helmet straps?

☐ To securely fasten the helmet

☐ To prevent the strap flapping in the wind

☐ To provide a quick-release fastening following a crash

☐ To stop draughts

Some helmet straps have a Velcro tab in addition to the main fastening, which is intended to secure the strap so that it doesn't flap in the wind. It mustn't be used on its own to fasten the helmet.

3.20   Mark one answer   RES s17

What does a catalytic converter reduce?

☐ Exhaust noise

☐ Fuel consumption

☐ Exhaust emissions

☐ Engine noise

Catalytic converters reduce the toxic and polluting gases given out by the engine. Never use leaded or lead-replacement petrol in a motorcycle with a catalytic converter; even one tankful can permanently damage the system.

3.21   Mark one answer   RES s15

Your motorcycle has a chain drive. What should you check after refitting the motorcycle's rear wheel?

☐ The steering damper

☐ The side stand

☐ The wheel alignment

☐ The suspension preload

After refitting the rear wheel or adjusting the drive chain, you should check your wheel alignment. Incorrect alignment will result in excessive tyre wear and poor roadholding.

3.22   Mark one answer   RES s15

You're checking your direction indicators. How many times per second must they flash?

☐ Between 1 and 2 times

☐ Between 3 and 4 times

☐ Between 5 and 6 times

☐ Between 7 and 8 times

You should check that all your lights work properly before every journey. If you aren't sure whether your signals can be seen, you can use arm signals as well to make your intentions clear; avoid this if you're riding at speed because it can upset your stability.

What should you check after adjusting the final drive chain?

☐ The rear wheel alignment

☐ The suspension adjustment

☐ The rear shock absorber

☐ The front suspension forks

Always check the rear wheel alignment after adjusting the final drive chain. Marks on the chain adjuster may be provided to make this easy. Incorrect alignment can cause instability and increased tyre wear.

What would cause your steering to feel wobbly?

☐ Tyre pressure is too high

☐ Incorrectly adjusted brakes

☐ Worn steering-head bearings

☐ A broken clutch cable

Worn bearings in the steering head can make your motorcycle very difficult to control. They should be checked for wear or correct adjustment and replaced if necessary.

Your motorcycle has a faulty oil seal on a shock absorber. Why is this a serious problem?

☐ The motorcycle will have excessive chain wear

☐ The motorcycle will be difficult to control

☐ The motorcycle will be harder to ride uphill

☐ The motorcycle won't accelerate so quickly

As well as making your motorcycle difficult to control, the leaking oil could find its way onto your tyres and brakes. This could result in a loss of control, putting you and other road users in danger.

Oil is leaking from your motorcycle's forks. Why is this dangerous?

☐ Your suspension will be ineffective

☐ Your steering is likely to seize up

☐ The forks will quickly begin to rust

☐ The motorcycle will become too noisy

If an oil seal on your forks or shock absorbers fails, fork oil will leak out, making the suspension ineffective and the motorcycle difficult to control. It can also be very dangerous if the oil gets onto brakes or tyres. Replace faulty oil seals without delay.

Section three | Questions

3.27   Mark one answer   RES s15

You've adjusted your motorcycle's drive chain. If this isn't done properly, what problem could it cause?

☐ Inaccurate speedometer reading
☐ Loss of braking power
☐ Incorrect rear wheel alignment
☐ Excessive fuel consumption

After carrying out drive-chain adjustment, you should always check the rear wheel alignment. Many motorcycles have alignment guides stamped onto the frame to help you do this correctly.

3.28   Mark one answer   RES s15, HC p129

What should you do if you find a cut in the sidewall of one of your motorcycle's tyres?

☐ Replace the tyre before riding the motorcycle
☐ Check regularly to see if it gets any worse
☐ Repair the cut before riding the motorcycle
☐ Reduce the tyre pressure before you ride

A cut in the sidewall can be very dangerous. The tyre is in danger of blowing out if you ride the motorcycle in this condition.

3.29   Mark one answer   RES s15

How would you find out the correct air pressure to use in your motorcycle's tyres?

☐ It will be shown on the tyre wall
☐ It will be stamped on the wheel
☐ By checking the vehicle handbook
☐ By checking the registration document

Tyre pressures should be checked regularly. Look in your vehicle handbook for the correct pressures to use.

3.30   Mark one answer   RES s15

What can you do to prevent a cable-operated clutch from becoming stiff?

☐ Keep the cable tight
☐ Keep the cable dry
☐ Keep the cable slack
☐ Keep the cable oiled

Keeping the clutch cable oiled will help it to move smoothly through its outer casing. This will extend the life of the cable and help prevent the clutch's operation from becoming stiff.

What can happen if your motorcycle's wheels are out of alignment?

☐ A serious loss of power

☐ Reduced braking performance

☐ Increased tyre wear

☐ Reduced ground clearance

If a motorcycle's wheels are incorrectly aligned, tyres may wear unevenly and the motorcycle can become unstable, especially when cornering.

Why should you wear specialist motorcycle clothing when you're riding?

☐ Because the law requires you to do so

☐ Because it looks better than ordinary clothing

☐ Because it gives the best protection from the weather

☐ Because it will reduce your insurance premium

If you become cold and wet when you're riding, your concentration and control of your motorcycle can be seriously affected. Proper motorcycle clothing can help protect you from the weather, as well as giving some protection in the event of a crash.

What should you do when you leave your motorcycle parked?

☐ Remove the battery lead

☐ Pull it onto the kerb

☐ Use the steering lock

☐ Leave the parking lights on

You should always use the steering lock when leaving your motorcycle. Also consider using additional locking devices, such as a U-lock, disc lock or chain. If possible, fasten the motorcycle to an immovable post or similar anchored structure.

You're parking your motorcycle. How can you reduce the chances of it being stolen?

☐ Park in a space marked for motorcycles only

☐ Chain it to an immovable object

☐ Switch off the engine cut-out switch

☐ Leave it on its side stand

Theft of motorcycles is a very common crime. If you can, secure your vehicle to a lamppost or other such object, to help reduce the chances of it being stolen.

3.35   Mark one answer   RES s8

What's the best way to stop a motorcycle and sidecar outfit rolling away if you park it on a hill?

☐ Leave it in neutral

☐ Put the rear wheel on the pavement

☐ Leave it in a low gear

☐ Park very close to another vehicle

To make sure a sidecar outfit doesn't roll away after you've parked it, you should leave it in a low gear and wedge it against the kerb or place a block behind the wheel.

3.36   Mark one answer   RES s5

When would you use the engine cut-out switch?

☐ To reduce speed in an emergency

☐ To prevent the motorcycle being stolen

☐ To stop the engine normally

☐ To stop the engine in an emergency

If you're involved in a collision, using the engine cut-out switch will help to reduce the risk of fire. When stopping the engine normally, use the ignition switch.

3.37   Mark one answer   RES s7, HC r153

What should you do when you ride along a road where there are road humps?

☐ Maintain a reduced speed throughout

☐ Accelerate quickly between each one

☐ Always keep to the maximum legal speed

☐ Ride slowly at school times only

The humps are there to reduce the speed of the traffic. Don't accelerate harshly between them, as you'll then have to brake sharply to negotiate the next hump. Harsh braking and acceleration uses more fuel, as well as causing wear and tear to your vehicle.

3.38   Mark one answer   RES s15

When should you check the engine oil level?

- ☐ Before a long journey
- ☐ When the engine is hot
- ☐ Early in the morning
- ☐ Before the MOT test

As well as the oil, you'll need to check other items. These include fuel, water and tyres.

3.39   Mark one answer   RES s17

You service your own motorcycle. How should you dispose of used engine oil?

- ☐ Take it to a local-authority site
- ☐ Pour it down a drain
- ☐ Tip it into a hole in the ground
- ☐ Put it into your dustbin

Never pour the oil down any drain. The oil is highly polluting and could harm wildlife. Put it in a container and dispose of it properly at an authorised site.

3.40   Mark one answer   RES s17

How could you safeguard your motorcycle against the risk of fire?

- ☐ Keep water levels above maximum
- ☐ Check out any strong smell of petrol
- ☐ Avoid riding with a full tank of petrol
- ☐ Use unleaded petrol

The fuel in your motorcycle can be a dangerous fire hazard. Don't use a naked flame if you can smell fuel, and don't smoke when refuelling.

3.41   Mark one answer   RES s4, HC r86

You're riding a motorcycle during the day. What would help to make you more visible to other road users?

- ☐ Wearing a black helmet
- ☐ Wearing a brightly coloured helmet
- ☐ Switching off your headlights
- ☐ Wearing a dark jacket

Wearing bright or fluorescent clothes will help other road users to see you. Wearing a light or brightly coloured helmet can also make you more visible.

3.42   Mark one answer   RES s4, HC r83

You're wearing a motorcycle safety helmet while riding your motorcycle. What would make the helmet illegal?

☐ If the helmet isn't fastened correctly

☐ If the helmet is more than four years old

☐ If the helmet is borrowed from a friend

☐ If the helmet doesn't have chin protection

A helmet that's incorrectly fastened or not fastened at all is likely to come off in a crash and will provide little or no protection. By law, you must wear a helmet when riding on the road, and it must be correctly fastened. (Members of the Sikh religion who wear a turban are exempt.)

3.43   Mark one answer   RES s15

When should you increase the tyre pressures on your motorcycle?

☐ When riding in hot weather

☐ After a long journey

☐ When carrying a heavy load

☐ When riding in wet weather

The vehicle handbook will explain when it's recommended that you increase tyre pressures – for example, when you're carrying extra weight from a passenger or a heavy load.

3.44   Mark one answer   RES s15, HC p128

What part of your motorcycle must be kept clean?

☐ The number plate

☐ The wheels

☐ The engine

☐ The fairing

Maintenance is a vital part of road safety. Lights, indicators, reflectors and number plates must all be kept clean.

3.45   Mark one answer   RES s5

When should you use your motorcycle's engine cut-out switch?

☐ When you want to save wear and tear on the battery

☐ When you want to stop the engine for a short time

☐ When you want to stop the engine in an emergency

☐ When you want to save wear and tear on the ignition

Only use the engine cut-out switch in an emergency. When stopping the engine normally, use the ignition switch. This will remind you to take your keys with you when parking. It could also prevent starting problems if you forget you've left the cut-out switch in the 'off' position.

What should you check after you've adjusted the tension on your motorcycle's drive chain?

☐ The rear wheel alignment

☐ The tyre pressures

☐ The valve clearances

☐ The sidelights

Drive chains wear and need frequent adjustment and lubrication. If the drive chain is worn or slack, it can jump off the sprocket and lock the rear wheel. When you've adjusted the chain tension, you need to check the rear wheel alignment. Marks by the chain adjusters may be provided to make this easier.

A friend offers you a second-hand safety helmet for you to use. Why may this be a bad idea?

☐ It may be damaged

☐ You'll be breaking the law

☐ You'll affect your insurance cover

☐ It may be a full-face type

A second-hand helmet may look in good condition but it could have received damage that isn't visible externally. A damaged helmet could be unreliable in a crash.

What would make a motorcycle tyre illegal?

☐ Tread less than 1.6 mm deep

☐ Tread less than 2 mm deep

☐ A large bulge in the sidewall

☐ A stone wedged in the tread

When checking tyres, check for bulges or cuts in the sidewalls. If there's any sign that the tyres have been damaged, they should be replaced.

How should you maintain cable-operated brakes?

☐ By removing all free play at the lever or pedal

☐ By checking them at normal operating temperature

☐ By always fitting new ones for the MOT

☐ By lubricating and adjusting them regularly

Cables will stretch with use and need checking and adjusting regularly. They also need lubricating to prevent friction and wear of the cables and pivots. Don't over-adjust brake cables or the brakes will bind, causing increased fuel consumption, risk of skidding and risk of the brakes overheating.

3.50   Mark one answer   RES s15

How will you benefit from having your motorcycle serviced regularly?

☐ Lower insurance premiums

☐ A refund on your vehicle tax

☐ Increased exhaust emissions

☐ Reduced risk of it breaking down

Your motorcycle will be most reliable if you have it serviced regularly. Check at what intervals you should have your motorcycle serviced – this can vary by model or manufacturer. Keeping the service record up-to-date can help the resale value too.

3.51   Mark one answer   RES s15

What could a loose drive chain cause?

☐ A locked rear wheel

☐ Wobbly wheels

☐ A braking fault

☐ Headlight misalignment

A motorcycle chain will stretch as it wears. It may need frequent checking and adjustment to keep the tension correct. In extreme cases, a loose chain can jump off the sprocket and become wedged in the rear wheel. This could cause serious loss of control and result in a crash.

3.52   Mark one answer   RES s12, HC r226

When must you use dipped headlights during the day?

☐ When you're riding on country roads

☐ When visibility is seriously reduced

☐ When the roads are wet

☐ When you're riding on a motorway

You must use dipped headlights during the day if visibility is seriously reduced; that is, when you can't see for more than 100 metres (328 feet).

3.53   Mark one answer   RES s14

When should you consider increasing your tyre pressures?

☐ When riding on a wet road

☐ When carrying a pillion passenger

☐ When travelling on an uneven surface

☐ When riding on twisty roads

Sometimes, manufacturers advise you to increase your tyre pressures for high-speed riding and when carrying extra weight, such as a pillion passenger. This information can be found in the vehicle handbook.

3.54 Mark one answer RES s15

What problem could be caused by putting too much oil in your engine?

☐ Low oil pressure
☐ Engine overheating
☐ Stiffer gear changes
☐ Oil leaks

Too much oil in the engine will create excess crankcase pressure. This could damage engine seals and cause oil leaks. Any excess oil should be drained off.

3.55 Mark one answer HC r123

You're leaving your motorcycle parked and unattended on a road. When may you leave the engine running?

☐ When parking for less than five minutes
☐ If the battery is flat
☐ When in a 20 mph zone
☐ Not on any occasion

When you leave your motorcycle parked and unattended on a road, switch off the engine, use the steering lock and remove the ignition key. Also take any tank bags, panniers or loose luggage with you, set the alarm if the motorcycle has one, and use an additional lock and chain, or cable lock.

3.56 Mark one answer RES s5

You're involved in a crash. What should you do to reduce the risk of fire?

☐ Keep the engine running
☐ Open the choke
☐ Turn the fuel tap to reserve
☐ Use the engine cut-out switch

The engine cut-out switch is used to stop the engine in an emergency. In the event of a crash, this may help to reduce any fire risk.

3.57 Mark one answer RES s4, 13, HC r87

What should you do when riding at night?

☐ Give arm signals
☐ Wear reflective clothing
☐ Wear a tinted visor
☐ Ride in the centre of the road

At night, you should wear clothing with reflective material, to help other road users to see you. If your jacket doesn't have reflective patches, you could wear garments that do, such as

• a hi-visibility vest or tabard
• a reflective belt.

Also use your headlights on dipped or main beam, as appropriate.

3.58 — Mark one answer — RES s15, HC p129

How would under-inflated tyres affect your vehicle?

☐ The vehicle's stopping distance would increase

☐ The flash rate of the vehicle's indicators would increase

☐ The vehicle's gear change mechanism would become stiff

☐ The vehicle's headlights would aim high

Your tyres are your only contact with the road. To prevent problems with braking and steering, keep your tyres free from defects; they must have sufficient tread depth and be correctly inflated. Correct tyre pressures help reduce the risk of skidding and provide a safer and more comfortable drive or ride.

3.59 — Mark one answer — RES s5, HC r112

When are you not allowed to sound your vehicle's horn?

☐ Between 10.00 pm and 6.00 am in a built-up area

☐ At any time in a built-up area

☐ Between 11.30 pm and 7.00 am in a built-up area

☐ Between 11.30 pm and 6.00 am on any road

Every effort must be made to prevent excessive noise, especially in built-up areas at night. Don't rev your engine or sound the horn unnecessarily. It's illegal to sound your horn in a built-up area between 11.30 pm and 7.00 am, except when another road user poses a danger.

3.60 — Mark one answer — RES s8

What makes the vehicle in the picture 'environmentally friendly'?

☐ It's powered by gravity

☐ It's powered by diesel

☐ It's powered by electricity

☐ It's powered by unleaded petrol

Trams are powered by electricity and therefore don't emit exhaust fumes. They ease traffic congestion by offering drivers an alternative to using their car, particularly in busy cities and towns.

3.61 | Mark one answer | RES s18, HC p115

Why have 'red routes' been introduced in major cities?

☐ To raise the speed limits

☐ To help the traffic flow

☐ To provide better parking

☐ To allow lorries to load more freely

Inconsiderate parking can obstruct the flow of traffic and so make traffic congestion worse. Red routes are designed to prevent this by enforcing strict parking restrictions. Driving slowly in traffic increases fuel consumption and causes a build-up of exhaust fumes.

3.62 | Mark one answer | RES s7, HC r153

What's the purpose of road humps, chicanes and narrowings?

☐ To separate lanes of traffic

☐ To increase traffic speed

☐ To allow pedestrians to cross

☐ To reduce traffic speed

Traffic-calming measures help to keep vehicle speeds low in congested areas where there are pedestrians and children. A pedestrian is much more likely to survive a collision with a vehicle travelling at 20 mph than they are with a vehicle travelling at 40 mph.

3.63 | Mark one answer | RES s17

What's the purpose of a catalytic converter?

☐ To reduce fuel consumption

☐ To reduce the risk of fire

☐ To reduce harmful exhaust gases

☐ To reduce engine wear

Catalytic converters reduce a large percentage of harmful exhaust emissions. They work more efficiently when the engine has reached its normal working temperature.

3.64 | Mark one answer | RES s15, HC p129

When should tyre pressures be checked?

☐ After any lengthy journey

☐ After travelling at high speed

☐ When tyres are hot

☐ When tyres are cold

Check the tyre pressures when the tyres are cold. This will give you a more accurate reading. The heat generated on a long journey will raise the pressure inside the tyre.

3.65 — Mark one answer — RES s15, 17

When will your vehicle use more fuel?

☐ When its tyres are under-inflated
☐ When its tyres are of different makes
☐ When its tyres are over-inflated
☐ When its tyres are new

Check your tyre pressures frequently – normally once a week. If they're lower than those recommended by the manufacturer, there will be more 'rolling resistance'. The engine will have to work harder to overcome this, leading to increased fuel consumption.

3.66 — Mark one answer — RES s17

How should you dispose of a used vehicle battery?

☐ Bury it in your garden
☐ Put it in the dustbin
☐ Take it to a local-authority disposal site
☐ Leave it on waste land

Batteries contain acid, which is hazardous, and they must be disposed of safely. This means taking them to an appropriate disposal site.

3.67 — Mark one answer — RES s17, HC r123

What's most likely to increase fuel consumption?

☐ Poor steering control
☐ Accelerating around bends
☐ Staying in high gears
☐ Harsh braking and accelerating

Accelerating and braking gently and smoothly will help to save fuel and reduce wear on your vehicle. This makes it better for the environment too.

3.68 — Mark one answer — RES s15

The fluid level in your battery is low. What fluid should you use to top it up?

☐ Battery acid
☐ Distilled water
☐ Engine oil
☐ Engine coolant

Some modern batteries are maintenance free. Check your vehicle handbook and, if necessary, make sure that the plates in each battery cell are covered with fluid.

3.69 Mark one answer RES s13

You're parked on the road at night. When must you use parking lights?

- ☐ When there are continuous white lines in the middle of the road
- ☐ When the speed limit exceeds 30 mph
- ☐ When you're facing oncoming traffic
- ☐ When you're near a bus stop

When parking at night, park in the direction of the traffic. This will enable other road users to see the reflectors on the rear of your vehicle. Use your parking lights if the speed limit is over 30 mph.

3.70 Mark one answer RES s17

How can you reduce the environmental harm caused by your motor vehicle?

- ☐ Only use it for short journeys
- ☐ Don't service it
- ☐ Drive faster than normal
- ☐ Keep engine revs low

Engines that burn fossil fuels produce exhaust emissions that are harmful to health. The harder you make the engine work, the more emissions it will produce. Engines also use more fuel and produce higher levels of emissions when they're cold. Anything you can do to reduce your use of fossil fuels will help the environment.

3.71 Mark one answer RES s15, HC p129

What can cause excessive or uneven tyre wear?

- ☐ A faulty gearbox
- ☐ A faulty braking system
- ☐ A faulty electrical system
- ☐ A faulty exhaust system

If you see that parts of the tread on your tyres are wearing before others, it may indicate a brake, suspension or wheel-alignment fault. Regular servicing will help to detect faults at an early stage and this will avoid the risk of minor faults becoming serious or even dangerous.

3.72 Mark one answer RES s15

You need to top up your battery with distilled water. What level should you fill it to?

- ☐ The top of the battery
- ☐ Halfway up the battery
- ☐ Just below the cell plates
- ☐ Just above the cell plates

Top up the battery with distilled water and make sure each cell plate is covered.

3.73   Mark one answer   RES s18

How can you plan your route before starting a long journey?

☐ Check your vehicle handbook

☐ Ask your local garage

☐ Use a route planner on the internet

☐ Consult a travel agent

Various route planners are available on the internet. Most of them give you several options, allowing you to choose between the most direct route and quieter roads. They may also identify rest and fuel stops. Print off the directions and take them with you.

3.74   Mark one answer   RES s18

Why is it a good idea to plan your journey to avoid busy times?

☐ You'll have an easier journey

☐ You'll have a more stressful journey

☐ Your journey time will be longer

☐ It will cause more traffic congestion

No-one likes to spend time in traffic queues. Try to avoid busy times related to school or work travel.

3.75   Mark one answer   RES s18

How will your journey be affected by travelling outside the busy times of day?

☐ Your journey will use more fuel

☐ Your journey will take longer

☐ Your journey will be more hazardous

☐ Your journey will have fewer delays

If possible, avoid the early morning, late afternoon and early evening 'rush hour'. Doing this should allow you to have a better journey, with fewer delays. This should help you to arrive at your destination feeling less stressed.

3.76   Mark one answer   RES s18

You plan your route before starting a journey. Why should you also plan an alternative route?

☐ Your original route may be blocked

☐ Your maps may have different scales

☐ You may find you have to pay a congestion charge

☐ You may get held up by a tractor

It can be frustrating and worrying to find your planned route is blocked by roadworks or diversions. If you've planned an alternative, you'll feel less stressed and more able to concentrate fully on your driving or riding. If your original route is mostly on motorways, it's a good idea to plan an alternative using non-motorway roads. Always carry a map with you just in case you need to refer to it.

3.77 Mark one answer RES s18

You have to arrive on time for an appointment. How should you plan for the journey?

- ☐ Allow plenty of time for the trip
- ☐ Plan to travel at busy times
- ☐ Avoid roads with the national speed limit
- ☐ Prevent other drivers from overtaking

Always allow plenty of time for your journey in case of unforeseen problems. Anything can happen; for example, punctures, breakdowns, road closures, diversions and delays. You'll feel less stressed and less inclined to take risks if you aren't 'pushed for time'.

3.78 Mark one answer RES s17

What can you expect if you drive using rapid acceleration and heavy braking?

- ☐ Reduced pollution
- ☐ Increased fuel consumption
- ☐ Reduced exhaust emissions
- ☐ Increased road safety

Using the controls smoothly can reduce fuel consumption by about 15%, as well as reducing wear and tear on your vehicle. Plan ahead and anticipate changes of speed well in advance. This will reduce the need to accelerate rapidly or brake sharply.

What could cause you to crash if the level is allowed to get too low?

☐ Anti-freeze level

☐ Brake-fluid level

☐ Battery-water level

☐ Radiator-coolant level

You should carry out frequent checks on all fluid levels but particularly brake fluid. As the brake pads or shoes wear down, the brake-fluid level will drop. If it drops below the minimum mark on the fluid reservoir, air could enter the hydraulic system and lead to a loss of braking efficiency or even complete brake failure.

Case study practice – 3 Safety and your motorcycle

You're riding your motorcycle to work. It's winter and the weather is dry, but cold.

You're wearing leather motorcycle clothing, boots, gloves, a fluorescent safety vest with reflective panels and a brightly coloured helmet.

At the service station, you buy fuel. You clean both handlebar mirrors, which have longer stems.

You also make your weekly check of tyre pressures and tread depths. The rear tyre is worn down to the legal limit.

3.1 What could affect your concentration on your ride to work?

Mark **one** answer

☐ Getting cold

☐ Getting wet

☐ Getting hot

☐ Getting blown off course

RES s12

3.2 How does your helmet's colour help?

Mark **one** answer

- ☐ It matches your motorcycle
- ☐ It won't show the dirt
- ☐ It makes you easier to see
- ☐ It helps you to blend in

RES s4 **HC r86**

3.3 How can being dressed in this way help you while you're riding?

Mark **one** answer

- ☐ It helps to keep you cool
- ☐ It helps to lower your insurance premiums
- ☐ It helps your friends to recognise you
- ☐ It helps to improve your safety

RES s4 **HC r86**

3.4 Why might you have this adaptation to your mirrors?

Mark **one** answer

- ☐ Because they look very cool and fashionable
- ☐ To give you an unobstructed view behind
- ☐ So that other vehicles will allow you more room
- ☐ To help balance and control the motorcycle

RES s5

3.5 What depth is the tread on your rear tyre?

Mark **one** answer

- ☐ 1 mm across three-quarters of the tread breadth and all around
- ☐ 2 mm across the entire tread breadth and all around
- ☐ 2 mm across three-quarters of the tread breadth and all around
- ☐ 1 mm across the entire tread breadth and all around

RES s15 **HC p129**

Section four

❄ Safety margins

In this section, you'll learn about

- keeping yourself and others safe by staying within safety margins
- stopping, thinking and braking distances
- risks caused by different weather conditions and road surfaces
- the risk of skidding
- contraflow systems.

Safety margins

It's essential that you always keep in mind your safety, and that of your passenger and other road users, as you're riding.

You can reduce your chances of being involved in an incident on the road by knowing the safety margins and what can happen if you don't ride within them. Never take risks.

Keep control of your motorcycle by using the correct procedures. For instance, control your speed before you reach a bend so that you aren't still braking while you're cornering.

HC r160 RES s6, 8

Don't 'coast' – this means travelling in neutral or with the clutch disengaged – as this can reduce your control over the machine.

HC r122

Stopping distance

Leave enough room between your motorcycle and the vehicle in front so that you can pull up safely if it slows down or stops suddenly.

Your overall stopping distance is the distance your motorcycle travels from the moment you realise that you must brake to the moment your motorcycle stops.

HC r126 RES s8

Thinking distance
(distance travelled in the time it takes to react to a situation)

+

Braking distance
(distance travelled from when you start to use the brakes to when your motorcycle completely stops)

=

Stopping distance

Typical stopping distances

Look at the typical stopping, thinking and braking distances given in *The Official Highway Code*. Remember that these are based on vehicles travelling

- with good tyres and brakes
- on a dry road
- in good conditions.

HC r126 RES s8

20 mph (32 km/h) | 6 m | 6 m | = **12 metres (40 feet)** or three car lengths

30 mph (48 km/h) | 9 m | 14 m | = **23 metres (75 feet)** or six car lengths

40 mph (64 km/h) | 12 m | 24 m | = **36 metres (118 feet)** or nine car lengths

50 mph (80 km/h) | 15 m | 38 m | = **53 metres (175 feet)** or thirteen car lengths

60 mph (96 km/h) | 18 m | 55 m | = **73 metres (240 feet)** or eighteen car lengths

70 mph (112 km/h) | 21 m | 75 m | = **96 metres (315 feet)** or twenty-four car lengths

The distances shown are a general guide. The distance will depend on your attention (thinking distance), the road surface, the weather conditions and the condition of your vehicle at the time.

Thinking Distance | **Braking Distance**

Average car length = 4 metres (13 feet)

Don't just learn the stopping distance figures: you need to be able to judge the distance when you're riding.

HC r126 RES s12

Tip

In good conditions, leave a two-second gap between your motorcycle and the vehicle in front. Use a fixed point, like a road sign, to measure the time gap between your motorcycle and the vehicle in front. You can measure two seconds by saying the sentence 'Only a fool breaks the two-second rule.'

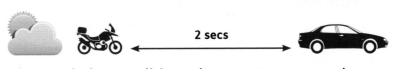

In good, dry conditions, leave a two-second gap.

In other conditions, you need to increase this distance.

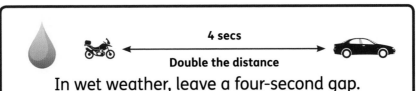

In wet weather, leave a four-second gap.

In icy weather, leave a 20-second gap.

Keeping a safe distance from the vehicle in front will help to lower your risk of having a collision. If someone overtakes you and pulls into the gap in front, drop back to keep a safe distance from them.

HC r126 RES s12

Remember, your overall stopping distance may be longer when carrying a passenger.

RES s14

Your personal safety margin is the space you maintain around your motorcycle.

Think about your personal safety margin the next time you ride.

Are you getting too close to other vehicles?

117

Weather conditions

Weather conditions have a major effect on your safety margins. If there's bad weather, such as snow, ice or thick fog, think about whether you really need to make your journey. Never underestimate the dangers and always wear suitable clothing.

HC r228–231 RES s4

 Read more about protective clothing at this website.

www.gov.uk

Weather	Actions to take
Heavy rain/wet road	When there's heavy rainfall, water can collect on the road surface and may cause aquaplaning. This is where the tyres lift off the road surface and skate on a film of water.

If this happens

- ease off the throttle smoothly
- don't brake or try to change direction until you can feel the tyres gripping again.

HC r121, 227 RES s12

Use a low gear when riding through a ford or flood water, and test your brakes afterwards. If necessary, dry them out by applying the brakes lightly as you go along.

HC r121 RES s12

If it rains after a long dry spell, the road surface can be unusually slippery and requires extra care.

HC r237

Weather	Actions to take

Hot and/or bright

Hot weather can also be dangerous. The road surface can become soft. This could affect your braking and steering.

Bright sunlight can dazzle. Other drivers might not be able to see your indicators flashing. Give an arm signal if you think it will be helpful.

HC r237 RES s12

Fog

Fog reduces your visibility. Remember to

- think about whether you could use a different form of transport or delay your journey until conditions improve
- allow more time for your journey
- slow down, because you can't see as far ahead as usual
- increase the gap between your motorcycle and the vehicle in front
- keep your visor or goggles clear
- beware of other road users not using their headlights
- use dipped headlights, even in daylight.

If visibility falls below 100 metres (328 feet), use fog lights if you've got them. You **MUST** switch them off when the fog lifts.

HC r234–236 RES s12

 Riding in bad weather can be a challenge. If this makes you anxious, affects your judgement or your ability to ride, then talk to your trainer before and after your lesson. They will be able to observe your behaviour and give you feedback and encouragement. Remember to review their feedback before your next lesson.

Weather	Actions to take

Weather

Wind

Freezing

Actions to take

High wind can blow you off course, especially on an open stretch of road. The wind can affect all road users but those worst affected include

- high-sided vehicles
- other motorcyclists
- vehicles towing trailers or caravans
- cyclists.

Take care and allow extra room if you pass these road users, as they may be blown off course by a sudden gust of wind.

HC r232–233 RES s12

Freezing conditions can make roads very slippery, which will make your motorcycle harder to control.

Before starting a journey, think about

- whether your journey is necessary
- whether you could use a different form of transport.

If you must travel, clear ice and snow from your lights, mirrors and number plate.

RES s12

When riding

- try and keep to main roads
- keep your speed down
- brake gently and in plenty of time.

HC r234–236 RES s12

Tip

Take extra care when there's a side wind from your left. It can blow you off course and into the path of oncoming vehicles.

At night

When riding at night

- wear reflective clothing
- use dipped headlights (you can also use these in the daytime to become more visible to others)
- don't use tinted glasses, lenses or visors.

RES s13

 If riding in the dark worries you, ask your trainer about getting some additional practice at night. Once you've ridden safely in the dark a few times, you'll become less anxious about it.

Skidding

Skidding is when the tyres lose grip on the road, and it's caused by the rider. Road surface and tyre conditions can increase the risk of skidding, but skids are the result of how the rider controls acceleration, braking, speed and steering.

There's a greater risk of skidding in wet or icy conditions. To reduce the risk of skidding in slippery conditions, ride

- at a low speed
- in the highest gear you can use effectively.

Skidding can be caused by

- heavy or uncoordinated braking, which can lock one or both wheels
- too much acceleration, causing rear wheel spin
- steering harshly – making a sudden change of direction
- travelling too fast and leaning over too far when cornering, which may cause tyres to lose grip.

If you accelerate too harshly and start to skid

- ease off the throttle to regain control
- steer in the direction of the skid; for example, if the back of the motorcycle skids to the right, steer to the right.

If the skid is caused by braking, release the brakes to allow the wheels to turn again, then apply the brakes again as firmly as you can in the riding conditions.

HC r119, 231 RES s8, 12

121

To reduce the risk of skidding, look at the road ahead for clues such as road signs and markings, and hazards like potholes, debris, drain covers, oil patches or loose gravel. You can then plan your riding so that you can

- slow down gradually before you reach a hazard, such as a bend
- avoid sudden steering movements.

HC r119, 231 RES s6, 8, 12

Anti-lock braking systems

An anti-lock braking system (ABS) will help to prevent wheel lock caused by excessive braking, such as in an emergency. The sensor will keep the wheel at the point of lock-up for as long as the rider continues to brake hard enough to activate the system, or until the motorcycle stops. Refer to your motorcycle handbook for details of the manufacturer's recommended method of use.

HC r120 RES s5

ABS doesn't necessarily reduce your stopping distance, but you can continue to steer while braking because the wheels are prevented from locking. It may not work as well if there's

- surface water, such as when there's been heavy rainfall
- a loose road surface, such as gravel.

Contraflow systems

contraflow system
where one or more lanes have a direction of traffic against that of the rest of the carriageway

When you enter a **contraflow system**, you should

- reduce your speed in good time
- choose a suitable lane in good time: look for signs advising you to use a particular lane if you want to take an exit that will be coming up soon
- keep a safe distance behind the vehicle in front.

HC r290 RES s11

Meeting the standards

You must be able to

keep a safe distance from the vehicle in front

use the throttle and brakes correctly to
- regulate your speed
- bring the machine to a stop safely

always use a safe, systematic approach to keep you and other road users safe. For example, **observation, signal, manoeuvre, position, speed, look.**

You must know and understand

the importance of keeping a safe separation distance in all weather and traffic conditions

about skidding
- why a skid may occur
- how to avoid skids
- how to correct them if they do occur

the distance that a machine needs to stop
- from different speeds
- in different road conditions
- in different weather conditions

how traffic and weather conditions may affect other road users and what to do. For example, their visibility may be reduced.

Notes

You can use this page to make your own notes or diagrams about the key points you need to remember.

Think about

- What are typical stopping distances and how do wet or icy roads affect them?
- What extra considerations or precautions might you need to take if the weather is

  - snowy or icy
  - wet
  - foggy
  - hot
  - bright and dazzling
  - windy?

- How can you reduce the risk of skidding and what should you do if your motorcycle starts to skid?
- How does the manufacturer recommend using ABS on your motorcycle?
- Picture yourself entering a contraflow system. What actions can you take to reduce risk?

Your notes

_____

_____

_____

_____

_____

_____

_____

_____

_____

_____

_____

_____

_____

_____

_____

_____

_____

 # Things to discuss and practise with your trainer

These are just a few examples of what you could discuss and practise with your trainer. Read more about safety margins to come up with your own ideas.

Discuss with your trainer

- how you should ride when you see various road markings; for example, bus-stop markings
- what lights you may use in foggy conditions
- stopping distances on dry, wet and icy roads.

Practise with your trainer

- riding in different weather conditions to practise vehicle handling; for example, in high winds or heavy rain
- leaving a two-second gap between yourself and the vehicle in front on dry roads.

Mark one answer

When will your overall stopping distance be increased?

☐ When you're riding at night

☐ When you're riding in fog

☐ When you're riding with a passenger

☐ When you're riding up a hill

When you're carrying a passenger on a motorcycle, the overall weight will be much more than when you're riding alone. This additional weight will make it harder for you to stop quickly in an emergency, so you'll need to increase the distance between your motorcycle and the vehicle in front.

Mark one answer

What's the safest way to stop when the road is wet?

☐ Change gear without braking

☐ Use the back brake only

☐ Use the front brake only

☐ Use both brakes

Motorcyclists need to take extra care when stopping on wet road surfaces. Plan well ahead so that you're able to brake in good time. For maximum stability, you should use both brakes, and brake when your motorcycle is upright and travelling in a straight line.

Mark one answer

You're riding in heavy rain. Your rear wheel skids as you accelerate. What must you do to regain control?

☐ Change down to a lower gear

☐ Ease off the throttle

☐ Brake to reduce speed

☐ Put your feet down

If you feel your back wheel beginning to skid as you accelerate, ease off the throttle. This will give your rear tyre the chance to grip the road and stop the skid.

Mark one answer

What should you do before starting a journey in the snow?

☐ Consider whether your journey is essential

☐ Try to avoid taking a passenger

☐ Plan a route avoiding towns

☐ Have a hot drink and a meal

Don't ride in snowy or icy conditions unless your journey is essential. If you must go out, try to keep to main roads, which are more likely to be treated and clear.

4.5   Mark one answer   RES s4, HC r86

Why should you ride with dipped headlights on in the daytime?

- [ ] They help other road users to see you
- [ ] They mean that you can ride faster
- [ ] Other vehicles will get out of the way
- [ ] So that they're already on when it gets dark

Making yourself as visible as possible is a positive step towards defensive riding. Having your headlights on, even in good daylight, makes it easier for other road users to see you approaching.

4.6   Mark one answer   RES s12, HC r114, 226, 236

When are motorcyclists allowed to use high-intensity rear fog lights?

- [ ] When a pillion passenger is being carried
- [ ] When they ride a large touring machine
- [ ] When visibility is 100 metres (328 feet) or less
- [ ] When they're riding on the road for the first time

If your motorcycle is fitted with high-intensity rear fog lights, you must only use them when visibility is seriously reduced. That's when you can see no further than 100 metres (328 feet). This rule about high-intensity rear fog lights applies to all motor vehicles.

4.7   Mark one answer   RES s13, HC r113–114, 226

When must you use your headlights?

- [ ] When riding in a group
- [ ] When visibility is poor
- [ ] When carrying a passenger
- [ ] When parked on an unlit road

Your headlights help you to see in the dark, and help other road users to see you. Use your headlights whenever visibility is poor. Using them at other times may also help other road users to see you. On modern motorcycles, the headlights are switched on automatically when you start the engine.

4.8   Mark one answer   RES s13

You're riding in town at night. The roads are wet after rain. How will the reflections from wet surfaces affect your safety?

- [ ] They'll make it easier to stop
- [ ] They'll make it harder to accelerate
- [ ] They'll make it easier to see unlit objects
- [ ] They'll make it harder to see unlit objects

After rain, the reflections from wet surfaces will make it hard to see unlit objects. Make sure that your visor or goggles are clean, so your vision is as clear as possible. Pedestrians will be difficult to see, especially if they're wearing dark clothing.

Mark one answer

What should you test when you've just ridden through shallow flood water?

☐ The starter motor

☐ The headlights

☐ The steering

☐ The brakes

Water can make your brakes less effective. When you're clear of the water, ride slowly while gently applying the brakes; this will dry the brakes and normal braking performance will be restored. Never ride into deep flood water because unseen hazards and strong currents can be dangerous.

Mark one answer

What should you do if you ride through shallow flood water?

☐ Ride quickly, in a high gear

☐ Ride slowly, in a high gear

☐ Ride quickly, in a low gear

☐ Ride slowly, in a low gear

If you have to ride through a flood, first check it's not too deep. Deep water is dangerous due to unseen hazards and strong currents. To ride through shallow flood water, ride slowly in a low gear. Keep the engine running fast enough to keep water out of the exhaust. You may need to slip the clutch to do this.

Mark one answer

What lights should you use if you're riding at night on a busy main road?

☐ Main-beam headlights

☐ Daytime running lights

☐ Dipped-beam headlights

☐ Rear fog lights

If there's other traffic on the road at night, use your headlights on dipped beam. Only switch to main beam when you won't dazzle other road users. At night, don't wear tinted glasses or contact lenses, or use a tinted visor, because these make it more difficult to see the road ahead.

Mark one answer

What should you do to help stay safe when you're riding in fog?

☐ Keep close to the vehicle in front

☐ Keep the vehicle in front in view

☐ Keep close to the centre of the road

☐ Keep your visor or goggles clear

You must use your dipped headlights when visibility is seriously reduced. In fog, a film of mist can form over the outside of your visor or goggles. This can further reduce your ability to see. Be aware of this hazard and keep your visor or goggles clear; anti-mist sprays can help.

4.13   Mark one answer   RES s7, 8

You're riding in heavy rain. Why should you try to avoid this marked area?

Painted lines and road markings can be very slippery, especially for motorcyclists. Try to avoid them if you can do so safely.

- ☐ It's illegal to ride over bus stops
- ☐ The painted lines may be slippery
- ☐ Cyclists may be using the bus stop
- ☐ Only emergency vehicles may drive over bus stops

4.14   Mark one answer   RES s4, HC r87

What should you do to make yourself more visible when riding at night?

- ☐ Wear reflective clothing
- ☐ Wear a tinted visor
- ☐ Ride in the middle of the road
- ☐ Give arm signals

You need to make yourself as visible as possible - from the front and back, and also from the side. Don't just rely on your headlight and tail light. Wear clothing with reflective material, as this stands out in other vehicles' headlights.

4.15   Mark one answer   RES s4

What should you do to keep warm when you're riding in extremely cold conditions?

- ☐ Stay close to the vehicles in front
- ☐ Wear suitable clothing
- ☐ Lie flat on the tank
- ☐ Put one hand on the exhaust pipe

Motorcyclists are exposed to the elements and can become very cold when riding in wintry conditions. It's important to keep warm or your concentration could be affected. The only way to stay warm is to wear suitable clothing. If you do find yourself getting cold, then stop at a suitable place to warm up.

4.16　Mark one answer　RES s4, HC r87, 115

What can you do to be seen more easily when you're riding at night?

☐ Wear reflective clothing
☐ Wear waterproof clothing
☐ Keep your motorcycle clean
☐ Stay well out to the right

It's vital to make yourself as visible as you can. Use the correct lights on your motorcycle. Wear reflective clothing and a light or brightly coloured helmet. Fluorescent clothing is effective in daytime but won't show up as well at night. Most high-visibility clothing will have a combination of fluorescent and reflective materials.

4.17　Mark one answer　RES s12

When will your overall stopping distance increase?

☐ When it's raining
☐ When it's sunny
☐ When it's dark
☐ When it's windy

Extra care should be taken in wet weather. Wet roads will affect the time it takes you to stop: your stopping distance could be as much as doubled.

4.18　Mark one answer　RES s8

Which road surface is most likely to reduce the stability of your motorcycle?

☐ Tarmac
☐ Shellgrip
☐ Concrete
☐ Loose gravel

Some road surfaces can affect the stability of a motorcycle far more than they affect other vehicles. Look out for loose or slippery road surfaces and be aware of any traffic around you. You may need to take avoiding action and change direction quickly.

4.19   Mark one answer   RES s8, HC r167

You're riding past queuing traffic. Why should you be more cautious when you approach this road marking?

When riding past queuing traffic, look out for 'keep clear' road markings, which will indicate a side road or entrance on the left. Vehicles may emerge or turn between gaps in the traffic.

☐ Lorries will be unloading here

☐ Schoolchildren will be crossing here

☐ Pedestrians will be standing in the road

☐ Traffic could be turning here

4.20   Mark one answer   RES s8

What can cause your motorcycle's tyres to lose their grip on the road surface and skid?

☐ Giving hand signals

☐ Riding one-handed

☐ Looking over your shoulder

☐ Heavy braking

You can cause your motorcycle to skid by heavy braking, as well as excessive acceleration, swerving or changing direction too sharply, and leaning over too far.

4.21   Mark one answer   RES s12, HC r227

Sometimes when you're riding in heavy rain your tyres can't displace the water fast enough. When this happens, water builds up between your tyres and the road - known as aquaplaning. What should you do to keep control when this happens?

☐ Use your rear brakes gently

☐ Steer to the crown of the road

☐ Ease off the throttle smoothly

☐ Change up to a higher gear

If your motorcycle starts to aquaplane, ease off the throttle smoothly. Don't brake or turn the steering until tyre grip has been restored.

4.22   Mark one answer   RES s12, HC r121

After riding through shallow flood water, you notice your motorcycle's brakes aren't working properly. What would be the best way to dry them out?

☐ Ride slowly, braking lightly

☐ Ride quickly, braking harshly

☐ Stop and dry them with a cloth

☐ Stop and wait for a few minutes

You can help to dry out brakes by riding slowly and applying light pressure to the brake pedal/lever. Don't ride at normal speeds until they're working normally again.

4.23   Mark one answer   RES s12, HC r226, 235

What should you do if you have to ride in foggy weather?

☐ Stay close to the centre of the road

☐ Switch on only your sidelights

☐ Switch on your dipped headlights

☐ Ride in the gutter so you can see the kerb

Only travel in fog if your journey is absolutely necessary. Fog is often patchy and visibility can reduce suddenly, without warning, so use your dipped headlights to help others to see you in these difficult conditions.

4.24   Mark one answer   RES s8, HC r126

What does the saying 'only a fool breaks the two-second rule' refer to?

☐ The time recommended when using the choke

☐ The time gap when following another vehicle in good conditions

☐ The time you should allow to restart a stalled engine

☐ The time you should keep your foot down at a junction

It's very important that you always leave a safe gap between your motorcycle and any vehicle you're following. In good conditions, you need to leave a two-second time interval.

4.25   Mark one answer   RES s9

What should a motorcyclist avoid at a mini-roundabout?

☐ Turning right

☐ Using signals

☐ Taking 'lifesavers'

☐ The painted area

Avoid riding over the painted area of a mini-roundabout, as this can become very slippery – especially when wet. At any given moment, only a small part of a motorcycle tyre makes contact with the road, so any reduction in grip can seriously affect stability.

4.26 — Mark one answer — RES s11

You're riding on an exposed stretch of motorway and there's a strong side wind. When should you anticipate the effect of the wind?

☐ As you approach a service area
☐ When you overtake a large vehicle
☐ When there's slow queuing traffic
☐ As you approach an exit slip road

Beware of side winds when riding on exposed stretches of road. Take care when overtaking large vehicles. As you pass them, you may emerge from their shelter into a gust of wind that can suddenly blow you off course. Bear in mind that strong winds can affect the stability of other road users too.

4.27 — Mark one answer — RES s8

Why should you take care when riding over this marked area?

Try to anticipate slippery road surfaces. Watch out for oil patches at places where vehicles stop for some time, such as bus stops, lay-bys and busy junctions.

☐ The next bus may be due
☐ It will alter your machine's centre of gravity
☐ Pedestrians may be waiting at the bus stop
☐ Waiting buses may have dripped oil onto the road

4.28 — Mark one answer — RES s8, HC r126

Your overall stopping distance comprises thinking distance and braking distance. You're on a good, dry road surface, with good brakes and tyres. What's the typical braking distance at 50 mph?

☐ 14 metres (46 feet)
☐ 24 metres (79 feet)
☐ 38 metres (125 feet)
☐ 55 metres (180 feet)

Various factors – such as weather and road conditions, vehicle condition and loading – affect how long it takes you to stop. You also need to add reaction time to this. The overall stopping distance at 50 mph includes a thinking distance of 15 metres (the reaction time before braking starts) plus your braking distance of 38 metres, giving a typical overall stopping distance of 53 metres (175 feet) in good conditions.

4.29   Mark one answer   RES s12, HC r126

How much can stopping distances increase in icy conditions?

☐ Two times

☐ Three times

☐ Five times

☐ Ten times

Tyre grip is greatly reduced in icy conditions. For this reason, you need to allow up to ten times the stopping distance you would allow on dry roads.

4.30   Mark one answer   RES s12, HC r232-233

What requires extra care when you're driving or riding in windy conditions?

☐ Using the brakes

☐ Moving off on a hill

☐ Turning into a narrow road

☐ Passing pedal cyclists

Always give cyclists plenty of room when overtaking them. You need to give them even more room when it's windy. A sudden gust could easily blow them off course and into your path.

4.31   Mark one answer   RES s9, HC r160

Why should you keep well to the left as you approach a right-hand bend?

Keeping to the left as you approach right-hand bends will give you an earlier view around the bend and enable you to see any hazards sooner. It also reduces the risk of collision with any oncoming vehicle that may have drifted over the centre line while taking the bend.

☐ To improve your view of the road

☐ To overcome the effect of the road's slope

☐ To let faster traffic from behind overtake

☐ To be positioned safely if you skid

4.32   **Mark one answer**   **RES s12, HC r121**

You've just gone through flood water. What should you do to make sure your brakes are working properly?

☐ Accelerate and keep to a high speed for a short time

☐ Go slowly while gently applying the brakes

☐ Avoid using the brakes at all for a few miles

☐ Stop for at least an hour to allow them time to dry

Water on the brakes will act as a lubricant, causing them to work less efficiently. Using the brakes lightly as you go along will quickly dry them out.

4.33   **Mark one answer**   **RES s12, HC r237**

What will be affected if the road surface becomes soft in very hot weather?

☐ The suspension

☐ The exhaust emissions

☐ The fuel consumption

☐ The tyre grip

If the road surface becomes very hot, it can soften. Tyres are unable to grip a soft surface as well as they can a firm dry one. Take care when cornering and braking.

4.34   **Mark one answer**   **RES s12, HC r232**

Where is your vehicle most likely to be affected by side winds?

☐ On a narrow country lane

☐ On an open stretch of road

☐ On a busy stretch of road

☐ On a long, straight road

In windy conditions, care must be taken on exposed roads. A strong gust of wind can blow you off course. Watch out for other road users who are particularly likely to be affected, such as cyclists, motorcyclists, high-sided lorries and vehicles towing trailers.

You're following a vehicle on a wet road. You stay a safe distance behind it. What should you do if a driver overtakes you and pulls into the gap you've left?

☐ Flash your headlights as a warning

☐ Try to overtake safely as soon as you can

☐ Drop back to regain a safe distance

☐ Stay close to the other vehicle until it moves on

Wet weather will affect the time it takes for you to stop and can affect your control. Your speed should allow you to stop safely and in good time. If another vehicle pulls into the gap you've allowed, ease back until you've regained your stopping distance.

You're travelling on the motorway. How can you lower the risk of a collision when the vehicle behind is following too closely?

☐ Increase your distance from the vehicle in front

☐ Brake sharply

☐ Switch on your hazard warning lights

☐ Move onto the hard shoulder and stop

On busy roads, traffic may still travel at high speeds. Don't follow the vehicle in front too closely. If a driver behind seems to be 'pushing' you, gradually increase your distance from the vehicle in front by slowing down gently. This will give you more space in front if you have to brake, and will reduce the risk of a collision involving several vehicles.

4.37 — Mark one answer — RES s12, HC r235

You're following other vehicles in fog. You have your headlights on dipped beam. What else can you do to reduce the chances of being in a collision?

- ☐ Keep close to the vehicle in front
- ☐ Use main beam instead of dipped headlights
- ☐ Keep up with the faster vehicles
- ☐ Keep a safe distance from the vehicle in front

When it's foggy, use your headlights on dipped beam. This will help you see and be seen by other road users. If visibility is seriously reduced, consider using front and rear fog lights if you have them. Keep to a sensible speed and don't follow the vehicle in front too closely. If the road is wet and slippery, you'll need to allow twice the normal stopping distance.

4.38 — Mark one answer — RES s11, HC r290

What should you do when you're using a contraflow system?

- ☐ Choose an appropriate lane in good time
- ☐ Switch lanes to make better progress
- ☐ Increase speed to get through the contraflow more quickly
- ☐ Follow other motorists closely to avoid long queues

In a contraflow system, you'll be travelling close to oncoming traffic and sometimes in narrow lanes. You should get into the correct lane in good time, obey any temporary speed-limit signs and keep a safe separation distance from the vehicle ahead.

Case study practice – 4 Safety margins

You're taking a pillion passenger to collect their new motorcycle. The weather is fine, with a strong side wind.

There's a cyclist in front and the road surface is cracked, with areas of loose and crumbled tarmac.

Further on, the traffic is heavier.

On reaching your destination, you turn right into the dealer's forecourt.

4.1 What might you need to adjust before the journey?
Mark **one** answer

☐ Tyre pressures and headlight aim

☐ Front forks and handlebar height

☐ Pillion seating and wheel alignment

☐ Passenger footrests and chain tension

RES s14

4.2 How would the weather conditions affect you?
Mark **one** answer

☐ It would be difficult to keep to the speed limits

☐ It would cause the motorcycle to use more fuel

☐ It would be difficult to hold a steady course

☐ It would reduce the overall stopping distance

RES s12 **HC r232**

4.3 How would the road surface affect the cyclist?

Mark **one** answer

- ☐ They would ride along the middle of the road
- ☐ They would get off and walk along the road
- ☐ They would try to avoid cracks and holes
- ☐ They would be able to ride faster

RES s10 **HC r213**

4.4 How would you need to ride on this road surface?

Mark **one** answer

- ☐ More slowly
- ☐ Using main-beam headlights
- ☐ More quickly
- ☐ In the highest gear possible

RES s8 **HC r213**

4.5 What should you do just before turning into the dealership?

Mark **one** answer

- ☐ Check over your right shoulder for overtaking vehicles
- ☐ Give a slowing-down arm signal
- ☐ Check over your left shoulder for overtaking vehicles
- ☐ Ask your passenger to give a right-turn arm signal

RES s3 **HC r180**

Section five

◔ Hazard awareness

In this section, you'll learn about

- static hazards; for example, parked cars, junctions, roundabouts
- moving hazards, such as pedestrians, cyclists, drivers
- road and weather conditions
- physical conditions that make someone unfit to ride.

Hazard awareness

When you start your compulsory basic training (CBT) to learn to ride, you'll be concentrating on the basic controls of your motorcycle. As your skills improve, so will your ability to recognise hazards on the road.

A hazard is a situation that may require you to respond by taking action, such as braking or steering.

Hazards can be …

static, such as parked cars, junctions or roundabouts

moving, such as pedestrians, cyclists or drivers

road and weather conditions

you, if you aren't alert and fit to ride

 The 'Perfect day' video shows what riding would be like in an ideal world.

youtube.com/thinkuk

Static hazards

There are many types of static hazard, including
- bends
- junctions
- roundabouts
- parked vehicles and obstructions in the road
- roadworks
- road surfaces
- different types of crossings
- traffic lights.

HC r153 RES s8, 9, 10

All of these may require you to respond in some way, so
- be aware that they're there
- slow down and be ready to stop if necessary.

Tip

At level crossings with traffic light signals, you **MUST** stop before the barrier when the red lights are flashing, even if the barrier isn't yet down.

HC r293

Road signs

Road signs and markings are there to give you clues about possible hazards, so it's vital that you learn their meanings. You can find them in *The Official Highway Code* (book, eBook, app and online) and *Know Your Traffic Signs* (book, eBook and online).

Watch out for signs and markings so that you can slow down in good time and are prepared for any action you may need to take. For example, if you see a sign for a bend, ask yourself 'What if there's a pedestrian or an obstruction just around the bend – could I stop in time? Could I do it safely?'

HC p106–116 RES s7 KYTS p10–71, 77–93

Parked vehicles

In busy areas, parked cars can cause a hazard – especially if they're parked badly or even illegally, for example on the zigzag lines by a pedestrian crossing.

Watch out for

- children running out from between parked vehicles
- vehicle doors opening
- vehicles moving away.

Would you be able to stop, or safely avoid them, in time?

HC r205–206 RES s8, 10

Junctions

Your view is often reduced at junctions, especially in built-up areas (for example, in towns). Take extra care and pull forward slowly until you can see well into the road. You may also be able to see reflections of traffic in the windows of buildings, such as shops.

In queuing traffic, be careful not to block a junction; leave it clear so that other vehicles can enter and emerge.

Where lanes are closed, be ready for vehicles cutting in front of you and keep a safe distance from the vehicle in front.

HC r151 RES s10

At a traffic-light-controlled junction where the lights aren't working, treat it as an unmarked junction and be prepared to stop. There may be police officers controlling traffic in these circumstances – make sure that you know and understand their signals.

HC r105, 176, p105 RES s10

Motorways and dual carriageways

If you're riding on a motorway or dual carriageway and see a hazard or obstruction ahead, you may use your hazard warning lights briefly to warn the traffic behind.

Slow-moving or stationary vehicles with a large arrow displayed on the back show where you need to change lanes as you approach roadworks.

Breakdowns

If your motorcycle breaks down and is causing an obstruction, switch on your hazard warning lights to warn other road users.

HC r116 RES s9, 11

 Find out more about what to do if you break down on a motorway at this link.

**survivegroup.org/pages/safety-information/
stopping-on-the-hard-shoulder**

Moving hazards

Moving hazards tend to be hazards caused by other types of road user.

Road user	What to do
Pedestrians	If you see pedestrians in the road, be patient and wait for them to finish crossing. On country roads there may be no pavement, so look out for pedestrians in the road. They may be walking towards you on your side of the road. **HC r205–206** RES s8, 10
Cyclists	Be aware of cyclists and give them plenty of room. They may wobble or swerve to avoid drains or potholes. At junctions or traffic lights, give cyclists time to turn or pull away. When travelling in slow traffic, before you turn left, check for cyclists filtering through the traffic on your left. **HC r211–213** RES s10

Road user	What to do

Horse riders

Horses can be unpredictable and easily spooked. Reduce your speed and give them plenty of room when you're overtaking them.

HC r215 RES s10

Drivers of large vehicles

If you see a bus at a bus stop, remember that

- people may get off and then cross the road
- the bus may be about to move off.

HC r223 RES s10

School buses might stop at places other than bus stops.

Large goods vehicles over 13 metres long have red and yellow markings at the back of the vehicle.

HC p117

At some bridges, high vehicles may need to use the centre of the road to be able to pass underneath.

HC r221 RES s10

Drivers of vehicles carrying hazardous loads

Some vehicles have information signs on the back, to show that they contain a hazardous load. Learn what the signs mean.

HC p117

Road user	What to do
Drivers overtaking you	Watch out for vehicles, especially other motorcyclists, overtaking and cutting in front of you. If you need to, drop back to keep a safe distance from the vehicle in front. When turning right, don't forget the 'lifesaver' look to your right to check for vehicles overtaking you before you make the turn. **HC r211–213** RES s10
Disabled people using powered vehicles	Reduce your speed and be careful. People using these small vehicles are extremely vulnerable on the road because • they're difficult to see • they travel slowly.
Older drivers	Older drivers may not react very quickly, so be patient with them. **HC r216** RES s10

A vehicle driving too closely behind you can be dangerous and intimidating. Move over and let the vehicle through if you can. If there's no room and the driver behind seems to be 'pushing' you, increase your distance from the vehicle in front. This will make an incident involving several vehicles less likely.

RES s10

 Tip

If it looks like the road user in front has forgotten to cancel their right indicator, be careful. Stay behind and don't overtake – they may be unsure of the position of a junction and turn suddenly.

HC r104

Find out about the hazard perception test on DVSA's YouTube channel.

youtube.com/dvsagovuk

If you have a provisional licence, you **MUST NOT**

- ride on public roads until you've successfully completed compulsory basic training (CBT)
- carry a pillion passenger
- tow a trailer
- ride on a motorway.

Until you've passed your practical riding tests, you can only ride unaccompanied on a motorcycle displaying red L plates, with an engine capacity less than 125 cc. To ride a larger machine displaying red L plates you must be

- at least 19 years old
- accompanied by a direct access scheme (DAS) trainer who's in radio contact with you
- wearing fluorescent safety clothing.

HC r253, p118–120

Road and weather conditions

Different types of weather – rain, ice, fog and even bright sunlight – can create extra hazards by making it harder to see the road or affecting your control of the vehicle. Change the way you ride to suit the weather conditions, and be aware of the added dangers.

Find out more about winter riding at this link.

bikesafe.co.uk/advice-centre/winter-riding

In these conditions...	remember to do this
Rain	Double your distance from the vehicle in front to four seconds.
Ice	Slow down and increase your separation distance: allow up to 10 times the gap you'd leave in the dry.
Fog	Slow down and use dipped headlights.
Bright sunlight	Be aware that sunlight can dazzle you or other drivers.

HC r227 RES s12

Remember that if you're wet and cold, you could lose concentration and it may take you longer to react to a hazard. Always wear proper protective clothing and footwear when riding.

Yourself

Don't allow yourself to become a hazard on the road. You need to be alert and concentrate on your riding at all times.

Awareness

Make sure you use your mirrors so that you're aware of what's going on around you at all times. These may be convex (curved outwards slightly) to give a wider field of vision.

HC r161

Tiredness

Don't ride if you're tired. Plan your journey so that you have enough rest and refreshment breaks. Try to stop at least once every two hours.

If you feel tired

- pull over at a safe and legal place to rest
- on a motorway, leave at the next exit or services.

HC r91 RES s1, 11

See the GEM Motoring Assist website for more information about riding and tiredness.

blog.motoringassist.com/road-safety/road-safety-general/dangers-fatigue

Distractions

Your concentration can be affected by

- using a hands-free phone headset
- listening to loud music
- looking at navigation equipment
- how you're feeling.

It's important to avoid being distracted by these things while you're riding.

- Turn off your mobile phone or switch it to voicemail.
- Before setting or adjusting navigation equipment or using your phone, find somewhere safe and legal to stop.
- Keep music at a reasonable volume.
- If you're upset or angry, take time to calm down before you begin riding.

When you're riding for long distances at speed, noise can make you feel tired and can damage your hearing. It's a good idea to wear ear plugs to protect your hearing when you ride.

HC r148–150 RES s1, 11

Alcohol

Never ride if you've been drinking alcohol: it's not worth taking the chance. If you ride to a social event, don't drink alcoholic drinks. If you've had a drink, find another way to get home, such as public transport, taxi, walking or getting a lift.

HC r95

Did you know?

Alcohol can

- reduce your concentration, coordination and control
- give you a false sense of confidence
- reduce your judgement of speed
- slow down your reactions.

 See the Think! road safety information on drink-driving.

think.gov.uk/road-safety-laws/#drink-driving

See the Think! road safety information on drug driving.

think.gov.uk/road-safety-laws/#drug-driving

Medicines and drugs

You must be fit to ride. Some medicines can make you sleepy: check the label or ask your doctor or pharmacist if it's safe for you to ride your motorcycle after you've taken the medicine.

HC r90, 95–96 RES s1

Using illegal drugs is highly dangerous and the effects of some can last up to 72 hours. Never take them before riding.

If you've been convicted of riding while unfit through drink or drugs, the cost of your insurance will rise considerably. Riding while under the influence of drink or drugs may even invalidate your insurance.

RES s1

 The consequences of drink and drug riding can be devastating. If you plan to ride on a night out, talk to your friends and ask them to help you stay sober. If you're caught riding over the alcohol limit you could face six months' imprisonment, an unlimited fine and a ban of at least a year.

Eyesight

Your eyesight **MUST** be of the required legal standard; if you need glasses or contact lenses to bring your eyesight up to this standard, you **MUST** wear them every time you ride. Tinted glasses, visors and goggles can restrict your vision, so you mustn't wear them for riding at night.

You **MUST** tell the licensing authority if you suffer from any medical condition that may affect your ability to ride a motorcycle.

HC r90, 92–94 RES s1

 Find out about the eyesight rules for riding at this website.

www.gov.uk

Meeting the standards

You must be able to

use visual clues to prepare you for possible hazards; for example, reflections in shop windows

judge which possible hazards are most likely to affect you, so that you can plan what to do

respond to hazards safely.

You must know and understand

methods that you can use to scan around you, both close and into the distance

which kinds of hazard you may find on different roads; for example

- tractors on country roads
- deer on forest roads
- children crossing near schools.

151

Notes

You can use this page to make your own notes or diagrams about the key points you need to remember.

Think about

- What are some examples of static hazards and why are they potentially dangerous?
- What kinds of moving hazards do you need to look out for when riding?
- What types of weather conditions can be hazardous and what can you do to reduce the risks?
- Think of the physical conditions that can make you unfit to ride. Have you experienced any? How did it affect you?

Your notes

_____

_____

_____

_____

_____

_____

_____

_____

_____

 ## Things to discuss and practise with your trainer

These are just a few examples of what you could discuss and practise with your trainer. Read more about hazard awareness to come up with your own ideas.

Discuss with your trainer

- the effects that alcohol and drugs can have on your riding
- how your riding is affected by tiredness and what you can do to help stay alert
- how to deal with other people's bad driving and riding behaviour.

Practise with your trainer

- riding through a busy town centre and identifying all the potential hazards; for example, wobbling cyclists, pedestrians, vans pulling out of junctions, etc. Discuss these after your lesson
- riding
  - up to blind junctions
  - along roads where many vehicles are parked
- identifying road markings.

What's likely to happen if you get cold and wet when you're riding a motorcycle?

☐ Your concentration will be impaired

☐ Your riding will improve

☐ Your visor will freeze up

☐ Your reactions will be quicker

When riding, make sure you wear suitable clothing for the conditions. Getting cold and wet will make you uncomfortable. This can cause you to lose concentration and considerably slow down your reaction time. Stop in a safe place to have a hot drink and warm up before this happens.

Which arm signal means 'I intend to slow down or stop'?

☐ ☐ ☐ ☐

Give your signal in good time and return your hand to the handlebars before changing speed or direction. While you're giving an arm signal you have reduced steering control and you're unable to operate some controls. If you're travelling at speed, it's generally safer to rely on your direction indicators and brake lights.

What should you do if you're about to ride home, but you can't find the glasses you need to wear?

☐ Ride home slowly, keeping to quiet roads

☐ Borrow a friend's glasses and use those

☐ Ride home at night, so that the lights will help you

☐ Find a way of getting home without riding

If you need glasses to bring your eyesight up to the legal standard for driving or riding, you must wear them whenever you ride. Don't be tempted to ride if you've lost or forgotten your glasses; you'll endanger yourself and other road users, and you'll be breaking the law.

5.4   Mark one answer   RES s1, HC r95

What is a known effect of drinking alcohol?

☐ Faster reactions

☐ Colour blindness

☐ Poor judgement

☐ Increased concentration

Even a small amount of alcohol will impair a person's judgement. It can increase confidence to a point where a person's behaviour may become 'out of character'. Someone who normally behaves sensibly may take risks and could endanger themselves and others. Don't drink and ride, or accept a lift from anyone who's been drinking.

5.5   Mark one answer   RES s4, HC r92

When must you wear your glasses if you need them to read vehicle number plates at the required distance?

☐ Only in bad weather conditions

☐ At all times when riding

☐ Only when you think it's necessary

☐ Only in bad light or at night time

Have your eyesight tested before you start your practical training. Then have checks periodically throughout your riding life, as your vision may change.

5.6   Mark one answer   RES s1, HC r95

How are you likely to be affected by drinking alcohol?

☐ You'll be more cautious and perceptive

☐ The speed of your reactions will increase

☐ Your judgement of speed will be worse

☐ Your awareness of danger will improve

Never drink if you're going to drive or ride. Your judgement can be seriously affected, even if you aren't over the drink-drive limit. Don't take risks; it isn't worth it.

5.7   Mark one answer   RES s4, HC r94

Which type of glasses shouldn't be worn when riding at night?

☐ Half-moon

☐ Round

☐ Bifocal

☐ Tinted

If you're riding at night or in poor visibility, tinted lenses or a tinted visor will reduce the amount of available light reaching your eyes, making you less able to see clearly.

When may you use your motorcycle's hazard warning lights?

☐ When you're riding on a motorway, to warn traffic behind of a hazard ahead

☐ When you're double parked on a two-way road

☐ When your direction indicators aren't working

☐ When you're riding in town, to warn oncoming traffic that you intend to stop

Hazard warning lights are an important safety feature. Use them when you're riding on a motorway to warn following traffic of danger ahead. You should also use them if your motorcycle has broken down and is causing an obstruction.

Why should you wear ear plugs when you're riding a motorcycle?

☐ To help prevent hearing damage

☐ To make you less aware of traffic

☐ To help keep you warm

☐ To make your helmet fit better

The use of ear plugs is recommended to protect your hearing from being damaged by the noise of air turbulence around your helmet. Staying within the national speed limit, a rider may experience noise levels in excess of 100 decibels.

You're going to a social event and alcohol will be available. What's the safest thing to do if you'll be riding your motorcycle shortly afterwards?

☐ Stay just below the legal limit

☐ Have soft drinks and alcohol in turn

☐ Don't go beyond the legal limit

☐ Stick to non-alcoholic drinks

Drinking even the smallest amount of alcohol can affect your judgement and reactions. The safest and best option is to avoid any alcohol at all when you know you'll be riding or driving afterwards.

How could your insurance be affected if you're convicted of riding after drinking too much alcohol?

☐ Your insurance may become invalid

☐ The amount of excess you pay will be reduced

☐ You'll only be able to get third-party cover

☐ Cover will only be given for riding smaller motorcycles

Riding while under the influence of drink or drugs can invalidate your insurance. It also endangers yourself and others. The risk isn't worth taking.

5.12	Mark one answer	RES s8

Why should you check over your shoulder before turning right into a side road?

☐ To make sure the side road is clear

☐ To check for emerging traffic

☐ To check for overtaking vehicles

☐ To confirm your intention to turn

Take a check over your shoulder before committing yourself to a manoeuvre. This is especially important when turning right, as other road users may not have seen your signal or may not understand your intentions.

5.13	Mark one answer	RES s1, HC r96

What should you do if you aren't sure whether your cough medicine will affect your ability to ride safely?

☐ Ask your doctor

☐ Don't take the medicine

☐ Ride if you feel all right

☐ Ask a friend or relative for advice

If you're taking medicine or drugs prescribed by your doctor, check to make sure they won't make you drowsy. If you forget to ask when you're at the surgery, check with your pharmacist.

5.14	Mark one answer	HC r116

When should you use hazard warning lights?

☐ When you're double-parked on a two-way road

☐ When your direction indicators aren't working

☐ When warning oncoming traffic that you intend to stop

☐ When your motorcycle has broken down and is causing an obstruction

Hazard warning lights are an important safety feature and should be used if you've broken down and are causing an obstruction. Don't use them as an excuse to park illegally, even for a short time. You may also use them on motorways to warn following traffic of danger ahead.

5.15	Mark one answer	RES s12

What hazard would you expect if you ride on a very hot day?

☐ Mud on the road

☐ A soft road surface

☐ Queuing traffic

☐ Brake fade

In very hot weather, the road surface can become soft and may melt. Take care when braking and cornering on soft tarmac, as this can lead to reduced grip and cause skidding.

Where would you expect to see these markers?

These markers must be fitted to vehicles over 13 metres long, large goods vehicles, and rubbish skips placed in the road. They're reflective to make them easier to see in the dark.

☐ On a motorway sign

☐ On a railway bridge

☐ On a large goods vehicle

☐ On a diversion sign

What's the main hazard shown in this picture?

Look at the picture carefully and try to imagine you're there. The cyclist in this picture appears to be trying to cross the road. You must be able to deal with the unexpected, especially when you're approaching a hazardous junction. Look well ahead to give yourself time to deal with any hazards.

☐ Vehicles turning right

☐ Vehicles doing U-turns

☐ The cyclist crossing the road

☐ Parked cars around the corner

5.18
Mark one answer   RES s8, HC r191

Which road user has caused a hazard?

☐ The parked car (arrowed A)

☐ The pedestrian waiting to cross
(arrowed B)

☐ The moving car (arrowed C)

☐ The car turning (arrowed D)

The car arrowed A is parked within the area marked by zigzag lines at the pedestrian crossing. Parking here is illegal. It also

• blocks the view for pedestrians wishing to cross the road

• restricts the view of the crossing for approaching traffic.

5.19
Mark one answer   RES s8, HC r195

What should the driver of the car approaching the crossing do?

☐ Continue at the same speed

☐ Sound the horn

☐ Drive through quickly

☐ Slow down and get ready to stop

Look well ahead to see whether any hazards are developing. This will give you more time to deal with them in the correct way. The man in the picture is clearly intending to cross the road. You should be travelling at a speed that allows you to check your mirror, slow down and stop in good time. You shouldn't have to brake harshly.

What should the driver of the grey car be especially aware of?

When passing parked cars, there's a risk that a driver or passenger may not check before opening the door into the road. A defensive driver will drive slowly and be looking for people who may be about to get out of their car.

☐ The uneven road surface

☐ Traffic following behind

☐ Doors opening on parked cars

☐ Empty parking spaces

What should you expect if you see this sign ahead?

This sign indicates that the road will bend sharply to the left. Slow down in plenty of time and select the correct gear before you start to turn. Braking hard and late, while also sharply changing direction, is likely to cause a skid.

☐ The road will go steeply uphill

☐ The road will go steeply downhill

☐ The road will bend sharply to the left

☐ The road will bend sharply to the right

5.22   **Mark one answer**   **RES s10, HC r211-213**

What should you do as you approach this cyclist?

Keep well back and give the cyclist time and room to turn safely. Don't intimidate them by getting too close or trying to squeeze past.

☐ Try to overtake before the cyclist gets to the junction

☐ Flash your headlights at the cyclist

☐ Slow down and allow the cyclist to turn

☐ Rev your engine so the cyclist knows you're following behind

5.23   **Mark one answer**   **RES s10, HC r146**

Why must you take great care when emerging from this junction?

You may have to pull forward slowly until you can see up and down the road. Be aware that the traffic approaching the junction can't see you either. If you don't know that it's clear, don't go.

☐ The road surface is poor

☐ The footpath is narrow

☐ The kerbs are high

☐ The view is restricted

Which type of vehicle should you be ready to give way to as you approach this bridge?

A bus or high-sided lorry will have to take a position in the centre of the road to clear the bridge. There's normally a sign to show this. Look well ahead, past the bridge and be ready to stop and give way to large oncoming vehicles.

- ☐ Bicycles
- ☐ Buses
- ☐ Motorcycles
- ☐ Cars

What type of vehicle could you expect to meet in the middle of the road?

The highest point of the bridge is in the centre, so a large vehicle might have to move to the centre of the road to have enough room to pass safely under the bridge.

- ☐ Lorry
- ☐ Bicycle
- ☐ Car
- ☐ Motorcycle

5.26

Mark one answer   RES s7, HC r171

What must you do at this junction?

The 'stop' sign has been put here because the view into the main road is poor. You must stop because it won't be possible to take proper observation while you're moving.

☐ Stop behind the line, then edge forward to see clearly

☐ Stop beyond the line, at a point where you can see clearly

☐ Stop only if there's traffic on the main road

☐ Stop only if you're turning right

5.27

Mark one answer   RES s1, HC r147

What should you do if a driver pulls out of a side road in front of you, causing you to brake hard?

☐ Ignore the error and stay calm

☐ Flash your lights to show your annoyance

☐ Sound your horn to show your annoyance

☐ Overtake as soon as possible

Be tolerant if a vehicle emerges and you have to brake quickly. Anyone can make a mistake, so don't react aggressively. Be alert where there are side roads and be especially careful where there are parked vehicles, because these can make it difficult for emerging drivers to see you.

5.28

Mark one answer   RES s1, HC r216

How would age affect an older person's driving ability?

☐ They won't be able to obtain car insurance

☐ They'll need glasses to read road signs

☐ They'll take longer to react to hazards

☐ They won't signal at junctions

As people age, their reaction time gets slower. The rate of decline varies from person to person but you can expect them to take longer to react to a hazard and they may be hesitant in some situations – for example, at a junction.

5.29
Mark one answer
RES s1, 11, HC r91

Do you need to plan rest stops when you're planning a long journey?

☐ Yes, you should plan to stop every half an hour

☐ Yes, regular stops help concentration

☐ No, you'll be less tired if you get there as soon as possible

☐ No, only fuel stops will be needed

Try to plan your journey so that you can take rest stops. It's recommended that you take a break of at least 15 minutes after every two hours of driving or riding. This should help to maintain your concentration.

5.30
Mark one answer
RES s7, HC r291-299

What should you do if the red lights start flashing as you approach a level crossing?

☐ Go over it quickly

☐ Go over it carefully

☐ Stop before the barrier

☐ Switch on your hazard warning lights

At level crossings, the red lights flash before and while the barrier is down. At most crossings, an amber light will precede the red lights. You must stop behind the white line unless you've already crossed it when the amber light comes on. Don't be tempted to zigzag around half-barriers.

5.31
Mark one answer
RES s7, HC r176

You're approaching a crossroads. What should you do if the traffic lights have failed?

☐ Brake and stop only for large vehicles

☐ Brake sharply to a stop before looking

☐ Be prepared to brake sharply to a stop

☐ Be prepared to stop for any traffic

When approaching a junction where the traffic lights have failed, you should proceed with caution. Treat the situation as an unmarked junction and be prepared to stop.

5.32 Mark one answer RES s10, HC r206-207

What should the driver of the red car (arrowed) do?

☐ Wave towards the pedestrians who are waiting to cross

☐ Wait for the pedestrian in the road to cross

☐ Quickly drive behind the pedestrian in the road

☐ Tell the pedestrian in the road she shouldn't have crossed

Some people might take a long time to cross the road. They may be older or have a disability. Be patient and don't hurry them by showing your impatience. If pedestrians are standing at the side of the road, don't signal or wave them to cross. Other road users might not have seen your signal and this could lead the pedestrians into a hazardous situation.

5.33 Mark one answer RES s8, HC r154

You're following a slower-moving vehicle. What should you do if there's a junction just ahead on the right?

☐ Overtake after checking your mirrors and signalling

☐ Only consider overtaking when you're past the junction

☐ Accelerate quickly to overtake before reaching the junction

☐ Slow down and prepare to overtake on the left

You should never overtake as you approach a junction. If a vehicle emerged from the junction while you were overtaking, a dangerous situation could develop very quickly.

What should you do as you approach this overhead bridge?

Oncoming large vehicles may need to move to the middle of the road to pass safely under the bridge. There won't be enough room for you to continue, so you should be ready to stop and wait.

☐ Move out to the centre of the road before going through

☐ Find another route; this one is only for high vehicles

☐ Be prepared to give way to large vehicles in the middle of the road

☐ Move across to the right-hand side before going through

Why are vehicle mirrors often slightly curved (convex)?

☐ They give a wider field of vision

☐ They totally cover blind spots

☐ They make it easier to judge the speed of the traffic behind

☐ They make the traffic behind look bigger

Although a convex mirror gives a wide view of the scene behind, you should be aware that it won't show you everything behind or to the side of your vehicle. Before you move off, you'll need to look over your shoulder to check for anything not visible in the mirrors.

5.36 Mark one answer RES s11, HC p113, 117, KYTS p135

You're travelling on a three-lane motorway. How should you overtake a slow-moving lorry in the middle lane if it's showing this sign?

This sign is found on slow-moving or stationary works vehicles. If you wish to overtake it, do so on the left, as indicated. Be aware that there might be workmen in the area.

☐ Cautiously approach the lorry, then overtake on either side

☐ Follow the lorry until you can leave the motorway

☐ Use the right-hand lane and overtake the lorry normally

☐ Approach with care and overtake on the left of the lorry

5.37 Mark one answer HC r104

What should you do if you think the driver of the vehicle in front has forgotten to cancel their right indicator?

Be cautious and don't attempt to overtake. The driver may be unsure of the location of a junction and may turn suddenly.

☐ Flash your lights to alert the driver

☐ Sound your horn before overtaking

☐ Overtake on the left if there's room

☐ Stay behind and don't overtake

What's the main hazard the driver of the red car (arrowed) should be aware of?

If you can do so safely, give way to buses signalling to move off at bus stops. Try to anticipate the actions of other road users around you. The driver of the red car should be prepared for the bus pulling out. As you approach a bus stop, look to see how many passengers are waiting to board. If the last one has just got on, the bus is likely to move off.

☐ Glare from the sun may affect the driver's vision

☐ The black car may stop suddenly

☐ The bus may move out into the road

☐ Oncoming vehicles will assume the driver is turning right

What type of vehicle displays this yellow sign?

Buses which carry children to and from school may stop at places other than scheduled bus stops. Be aware that they might pull over at any time to allow children to get on or off. This will normally be when traffic is heavy during rush hour.

☐ A broken-down vehicle

☐ A school bus

☐ An ice-cream van

☐ A private ambulance

5.40   Mark one answer   RES s10, HC r205-206

What hazard should you be aware of when travelling along this street?

On roads where there are many parked vehicles, you might not be able to see children between parked cars and they may run out into the road without looking.

- ☐ Glare from the sun
- ☐ Lack of road markings
- ☐ Children running out between vehicles
- ☐ Large goods vehicles

5.41   Mark one answer   RES s10, HC r213

What's the main hazard you should be aware of when following this cyclist?

When following a cyclist, be aware that they have to deal with the hazards around them. They may wobble or swerve to avoid a pothole in the road or see a potential hazard and change direction suddenly. Don't follow them too closely or rev your engine impatiently.

- ☐ The cyclist may move to the left and dismount
- ☐ The cyclist may swerve into the road
- ☐ The cyclist may get off and push their bicycle
- ☐ The cyclist may wish to turn right at the end of the road

A driver's behaviour has upset you. How can you get over this incident safely?

☐ Stop and take a break

☐ Shout abusive language

☐ Gesture to them with your hand

☐ Follow them, flashing your headlights

If you feel yourself becoming tense or upset, stop in a safe place and take a break. Tiredness can make things worse and may cause a different reaction to upsetting situations.

How should you drive in areas with traffic-calming measures?

Traffic-calming measures such as road humps, chicanes and narrowings are intended to slow drivers down to protect vulnerable road users. Don't speed up until you reach the end of the traffic-calmed zone.

☐ At a reduced speed

☐ At the speed limit

☐ In the centre of the road

☐ With headlights on dipped beam

Why should you slow down as you approach this hazard?

You should be slowing down and selecting the correct gear in case you have to stop at the level crossing. Look for the signals and be prepared to stop if necessary.

☐ Because of the level crossing

☐ Because it's hard to see to the right

☐ Because of approaching traffic

☐ Because of animals crossing

5.45 — Mark one answer — RES s7, HC p116, KYTS p70-71

Why are place names painted on the road surface?

- ☐ To restrict the flow of traffic
- ☐ To warn of oncoming traffic
- ☐ To help you select the correct lane in good time
- ☐ To prevent you from changing lanes

The names of towns and cities may be painted on the road at busy junctions and complex road systems. They guide you into the correct lane in good time, allowing traffic to flow more freely.

5.46 — Mark one answer — HC r135

Some two-way roads are divided into three lanes. Why are they particularly dangerous?

- ☐ Traffic in both directions can use the middle lane to overtake
- ☐ Traffic can travel faster in poor weather conditions
- ☐ Traffic can overtake on the left
- ☐ Traffic uses the middle lane for emergencies only

If you intend to overtake, you must consider that approaching traffic could be planning the same manoeuvre. When you've considered the situation and decided it's safe, indicate your intentions early. This will show the approaching traffic that you intend to pull out.

5.47 — Mark one answer — RES s10, HC r220

What type of vehicle uses an amber flashing beacon on a dual carriageway?

- ☐ An ambulance
- ☐ A fire engine
- ☐ A doctor on call
- ☐ A tractor

An amber flashing beacon on a vehicle indicates that it's moving slowly or stopped and a possible hazard. Look well ahead on a dual carriageway and you should be able to see and respond to these vehicles in good time.

What does this signal from a police officer mean to oncoming traffic?

Police officers may need to direct traffic; for example, at a junction where the traffic lights have broken down. Check your copy of The Highway Code for the signals that they use.

☐ Go ahead
☐ Stop
☐ Turn left
☐ Turn right

Why should you be cautious when going past this bus waiting at a bus stop?

A bus at a bus stop can hide pedestrians who might try to cross the road just in front of it. Drive at a speed that will enable you to respond safely if you have to.

☐ There's a zebra crossing ahead
☐ There are driveways on the left
☐ People may cross the road in front of it
☐ The road surface will be slippery

5.50
Mark one answer   RES s8, HC r162-167

Where would it be unsafe to overtake?

☐ On a single carriageway

☐ On a one-way street

☐ Approaching a junction

☐ Travelling up a long hill

You should overtake only when it's really necessary and you can see it's clear ahead. Look out for road signs and markings that show it's illegal or would be unsafe to overtake; for example, approaching junctions or bends. In many cases, overtaking is unlikely to significantly improve your journey time.

5.51
Mark one answer   HC r95

How can drinking alcohol affect your ability to drive?

☐ Your ability to judge speed will be reduced

☐ Your confidence will be reduced

☐ Your reactions will be faster

☐ Your awareness of danger will be improved

Alcohol will severely reduce your ability to drive or ride safely and there are serious consequences if you're caught over the drink-drive limit. It's known that alcohol can

• affect your judgement
• cause overconfidence
• reduce coordination and control.

Case study practice – 5 Hazard awareness

Your rear-view mirrors are convex and give a wide-angle field of view.

You're travelling to a local pub to see some friends, and you stay for several hours.

At the end of the evening, you ride home. The weather has changed and it's raining steadily.

There's a skip parked on the road ahead, showing a flashing beacon and vertical markings.

5.1 How would the reflections in your mirrors differ from those in a normal mirror?

Mark **one** answer

☐ They would be larger

☐ They would be brighter

☐ They would be smaller

☐ They would be dimmer

RES s5

5.2 What's the safest thing to do while you're with your friends?

Mark **one** answer

☐ Drink pints of shandy

☐ Alternate soft drinks with alcoholic drinks

☐ Drink shorts with lots of water

☐ Drink soft drinks the whole time

RES s1 **HC r95**

5.3 How would the conditions affect visibility during your journey home?

Mark **one** answer

☐ By making you less visible to others

☐ By making it easier for you to see others

☐ By making the street lights seem brighter

☐ By making it easier for others to see you

RES s10 **HC r126**

5.4 On the ride home, how large a time gap should you leave between your motorcycle and any vehicle you're following?

Mark **one** answer

☐ Two seconds

☐ Three seconds

☐ Four seconds

☐ Five seconds

RES s11 **HC r227**

5.5 What colour is the flashing beacon?

Mark **one** answer

☐ Amber

☐ Blue

☐ Green

☐ White

HC p117

Section six

Vulnerable road users

In this section, you'll learn about

- who is particularly vulnerable on the road
- how to help keep other road users safe.

Vulnerable road users

As a motorcyclist, you'll share the road with many other road users. Some of these are more vulnerable than you, because of their

- inexperience or lack of judgement
- size
- speed
- unpredictable behaviour.

Among the most vulnerable road users are

- pedestrians – especially children and older people
- cyclists
- other motorcyclists
- horse riders.

Remember to treat all road users with courtesy and consideration. It's particularly important to be patient when there are children, older or disabled people using the road.

The most vulnerable drivers and riders are those who are still learning, inexperienced or older. Keep calm and make allowances for them.

Pedestrians

People walking on or beside the road – pedestrians – are vulnerable because they move more slowly than other road users and have no protection if they're involved in a collision. Everybody is a pedestrian at some time, but not every pedestrian has the understanding of how to use roads safely.

Pedestrians normally use a pavement or footpath. Take extra care if they have to walk in the road – for example, when the pavement is closed for repairs or on country roads where there's no pavement. Always check for road signs that indicate people may be walking in the road.

HC r206 RES s10 KYTS p13

177

On country roads, it's usually safest for pedestrians to walk on the right-hand side of the road, so that they're facing oncoming traffic and can see the vehicles approaching.

HC r2

A large group of people, such as those on an organised walk, may walk on the left-hand side. At night, the person at the front of the group should show a white light while the person at the back of the group should show a bright red light to help approaching drivers to see them.

HC r5

Watch out for pedestrians already crossing when you're turning into a side road. They have priority, so allow them to finish crossing.

HC r170 RES s9

 Tip
When you see a bus stopped on the other side of the road, watch out for pedestrians who may come from behind the bus and cross the road, or dash across the road from your left to catch the bus.

HC r223 RES s10

Pedestrian crossings

Pedestrian crossings allow people to cross the road safely: be ready to slow down and stop as you approach them. Make sure you know how different types of crossing work. See section 2, Attitude, for more details.

Remember that you should never park on or near a pedestrian crossing; for example, on the zigzag lines either side of a zebra crossing.

HC r195–199 RES s8

 Do you find that riding near vulnerable road users makes you anxious? Focusing on what *might* happen means that your concentration is taken away from the road. Ask your trainer to help you by talking through stress management techniques. And don't be afraid to ask for additional practice!

Tip

Look for tell-tale signs that someone is going to cross the road between parked cars, such as

- seeing their feet when looking between the wheels of the parked cars
- a ball bouncing out into the road
- a bicycle wheel sticking out between cars.

Slow down and be prepared to stop.

HC r205 RES s10

Children

Children are particularly vulnerable as road users because they can be unpredictable. They're less likely than other pedestrians to look before stepping into the road.

See this link for information on teaching road safety to children.

http://think.gov.uk/education-resources/

Ride carefully near schools.

There may be flashing amber lights under a school warning sign, to show that children are likely to be crossing the road on their way to or from school. Slow down until you're clear of the area.

Be prepared for a school crossing patrol to stop the traffic by stepping out into the road with a stop sign. You **MUST** obey the stop signal given by a school crossing patrol.

Ride carefully near schools.

Don't wait or park on yellow zigzag lines outside a school. A clear view of the crossing area outside the school is needed by

- drivers and riders on the road
- pedestrians on the pavement.

HC r208–210, 238 RES s7, 10 KYTS p56

Buses and coaches carrying schoolchildren show a special sign in the back. This tells you that they may stop often, and not just at normal bus stops.

HC r209, p117 RES s10

Older and disabled pedestrians

If you see older people about to cross the road ahead, be careful as they may have misjudged your speed.

If they're crossing, be patient and allow them to cross in their own time: they may need extra time to cross the road.

HC r207 RES s10

A pedestrian with hearing difficulties may have a dog with a distinctive yellow or burgundy coat.

Take extra care as they may not be aware of vehicles approaching.

A person carrying a white stick with a red band is both deaf and blind. They may also have a guide dog with a red and white checked harness.

HC r207 RES s10

Cyclists

Cyclists should normally follow the same rules of the road as drivers, but they're slower and more vulnerable than other vehicles.

 Find out about cycling safely at this link.

bikeability.org.uk

Cycle routes

In some areas there may be special cycle or shared cycle and pedestrian routes, which are marked by signs.

KYTS p35–36

At traffic lights, advanced stop lines are sometimes marked on the road so that cyclists can stop in front of other traffic. When the lights are red or about to become red, you should stop at the first white line.

HC r178

Overtaking cyclists

If you're overtaking a cyclist, give them as much room as you would a car. They may swerve

- to avoid an uneven road surface
- if a gust of wind blows them off course.

HC r211–213 RES s8, 10

A cyclist travelling at a low speed, or glancing over their shoulder to check for traffic, may be planning to turn right. Stay behind and give them plenty of room.

Never overtake a slow-moving vehicle just before you turn left. Hold back and wait until it has passed the junction before you turn.

Cyclists at junctions

When you're emerging from a junction, look carefully for cyclists. They're not as easy to see as larger vehicles. Also look out for cyclists emerging from junctions.

HC r77, 187 RES s9

Be aware of cyclists at a roundabout. They travel at lower speeds and are more vulnerable than other road users, and may decide to stay in the left-hand lane whichever direction they're planning to take. Hold back and allow plenty of room.

Other motorcyclists

Motorcyclists can be hard to see because their vehicles are smaller than cars. They're usually fast-moving too, so they can be very vulnerable in a collision.

Remember to leave enough room while overtaking another motorcycle; the rider may swerve to avoid an uneven surface or be affected by a gust of wind. Look carefully for motorcyclists at junctions too, as they may be easily hidden by other vehicles, **street furniture** or other roadside features, such as trees.

street furniture
objects and pieces of equipment on roads and pavements; for example, street lights and signs, bus stops, benches, bollards, etc.

Before you turn right, always check for other traffic, especially other motorcyclists, who may be overtaking. Always use the 'lifesaver' look before making your manoeuvre.

HC r180

 See the Think! road safety information about riding safely near motorcyclists.

think.gov.uk/road-safety-laws/#motorcycling

When you're moving in queues of traffic, be aware that other motorcyclists may also

- filter between lanes
- cut in just in front of you
- pass very close to you.

Check your mirrors for motorcycles approaching from behind and give them space if possible.

If there's a slow-moving motorcyclist ahead and you're not sure what the rider is going to do, stay behind them in case they change direction suddenly.

HC r180 RES s9

If a motorcyclist is injured in an incident, get medical assistance. Don't remove their helmet unless it's essential.

HC r283 RES s16

Animals

Horses and other animals can behave in unpredictable ways on the road because they get frightened by the noise and speed of vehicles. Always ride carefully if there are animals on the road.

- Stay well back.
- Don't rev your engine or sound your horn near horses as this may startle them.
- Go very slowly and be ready to stop.

When it's safe to overtake

- ride past slowly
- leave plenty of room.

HC r214–215 RES s10

Take extra care when approaching a roundabout. Horse riders, like cyclists, may keep to the left, even if they're signalling right. Stay well back.

HC r187, 215 RES s9

 See the Think! road safety advice about horses on the road.

http://think.gov.uk/road-safety-laws/#horses

Visit this web page for more advice on passing horses safely.

bhs.org.uk/our-work/safety/dead-slow

Drivers

Drivers, especially those who are inexperienced or older, may not react as quickly as you to what's happening on the road. Learner drivers and riders may make mistakes, such as stalling at a junction. Be patient and be ready to slow down or stop if necessary.

HC r216–217 RES s1

 Tip
A flashing amber beacon on the top of a vehicle means it's a slow-moving vehicle. A powered wheelchair or mobility scooter **MUST** have a flashing amber light when travelling on a dual carriageway with a speed limit that exceeds 50 mph.

HC r220

If you find another vehicle is following you too closely in fast-moving traffic, slow down gradually to increase your distance from the vehicle in front. This gives you more room to slow down gradually or stop if necessary, and so reduces the risk of the vehicle behind crashing into you because the driver hasn't left enough room to stop safely.

Learner riders and drivers, and newly qualified riders and drivers

Statistics show that 17- to 25-year-olds are the most likely to be involved in a road traffic incident. Over-confidence, lack of experience and poor judgement are the main causes of incidents for young and new drivers and riders.

Newly qualified riders can decrease their risk of being involved in road traffic incidents by taking further training; for example, the enhanced rider scheme.

HC p134 RES s11

 Find out more about the enhanced rider scheme at this website.

www.gov.uk

Meeting the standards

You must be able to

look out for the effect of starting your engine near vulnerable road users. Passing cyclists or pedestrians may be affected

look for vulnerable road users at junctions, roundabouts and crossings. For example
- cyclists
- other motorcyclists
- horse riders.

You must know and understand

when other road users are vulnerable and how to allow for them

the rules that apply to vulnerable road users, like cyclists, and the position that they may select on the road as a result

how vulnerable road users may act on the road. For example
- cyclists may wobble
- children may run out
- older people may take longer to cross the road.

Notes

You can use this page to make your own notes or diagrams about the key points you need to remember.

Think about

- Which types of pedestrian crossing might you see, and what are the differences between them?
- When might you need to watch out for children near the road?
- Which disability might a person have if they're walking with a dog that has a red and white checked harness?
- What might a cyclist be about to do if they're checking over their shoulder?
- What mustn't you do when riding near horses or other animals on the road?

Your notes

_____

_____

_____

_____

_____

_____

_____

_____

_____

_____

_____

Things to discuss and practise with your trainer

These are just a few examples of what you could discuss and practise with your trainer. Read more about vulnerable road users to come up with your own ideas.

Discuss with your trainer

- which sticks are used by people with different disabilities; for example, a white stick with a red band
- what you think a cyclist's experience of riding through traffic may be? How can you make them feel safer?
- where pedestrians may have to walk in the road and what you should look out for.

Practise with your trainer

- riding near schools at times when students and parents are likely to be arriving or leaving
- riding up to different types of crossing to practise how to respond to their users and any lights
- identifying the signs warning you of vulnerable road users, such as a red triangle with a picture of a bicycle. Discuss these after your lesson.

6.1   Mark one answer   RES s10, HC r222

You're following a lorry. Why should you stay well back from these vehicles?

- ☐ So you don't breathe in the lorry's exhaust fumes
- ☐ So wind from the lorry won't slow you down
- ☐ So drivers behind can see you
- ☐ So your view ahead isn't obstructed

If you follow a large vehicle too closely, your view beyond it will be restricted. Drop back. This will help you to see more of the road ahead. It will also help the driver of the large vehicle to see you in their mirrors and will give you a safe separation distance if the lorry needs to stop suddenly.

6.2   Mark one answer   RES s10, HC r214

You're riding a motorcycle along a country lane. What should you do if you come across cattle on the road?

- ☐ Ride up close behind them
- ☐ Rev your engine
- ☐ Give them plenty of room
- ☐ Sound your horn

Try not to startle the animals. They can be easily frightened by noise or by traffic passing too closely. Slow down, give them plenty of room and be prepared to stop if necessary. Obey any directions given by people in charge of the animals.

6.3   Mark one answer   RES s10

What should you do if a driver begins to emerge into your path from a side road on the left?

- ☐ Slow down and be ready to stop
- ☐ Let them emerge, then ride close behind
- ☐ Turn into the side road
- ☐ Brake hard, then wave them out

You should always be looking for vehicles emerging from side roads as you approach them. If you see another vehicle begin to emerge into your path, be ready to slow down or stop if necessary.

6.4   Mark one answer   RES s10, HC r204, 217

What should you do when you're following a car that's being driven by a learner?

- ☐ Keep calm and be patient
- ☐ Ride close behind
- ☐ Put your headlights on main beam
- ☐ Sound your horn and overtake

Learner drivers might take longer to react to traffic situations, so be patient and give them time. Don't unnerve them by riding close behind or showing signs of impatience.

6.5 — Mark one answer — RES s8, HC r126

You're riding in fast-flowing traffic. What should you do if the vehicle behind is following too closely?

☐ Slow down gradually to increase the gap in front of you

☐ Slow down as quickly as possible by braking

☐ Accelerate to get away from the vehicle behind you

☐ Apply the brakes sharply to warn the driver behind

By increasing the separation distance between you and the vehicle in front, you have a greater safety margin. If the vehicle in front of you brakes suddenly to avoid a hazard, you'll have time to reduce speed gradually. This will reduce the risk of the close-following vehicle running into you.

6.6 — Mark one answer — RES s8, HC r195

You're riding towards a zebra crossing. What should you do if there's a person in a wheelchair waiting to cross?

☐ Continue on your way

☐ Wave to the person to cross

☐ Wave to the person to wait

☐ Be prepared to stop

As you would with any pedestrian, you should prepare to stop. Don't wave the person across, as other traffic may not slow down.

6.7 — Mark one answer — RES s12, HC r233

Why should you allow extra room when overtaking another motorcyclist on a windy day?

☐ The rider may turn off suddenly to get out of the wind

☐ The rider may be blown across in front of you

☐ The rider may stop suddenly

☐ The rider may be travelling faster than normal

On a windy day, be aware that the blustery conditions might blow you or other motorcyclists out of position. Think about this before deciding to overtake.

6.8　Mark one answer　RES s8, HC r198

You've stopped at a pelican crossing, where a disabled person is crossing very slowly in front of you. What should you do when the lights change to green?

☐ Allow the person to finish crossing
☐ Edge forward slowly
☐ Ride behind the person
☐ Sound your horn

At a pelican crossing, the green light means you may proceed as long as the crossing is clear. If someone hasn't finished crossing, be patient and wait until the road is clear.

6.9　Mark one answer　RES s9, HC r170

Where should you take particular care to look out for other motorcyclists and cyclists?

☐ On dual carriageways
☐ At junctions
☐ At zebra crossings
☐ On one-way streets

Other motorcyclists and cyclists may be difficult to see on the road, particularly at junctions. If your view is blocked by other traffic, you may not be able to see them approaching.

6.10　Mark one answer　RES s8

Why is it recommended for a rider to make a lifesaver check before turning right?

☐ To check for any overtaking traffic
☐ To confirm that they're about to turn
☐ To make sure the side road is clear
☐ To check that the rear indicator is flashing

The lifesaver glance makes you aware of what's happening behind and alongside you before you alter your course. This glance must be timed so that you still have time to react if it isn't safe to carry out your manoeuvre.

6.11　Mark one answer　RES s10, HC r214

You're about to overtake a group of horse riders. What's most likely to scare the horses?

☐ Your dipped headlights
☐ Giving arm signals
☐ Riding slowly
☐ Revving your engine

When passing horses, allow them plenty of space and slow down. Animals can be frightened by sudden or loud noises, so don't sound your horn or rev your engine.

6.12

Mark one answer

RES s1

Why are young and new motorcyclists involved in more incidents than other motorcyclists?

☐ They use borrowed equipment

☐ They lack experience and judgement

☐ They ride in bad weather conditions

☐ They don't maintain their motorcycles

Young and inexperienced motorcyclists are far more likely to be involved in incidents than more experienced riders. The reasons for this include natural exuberance, showing off, competitive behaviour and overconfidence. Don't overestimate your abilities and never ride too fast for the conditions.

6.13

Mark one answer

RES s1

Why is someone new to motorcycling especially vulnerable?

☐ They're not used to wearing motorcycling gear

☐ They're more alert than older riders

☐ They lack of experience

☐ They don't understand the rules of the road

Young and inexperienced motorcyclists often have more confidence than ability. It takes time to gain experience and become a good rider. Make sure you have the right attitude and put safety first.

6.14

Mark one answer

HC r236, p116, KYTS p56

The road outside this school is marked with yellow zigzag lines. What do these lines mean?

Parking here will block the view of the road, endangering the lives of children crossing the road on their way to and from school.

☐ You may park on the lines when dropping off schoolchildren

☐ You may park on the lines when picking up schoolchildren

☐ You must not wait or park your motorcycle here

☐ You must stay with your motorcycle if you park here

Which sign means that there may be people walking along the road?

Always check the road signs. Triangular signs are warning signs: they inform you about hazards ahead and help you to anticipate any problems. There are a number of different signs showing pedestrians. Learn the meaning of each one.

What should you do if you want to turn left at a junction where pedestrians have started to cross?

When you're turning into a side road, pedestrians who are crossing have priority. You should wait to allow them to finish crossing safely. Be patient if they're slow or unsteady. Don't try to rush them by sounding your horn, flashing your lights, revving your engine or giving any other inappropriate signal.

- ☐ Go around them, leaving plenty of room
- ☐ Stop and wave at them to cross
- ☐ Sound your horn and proceed
- ☐ Give way to them

What hazard should you be especially aware of if you're turning left into a side road?

- ☐ One-way street
- ☐ Pedestrians
- ☐ Traffic congestion
- ☐ Parked vehicles

Make sure that you've reduced your speed and are in the correct gear for the turn. Look into the road before you turn and always give way to any pedestrians who are crossing.

| 6.18 | Mark one answer | RES s9, HC r211 |

Why should you check for motorcyclists just before turning right into a side road?

☐ They may be overtaking on your left

☐ They may be following you closely

☐ They may be emerging from the side road

☐ They may be overtaking on your right

Never attempt to change direction to the right without first checking your right-hand mirror and blind spot. A motorcyclist might not have seen your signal and could be hidden by other traffic. This observation should become a matter of routine.

| 6.19 | Mark one answer | RES s8, HC r25 |

Why is a toucan crossing different from other crossings?

☐ Moped riders can use it

☐ It's controlled by a traffic warden

☐ It's controlled by two flashing lights

☐ Cyclists can use it

Toucan crossings are shared by pedestrians and cyclists, who are permitted to cycle across. They're shown the green light together. The signals are push-button-operated and there's no flashing amber phase.

| 6.20 | Mark one answer | RES s8, HC r210 |

How will a school crossing patrol signal you to stop?

☐ By pointing to children waiting to cross

☐ By displaying a red light

☐ By displaying a 'stop' sign

☐ By giving you an arm signal

If a school crossing patrol steps out into the road with a 'stop' sign, you must stop. Don't wave anyone across the road and don't get impatient or rev your engine.

Where would you see this sign?

Vehicles that are used to carry children to and from school will be travelling at busy times of the day. If you're following a vehicle with this sign, be prepared for it to make frequent stops. It might pick up or set down passengers in places other than normal bus stops.

☐ In the window of a car taking children to school

☐ At the side of the road

☐ At playground areas

☐ On the rear of a school bus or coach

What does this sign mean?

This sign shows a shared route for pedestrians and cyclists: when it ends, the cyclists will be rejoining the main road.

☐ No route for pedestrians and cyclists

☐ A route for pedestrians only

☐ A route for cyclists only

☐ A route for pedestrians and cyclists

6.23
Mark one answer   RES s10, HC r207

You see a pedestrian carrying a white stick that also has a red band. What does this mean?

When someone is deaf as well as blind, they may carry a white stick with a red reflective band or bands. They may not be aware that you're approaching and they may not be able to hear anything; so, for example, your horn would be ineffective as a warning to them.

☐ They have limited mobility

☐ They're deaf

☐ They're blind

☐ They're deaf and blind

6.24
Mark one answer   RES s10, HC r207

What would you do if you see older people crossing the road ahead?

Be aware that older people might take a long time to cross the road. They might also be hard of hearing and not hear you approaching. Don't hurry older people across the road by getting too close to them or revving your engine.

☐ Wave them across so they know that you've seen them

☐ Be patient and allow them to cross in their own time

☐ Rev the engine to let them know that you're waiting

☐ Tap the horn in case they're hard of hearing

6.25   Mark one answer   RES s10, HC r207

What should you do when you see an older person about to cross the road ahead?

☐ Expect them to wait for you to pass

☐ Speed up to get past them quickly

☐ Stop and wave them across the road

☐ Be careful; they may misjudge your speed

Older people may have impaired hearing, vision, concentration and judgement. They may also walk slowly and so could take a long time to cross the road.

6.26   Mark one answer   RES s9, HC r187

You're approaching a roundabout. What should you do if a cyclist ahead is signalling to turn right?

☐ Overtake on the right

☐ Give a warning with your horn

☐ Signal the cyclist to move across

☐ Give the cyclist plenty of room

If you're following a cyclist who's signalling to turn right at a roundabout, leave plenty of room. Give them space and time to get into the correct lane.

6.27   Mark one answer   RES s8, HC r163

Which vehicle should you allow extra room as you overtake them?

☐ Lorry

☐ Tractor

☐ Bicycle

☐ Road-sweeper

Don't pass cyclists too closely, as they may

- need to veer around a pothole, drain or other hazard
- be buffeted by side wind
- be made unsteady by your vehicle.

Always leave as much room as you would for a car, and don't cut in front of them.

6.28   Mark one answer   RES s10, HC r211

Why should you look carefully for motorcyclists and cyclists at junctions?

☐ They may want to turn into the side road

☐ They may slow down to let you turn

☐ They're harder to see

☐ They might not see you turn

Cyclists and motorcyclists are smaller than other vehicles and so are more difficult to see. They can easily be hidden from your view by cars parked near a junction.

6.29
Mark one answer   RES s10, HC r211

You're waiting to come out of a side road. Why should you look carefully for motorcycles?

☐ Motorcycles are usually faster than cars

☐ Police patrols often use motorcycles

☐ Motorcycles can easily be hidden behind obstructions

☐ Motorcycles have right of way

If you're waiting to emerge from a side road, look carefully for motorcycles: they can be difficult to see. Be especially careful if there are parked vehicles or other obstructions restricting your view.

6.30
Mark one answer   RES s4, HC r86

Why do motorcyclists use dipped headlights in daylight?

☐ So that the rider can be seen more easily

☐ To stop the battery overcharging

☐ To improve the rider's vision

☐ The rider is inviting you to proceed

A motorcycle can be lost from sight behind another vehicle. The use of headlights helps to make it more conspicuous and therefore more easily seen.

6.31
Mark one answer   RES s4, HC r86

Why do motorcyclists wear bright clothing?

☐ They must do so by law

☐ It helps keep them cool in summer

☐ The colours are popular

☐ To make them more visible

Motorcycles and scooters are generally smaller than other vehicles and can be difficult to see. Wearing bright clothing makes it easier for other road users to see a motorcyclist approaching, especially at junctions.

6.32
Mark one answer   RES s8, HC r212

Why do motorcyclists often look round over their right shoulder just before turning right?

☐ To listen for traffic behind them

☐ Motorcycles don't have mirrors

☐ It helps them balance as they turn

☐ To check for traffic in their blind area

When you see a motorcyclist take a glance over their shoulder, they're probably about to change direction. Recognising a clue like this helps you to anticipate their next action. This can improve road safety for you and others.

6.33

Mark one answer

RES s10, HC r207, 211

Which is the most vulnerable road user?

☐ Car driver

☐ Tractor driver

☐ Lorry driver

☐ Motorcyclist

Pedestrians and riders on two wheels can be harder to see than other road users. Make sure you look for them, especially at junctions. Effective observation, coupled with appropriate action, can save lives.

6.34

Mark one answer

RES s9, HC r187, 215

You're approaching a roundabout. What should you do if there are horses being ridden in front of you?

☐ Sound your horn as a warning

☐ Treat them like any other vehicle

☐ Give them plenty of room

☐ Accelerate past as quickly as possible

Horse riders often keep to the outside of the roundabout even if they're turning right. Give them plenty of room and remember that they may have to cross lanes of traffic.

6.35

Mark one answer

RES s8, HC r207

As you approach a pelican crossing, the lights change to green. What should you do if older people are still crossing?

☐ Wave them to cross as quickly as they can

☐ Rev your engine to make them hurry

☐ Flash your lights in case they haven't noticed you

☐ Wait patiently while they cross

If the lights turn to green, wait for any pedestrians to clear the crossing. Allow them to finish crossing the road in their own time, and don't try to hurry them by revving your engine.

6.36   **Mark one answer**   RES s7, 8, 10, HC r208

What action should you take when you see flashing amber lights under a school warning sign?

The flashing amber lights are switched on to warn you that children may be crossing near a school. Slow down and take extra care, as you may have to stop.

☐ Reduce speed until you're clear of the area

☐ Keep up your speed and sound the horn

☐ Increase your speed to clear the area quickly

☐ Wait at the lights until they stop flashing

6.37   **Mark one answer**   RES s7, HC r208, 238, KYTS p56

Why should these road markings be kept clear?

The markings are there to show that the area should be kept clear. This is to allow an unrestricted view for

• approaching drivers and riders
• children wanting to cross the road.

☐ To allow children to be dropped off at school

☐ To allow teachers to park

☐ To allow children to be picked up after school

☐ To allow children to see and be seen when they're crossing the road

Where would you see this sign?

School buses can stop to pick up or drop off schoolchildren at places that aren't designated bus stops. Watch out for children crossing the road to catch the bus or from the far side of the bus if they've just been dropped off.

☐ Near a school crossing

☐ At a playground entrance

☐ On a school bus

☐ At a 'pedestrians only' area

You're following two cyclists as they approach a roundabout in the left-hand lane. Where would you expect the cyclists to go?

Cyclists approaching a roundabout in the left-hand lane may be turning right but may not have been able to get into the correct lane due to heavy traffic. They may also feel safer keeping to the left all the way around the roundabout. Be aware of them and give them plenty of room.

☐ Left

☐ Right

☐ Any direction

☐ Straight ahead

You're travelling behind a moped. What should you do if you want to turn left a short distance ahead?

Passing the moped and turning into the junction could mean that you cut across the front of the rider. This might force them to slow down, stop or even lose control. Stay behind the moped until it has passed the junction and then you can turn without affecting the rider.

☐ Overtake the moped before the junction

☐ Pull alongside the moped and stay level until just before the junction

☐ Sound your horn as a warning and pull in front of the moped

☐ Stay behind until the moped has passed the junction

6.41   Mark one answer   RES s9, HC r187, 215

You see a horse rider as you approach a roundabout. What should you do if they're signalling right but keeping well to the left?

☐ Proceed as normal

☐ Keep close to them

☐ Cut in front of them

☐ Stay well back

Allow the horse rider to enter and exit the roundabout in their own time. They may feel safer keeping to the left all the way around the roundabout. Don't get up close behind or alongside them, because that would probably upset the horse and create a dangerous situation.

6.42   Mark one answer   RES s1, HC r217

How should you react to inexperienced drivers?

☐ Sound your horn to warn them of your presence

☐ Be patient and prepare for them to react more slowly

☐ Flash your headlights to indicate that it's safe for them to proceed

☐ Overtake them as soon as possible

Learners might not have confidence when they first start to drive. Allow them plenty of room and don't react adversely to their hesitation. We all learn from experience, but new drivers will have had less practice in dealing with all the situations that might occur.

6.43   Mark one answer   RES s1, HC r217

What should you do when you're following a learner driver who stalls at a junction?

☐ Be patient, as you expect them to make mistakes

☐ Stay very close behind and flash your headlights

☐ Start to rev your engine if they take too long to restart

☐ Immediately steer around them and drive on

Learning to drive is a process of practice and experience. Try to understand this and tolerate those who make mistakes while they're learning.

Mark one answer RES s10, HC r5, 154

You're travelling on a country road that has no pavement. What should you anticipate finding on your side of the road?

☐ Motorcycles

☐ Bicycles

☐ Pedestrians

☐ Horse riders

On a quiet country road, always be aware that there may be a hazard just around the next bend, such as a slow-moving vehicle or pedestrians. Pedestrians are advised to walk on the right-hand side of the road if there's no pavement, so they may be walking towards you on your side of the road.

6.45 **Mark one answer** RES s9, HC r182, 212

You're following a cyclist. What should you do when you wish to turn left a short distance ahead?

Make allowances for cyclists, and give them plenty of room. Don't overtake and then immediately turn left. Be patient and turn behind them when they've passed the junction.

☐ Overtake the cyclist before you reach the junction

☐ Pull alongside the cyclist and stay level until after the junction

☐ Hold back until the cyclist has passed the junction

☐ Go around the cyclist on the junction

6.46 **Mark one answer** RES s9, HC r187, 215

A horse rider is in the left-hand lane approaching a roundabout. Where should you expect the rider to go?

☐ In any direction

☐ To the right

☐ To the left

☐ Straight ahead

Horses and their riders move more slowly than other road users. They might not have time to cut across heavy traffic to take up a position in the right-hand lane. For this reason, a horse and rider may approach a roundabout in the left-hand lane even though they're turning right.

6.47   Mark one answer   RES s10, HC r220

Powered vehicles used by disabled people are small and can be hard to see. What must they display if they're travelling on a dual carriageway?

☐ Flashing red beacon

☐ Flashing green beacon

☐ Flashing blue beacon

☐ Flashing amber beacon

Powered vehicles used by disabled people are small and low making them hard to see on the road. They also travel very slowly. On an unrestricted dual carriageway, they must display a flashing amber beacon to warn other road users of their presence.

6.48   Mark one answer   HC r225

What does it mean when a moving vehicle is showing a flashing amber beacon?

☐ The vehicle is slow moving

☐ The vehicle has broken down

☐ The vehicle is a doctor's car

☐ The vehicle belongs to a school crossing patrol

Different coloured beacons warn of different types of vehicle needing special attention. Blue beacons are used on emergency vehicles that need priority. Green beacons are found on doctors' cars. Amber beacons generally denote slower moving vehicles, which are often large. These vehicles are usually involved in road maintenance or local amenities and make frequent stops.

6.49   Mark one answer   HC p107, KYTS p35

What does this sign mean?

Usually, a picture of a cycle will also be painted on the road, and sometimes the lane will have a different coloured surface. Leave these areas clear for cyclists and don't pass too closely when you overtake.

☐ Contraflow cycle lane

☐ With-flow cycle lane

☐ Cycles and buses only

☐ No cycles or buses

Mark one answer   RES s10, HC r215

What should you do when you see these horse riders in front?

Be particularly careful when approaching horse riders – slow down and be prepared to stop. Always pass wide and slowly, and look out for signals given by the riders. Horses are unpredictable: always treat them as potential hazards and take great care when passing them.

☐ Pull out to the middle of the road

☐ Slow down and be ready to stop

☐ Switch on your hazard warning lights

☐ Give a right-turn signal

Mark one answer   RES s7, HC r208, 238, KYTS p56

What's the purpose of these road markings?

These markings are found on the road outside schools. Don't stop or park on them, even to set down or pick up children. The markings are there to ensure that drivers, riders, children and other pedestrians have a clear view of the road in all directions.

☐ To ensure children can see and be seen when they're crossing the road

☐ To enable teachers to have clear access to the school

☐ To ensure delivery vehicles have easy access to the school

☐ To enable parents to pick up or drop off children safely

Mark one answer   RES s10, HC r2, 206

What should you do if the left-hand pavement is closed due to street repairs?

☐ Watch out for pedestrians walking in the road

☐ Use your right-hand mirror more often

☐ Speed up to get past the roadworks more quickly

☐ Position close to the left-hand kerb

Where street repairs have closed off pavements, proceed carefully and slowly, as pedestrians might have to walk in the road.

6.53   **Mark one answer**   **RES s10, HC r213**

What should you do when you're following a motorcyclist along a road that has a poor surface?

☐ Follow closely so they can see you in their mirrors

☐ Overtake immediately to avoid delays

☐ Allow extra room in case they swerve to avoid potholes

☐ Allow the same room as normal to avoid wasting road space

To avoid being unbalanced, a motorcyclist might swerve to avoid potholes and bumps in the road. Be prepared for this and allow them extra space.

6.54   **Mark one answer**   **HC p109, KYTS p36**

What does this sign mean?

☐ No cycling

☐ Cycle route ahead

☐ Cycle parking only

☐ End of cycle route

More people are cycling today and cycle routes are being extended in our towns and cities to provide safe cycling routes. Respect the presence of cyclists on the road and give them plenty of room if you need to pass.

You're approaching this roundabout. What should you do when a cyclist is keeping to the left while signalling to turn right?

Cycling in today's heavy traffic can be hazardous. Some cyclists may not feel safe crossing the path of traffic to take up a position in an outside lane. Be aware of this and understand that, although they're in the left-hand lane, the cyclist might be turning right.

- ☐ Sound your horn
- ☐ Overtake them
- ☐ Assume they're turning left
- ☐ Allow them space to turn

What should you do when you're approaching this crossing?

Be courteous and prepare to stop. Don't wave people across, because this could be dangerous if another vehicle is approaching the crossing.

- ☐ Prepare to slow down and stop
- ☐ Stop and wave the pedestrians across
- ☐ Speed up and pass by quickly
- ☐ Continue unless the pedestrians step out

6.57   Mark one answer   RES s10, HC r207

What does it mean if you see a pedestrian with a dog that has a yellow or burgundy coat?

- ☐ The pedestrian is an older person
- ☐ The pedestrian is a dog trainer
- ☐ The pedestrian is colour-blind
- ☐ The pedestrian is deaf

Dogs trained to help deaf people have a yellow or burgundy coat. If you see one, you should take extra care, as the pedestrian may not be aware of vehicles approaching.

6.58   Mark one answer   RES s8, HC r25

Who may use toucan crossings?

- ☐ Motorcyclists and cyclists
- ☐ Motorcyclists and pedestrians
- ☐ Only cyclists
- ☐ Cyclists and pedestrians

There are some crossings where cycle routes lead cyclists to cross at the same place as pedestrians. These are called toucan crossings. Always look out for cyclists, as they're likely to be approaching faster than pedestrians.

6.59   Mark one answer   HC r178

This junction, controlled by traffic lights, has a marked area between two stop lines. What's this for?

These are known as advanced stop lines. When the lights are red (or about to become red), you should stop at the first white line. However, if you've crossed that line as the lights change, you must stop at the second line even if it means you're in the area reserved for cyclists.

- ☐ To allow taxis to position in front of other traffic
- ☐ To allow people with disabilities to cross the road
- ☐ To allow cyclists and pedestrians to cross the road together
- ☐ To allow cyclists to position in front of other traffic

Mark one answer RES s8, HC r211–213

You're about to overtake a cyclist. Why should you leave them as much room as you would give to a car?

☐ The cyclist might speed up

☐ The cyclist might get off their bicycle

☐ The cyclist might be unsettled if you pass too near them

☐ The cyclist might have to make a left turn

Before overtaking, assess the situation. Look well ahead to see whether the cyclist will need to change direction. Be especially aware of a cyclist approaching parked vehicles, as they'll need to alter course. Don't pass too closely or cut in sharply as this could unsettle the rider.

Mark one answer RES s10, HC r214

What should you do when you're passing loose sheep on the road?

Slow down and be ready to stop if you see animals in the road ahead. Animals are easily frightened by noise and vehicles passing too close to them. Stop if you're signalled to do so by the person in charge.

☐ Briefly sound your horn

☐ Go very slowly

☐ Pass quickly but quietly

☐ Herd them to the side of the road

6.62	Mark one answer	HC r5

At night, what does it mean if you see a pedestrian wearing reflective clothing and carrying a bright red light?

☐ You're approaching roadworks

☐ You're approaching an organised walk

☐ You're approaching a slow-moving vehicle

☐ You're approaching a traffic danger spot

The people on the walk should be keeping to the left, but don't assume this. Pass carefully, making sure you have time to do so safely. Be aware that the pedestrians have their backs to you and may not know that you're there.

6.63	Mark one answer	HC p134

You've just passed your driving test. How can you reduce your risk of being involved in a collision?

☐ By always staying close to the vehicle in front

☐ By never going over 40 mph

☐ By staying in the left-hand lane on all roads

☐ By taking further training

New drivers and riders are often involved in a collision or incident early in their driving career. Due to a lack of experience, they may not react to hazards appropriately. Approved training courses are offered by driver and rider training schools for people who have passed their test but want extra training.

Case study practice – 6 Vulnerable road users

You live in a village and you're riding your motorcycle into town. As you leave the village, sheep are being herded across the road ahead.

Once in town, traffic is heavy. At a pelican crossing, amber lights are flashing and people are still crossing.

Later, you need to turn left into a side road where pedestrians are just beginning to cross.

Further along on your side of the road, there's a stationary refuse collection vehicle.

6.1 How should you behave as you leave the village?
Mark **one** answer

☐ Stop the motorcycle and wait until the animals have crossed

☐ Get off the motorcycle and wheel it past the animals

☐ Move slowly forward and ride through the herd

☐ Rev the engine to hurry the animals across

RES s10 HC r214

6.2 At the pelican crossing, what should you do?
Mark **one** answer

☐ Stop, but keep revving the engine to hurry the pedestrians up

☐ Stop and give way to the pedestrians crossing

☐ Keep moving slowly forward while the lights are flashing

☐ Keep going and ride slowly past the pedestrians

HC r196

6.3 What should you do at the left turn?

Mark **one** answer

☐ Get off and wheel the motorcycle on the pavement

☐ Indicate, then ride slowly round the pedestrians

☐ Flash your headlights and use the horn before turning

☐ Give way to the pedestrians crossing

RES s9 **HC r170**

6.4 What should you expect by the stationary vehicle?

Mark **one** answer

☐ Binmen

☐ Builders

☐ Cyclists

☐ Children

HC r225

6.5 What colour beacon does the vehicle at the end of your journey have?

Mark **one** answer

☐ Amber

☐ Red

☐ Blue

☐ Green

HC r225

Section seven

 Other types of vehicle

In this section, you'll learn about

- different types of vehicles
- safety when riding towards or following other types of vehicle.

Other types of vehicle

When you're riding towards or following another type of vehicle, such as a bus or a lorry, you need to be aware of that vehicle's capabilities and how they differ from those of your motorcycle.

Other motorcycles

Windy weather has a big effect on motorcyclists. Other motorcyclists can be blown into your path, so

- if you're overtaking another motorcyclist, allow extra room
- if a motorcyclist in front of you is overtaking a high-sided vehicle, keep well back, as they could be blown off course
- be particularly aware of other motorcyclists where there are side-wind warning signs.

HC r232–233, p109 RES s12

Tip

Side winds are likely to affect

- cyclists
- motorcyclists
- drivers towing caravans or trailers
- drivers of high-sided vehicles

more than car drivers. If you're following or overtaking, be aware that these vehicles might be blown off course, and give them extra room.

RES s12

Metal drain covers can become very slippery in wet weather and are particularly hazardous for two-wheeled vehicles. Take care to avoid uneven or slippery surfaces and watch out for other motorcyclists having to do so.

HC r213 RES s10

Large vehicles

Large vehicles can make it difficult for you to see the road ahead. Keep well back if you're following a large vehicle, especially if you're planning to overtake. If another vehicle fills the gap you've left, drop back further. This will improve your view of the road ahead.

HC r164, 222 RES s8

Overtaking a large vehicle is risky because it takes more time to overtake than a car.

Keep well back until you can see that the road ahead is clear. This also helps the driver of the large vehicle to see you in their mirrors.

HC r164 RES s8, 12

Never begin to overtake unless you're sure that you can complete the manoeuvre safely.

In wet weather, large vehicles throw up a lot of spray. This can affect your view, and your vision, if your visor becomes smeared or dirty. Drop back further until you can see better. If the conditions make it difficult for you to see or be seen, use dipped headlights. If visibility is reduced to less than 100 metres (328 feet), you may use fog lights (if fitted).

If your visor or goggles mist up, stop and clean them to make sure that your vision isn't restricted before continuing.

HC r226 RES s11, 12

Tip

If you're riding downhill and a large vehicle coming uphill needs to move out to pass a parked car, slow down and give way if possible. It's much more difficult for large vehicles to stop and then start up again if they're going uphill.

RES s8

Stay well back and give large vehicles plenty of room as they approach or negotiate

- road junctions
- crossroads
- mini-roundabouts.

To get around a corner, long vehicles may need to move in the opposite direction to the one they're indicating. If they want to turn left, they may indicate left but move over to the right before making the turn, and vice versa.

HC r221 RES s9

If you're waiting to turn left from a minor road and a large vehicle is approaching from the right, think. It may seem as if there's time to turn but there could be an overtaking vehicle hidden from view.

Buses

Bus drivers need to make frequent stops to pick up and set down passengers. If a bus pulls up at a bus stop, watch out for pedestrians who may get off and cross the road in front of or behind the bus. Be prepared to give way to a bus that's trying to move off from a bus stop, as long as it's safe to do so.

HC r223 RES s10

Trams

Some cities have trams. Take extra care around them because they

- are very quiet
- move quickly
- can't steer to avoid you.

HC r223–224 RES s7, 8

In these cities there may be extra white light signals at some traffic lights, which are for tram drivers. When you're riding in an area where trams run, take care when crossing tram tracks, particularly in bad weather, as they can become very slippery.

RES s7, 8

Powered vehicles used by disabled people

Powered vehicles used by disabled people, such as wheelchairs and mobility scooters, have a maximum speed limit of 8 mph (12 km/h) when used on the road.

HC r36, 220

Meeting the standards

You must be able to

look out for other road users and predict what they may do

monitor and manage your own reactions to other road users.

You must know and understand

the rules that apply to other road users and the positions they may select on the road as a result. For example

- drivers of large vehicles
- bus and coach drivers
- cyclists
- car drivers

the importance of predicting the actions of other road users, especially as many motorcycle crashes involve claims of 'I just didn't see you!' from others.

Notes

You can use this page to make your own notes or diagrams about the key points you need to remember.

Think about

- What conditions could make you or another motorcyclist swerve unexpectedly?
- When do you need to give large vehicles plenty of space?
- What should you watch out for when a bus has stopped at the side of the road?
- What do you need to be aware of when riding in an area that has trams?

Your notes

_____

_____

_____

_____

_____

_____

_____

_____

 ## Things to discuss and practise with your trainer

These are just a few examples of what you could discuss and practise with your trainer. Read more about other types of vehicle to come up with your own ideas.

Discuss with your trainer

- how windy weather can affect the way that motorcyclists ride. What can you do to allow for this when you encounter another motorcyclist in these conditions?
- the maximum speed of powered wheelchairs and how you should behave when you need to overtake one
- how trams operate and what to look out for if you encounter a tram system.

Practise with your trainer

- how to behave when you're following a large vehicle, particularly at junctions and roundabouts
- overtaking large vehicles and noting how this differs from overtaking a car
- how to react to buses in a busy town centre.

7.1 — Mark one answer — RES s9, HC r221

You're riding behind a long vehicle as it approaches a mini-roundabout. What should you do if the vehicle is signalling left, but is positioned to the right?

- ☐ Sound your horn
- ☐ Overtake on the left
- ☐ Keep well back
- ☐ Flash your headlights

Long vehicles need more room than other vehicles to turn at junctions. The driver may take up a position that seems strange, but they have to do this to ensure their rear wheels don't mount the kerb as they turn. Don't overtake on the left – the driver won't expect you to be there and may not see you. Staying well back will also give you a better view ahead.

7.2 — Mark one answer — RES s7, HC r302

Why should you be careful when you're riding on roads where trams also operate?

- ☐ Trams can't steer to avoid you
- ☐ Trams give off harmful exhaust fumes
- ☐ Trams are noisy and slow
- ☐ Trams can brake very quickly

Trams run on rails and can't deviate from the tracks. Keep a lookout for trams, as they move very quietly and you may not notice them approaching. Be particularly careful of the rails – they can be very slippery, especially when they're wet.

7.3 — Mark one answer — RES s12, HC r213, p109, KYTS p12

You're about to overtake a slow-moving motorcyclist. Which sign would make you take special care?

☐   ☐

☐   ☐

In windy weather, watch out for motorcyclists and also cyclists, as they can be blown sideways into your path. When you pass them, leave plenty of room and check their position in your mirror before pulling back in.

7.4 | Mark one answer | RES s9, HC r164, 222

You're waiting to turn right out of a minor road. It's clear to the left but a lorry is coming from the right. Why should you wait, even if you have enough time to turn?

☐ Anything overtaking the lorry will be hidden from view

☐ The lorry could suddenly speed up

☐ The lorry might be slowing down

☐ The load on the lorry might be unstable

Large vehicles can hide other vehicles that are overtaking – especially motorcycles. You need to be aware of the possibility of hidden vehicles and not assume that it's safe to turn.

7.5 | Mark one answer | RES s10, HC r221

You're following a long vehicle as it approaches a crossroads. What should you do if it signals left but moves out to the right?

☐ Get closer in order to pass it quickly

☐ Stay well back and give it room

☐ Assume the signal is wrong and that it's turning right

☐ Overtake it as it starts to slow down

A long vehicle may need to swing out in the opposite direction as it approaches a turn, to allow the rear wheels to clear the kerb. Don't try to filter through if you see a gap; as the lorry turns, the gap will close.

7.6 | Mark one answer | RES s10, HC r221

You're following a long vehicle approaching a crossroads. What should you do if the driver signals right but moves close to the left-hand kerb?

☐ Warn the driver about the wrong signal

☐ Wait behind the long vehicle

☐ Report the driver to the police

☐ Overtake on the right-hand side

When a long vehicle is going to turn right, it may need to keep close to the left-hand kerb. This is to prevent the rear end of the trailer cutting the corner. You need to be aware of how long vehicles behave in such situations. Don't overtake the lorry, because it could turn as you're alongside. Stay behind and wait for it to turn.

Mark one answer   RES s10, HC r187

You're approaching a mini-roundabout. What should you do if a long vehicle in front signals left but positions over to the right?

☐ Sound your horn

☐ Overtake on the left

☐ Follow the same course as the lorry

☐ Keep well back

At mini-roundabouts, there isn't much room for a long vehicle to manoeuvre. It will have to swing out wide so that it can complete the turn safely. Keep well back and don't try to move up alongside it.

7.8   Mark one answer   RES s10, HC r164, 222

You're travelling on a single carriageway road. Why should you keep well back while you're following a large vehicle?

☐ To give yourself acceleration space if you decide to overtake

☐ To get the best view of the road ahead

☐ To leave a gap in case the vehicle stops and rolls back

☐ To offer other drivers a safe gap if they want to overtake you

When following a large vehicle, keep well back. If you're too close, you won't be able to see the road ahead and the driver of the long vehicle might not be able to see you in their mirrors.

7.9   Mark one answer   RES s10, HC r223

You're travelling behind a bus. What should you do if it pulls up at a bus stop?

☐ Accelerate past the bus

☐ Look for pedestrians

☐ Sound your horn

☐ Pull in closely behind the bus

People may be running to catch the bus or passengers leaving the bus might wish to cross the road in front of the bus. Look out for them if you intend to go past it. Consider how many people are waiting to get on the bus – check the queue if you can. The bus might move off straight away if no-one is waiting to get on.

If a bus is signalling to pull out, give it priority if it's safe to do so.

7.10   Mark one answer   RES s10, HC r222, 227

You're following a lorry on a wet road. What should you do when spray makes it difficult to see the road ahead?

Large vehicles can throw up a lot of spray when it's wet. This makes it difficult for drivers behind to see the road ahead. You'll be able to see more by dropping back further, out of the spray. This will also increase your separation distance, giving you more room to stop if you have to.

☐ Drop back until you can see better

☐ Put your headlights on full beam

☐ Keep close to the lorry, away from the spray

☐ Speed up and overtake quickly

7.11   Mark one answer   RES s10, HC r164, 222

You're leaving a safe gap as you follow a large vehicle. What should you do if a car moves into this gap?

☐ Sound your horn

☐ Drop back further

☐ Flash your headlights

☐ Start to overtake

Sometimes your separation distance is shortened by a driver moving into the gap you've allowed. When this happens, react positively, stay calm and drop further back to re-establish a safe following distance.

7.12   Mark one answer   RES s10, HC r223

What should you do when you're approaching a bus that's signalling to move away from a bus stop?

☐ Get past before it moves

☐ Allow it to pull away, if it's safe to do so

☐ Flash your headlights as you approach

☐ Signal left and wave the bus on

Try to give way to buses if you can do so safely, especially when the driver signals to pull away from a bus stop. Look out for people getting off the bus or running to catch it, because they may cross the road without looking. Don't accelerate to get past the bus, and don't flash your lights, as this could mislead other road users.

What should you do if you want to overtake a long, slow-moving vehicle on a busy road?

- ☐ Follow it closely and keep moving out to see the road ahead
- ☐ Flash your headlights for the oncoming traffic to give way
- ☐ Stay behind until the driver waves you past
- ☐ Keep well back so that you get a good view of the road ahead

When you're following a long vehicle, stay well back so that you can get a better view of the road ahead. The closer you get, the less you'll be able to see of the road. Be patient and don't take a gamble. Only overtake when you're certain that you can complete the manoeuvre safely.

Which vehicles are least likely to be affected by side wind?

- ☐ Cyclists
- ☐ Motorcyclists
- ☐ High-sided vehicles
- ☐ Cars

Although cars are the least likely to be affected, side winds can take anyone by surprise. This is most likely to happen after overtaking a large vehicle, when passing gaps between hedges or buildings, and on exposed sections of road.

What should you do as you approach this lorry?

When turning, long vehicles need much more room on the road than other vehicles. At junctions, they may take up the whole of the road space, so be patient and allow them the room they need.

- ☐ Slow down and be prepared to wait
- ☐ Make the lorry wait for you
- ☐ Flash your lights at the lorry
- ☐ Move to the right-hand side of the road

7.16
Mark one answer
RES s9, HC r221

You're following a large vehicle as it approaches a crossroads. What should you do if the driver signals to turn left?

☐ Overtake if you can leave plenty of room

☐ Overtake if there are no oncoming vehicles

☐ Wait for the driver to cancel his signal

☐ Wait for the vehicle to finish turning

Hold back and wait until the vehicle has turned before proceeding. Don't overtake, because the vehicle turning left could hide another vehicle emerging from the same junction.

7.17
Mark one answer
RES s8, HC r164

Why is it more difficult to overtake a large vehicle than a car?

☐ It will take longer to overtake a large vehicle

☐ A large vehicle will be fitted with a speed limiter

☐ A large vehicle will have air brakes

☐ It will take longer for a large vehicle to accelerate

Depending on relative speed, it will usually take you longer to pass a lorry than other vehicles. Hazards to watch for include oncoming traffic, junctions ahead, bends or dips that could restrict your view, and signs or road markings that prohibit overtaking. Make sure you can see that it's safe to complete the manoeuvre before you start to overtake.

Case study practice – 7 Other types of vehicle

> You travel to work in the town centre on your 1000 cc motorcycle. It's a dull, wet day.
>
> There are many trams in town, and a bus is indicating to pull out from a bus stop.
>
> At the first junction, you have to cross tramlines.
>
> On the main high street, you see specifically shaped signs for tram drivers.
>
> Ahead, you see a large vehicle indicating to turn left.

7.1 How can you improve your visibility in this weather?

Mark **one** answer

☐ By using main-beam headlights

☐ By using hazard warning lights

☐ By using dipped headlights

☐ By using front and rear fog lights

RES s4 **HC r86**

7.2 How should you react to the bus?

Mark **one** answer

☐ Rev the engine and sound the horn

☐ Keep going past but slow down a little

☐ Speed up quickly to get past the bus

☐ Allow it to pull out if it's safe to do so

HC r223

7.3 Why should you take care at the first junction?

Mark **one** answer

☐ The tyres could get stuck between the tracks

☐ The lines could be very slippery

☐ The motorcycle's tyres could stick to the metal

☐ The gaps in the lines could be full of water

RES s8 **HC r306**

7.4 What shape are the signs you see?

Mark **one** answer

☐ Triangle

☐ Diamond

☐ Hexagon

☐ Rectangle

KYTS p31

7.5 What might the large vehicle do next?

Mark **one** answer

☐ Pull a little over to the right

☐ Use the horn to warn others

☐ Pull a little over to the left

☐ Run over the pavement area

RES s9 **HC r170, 221**

Section eight

 # Road conditions and motorcycle handling

In this section, you'll learn about

- how to ride safely in different weather conditions
- riding at night
- keeping control of your motorcycle
- traffic-calming measures and different road surfaces.

Road conditions and motorcycle handling

As well as being aware of other road users, you need to think about the conditions you're riding in and how they might affect your safety. The weather, the time of day, hills, traffic calming and different road surfaces can all change the way you need to ride.

Weather conditions

The weather makes a big difference to how you ride and how your motorcycle will handle.

Rain and wet conditions

When it's raining or the road is wet, leave at least double the normal stopping distance between you and the vehicle in front. If you're following a vehicle at a safe distance and another vehicle pulls into the gap you've left, drop back until you're at a safe distance again. See section 4, Safety margins, for more information on stopping distances.

If visibility becomes seriously reduced, you **MUST** use dipped headlights. 'Seriously reduced' means you can't see for more than about 100 metres (328 feet).

HC r226 RES s12

When there's been heavy rainfall, a ford is likely to flood and become difficult to cross. There may be a depth gauge to help you decide whether you should go through. If you decide to cross it

- use a low gear
- ride through slowly
- test your brakes afterwards: wet brakes are less effective.

HC r121 RES s12

Fog

When visibility is seriously reduced, you **MUST** use headlights and you may also use fog lights if you have them.

Remember to switch off your fog lights when conditions improve. Never use front or rear fog lights unless visibility is seriously reduced because

- they can dazzle other road users
- road users behind you won't be able to see your brake lights clearly, so they may not react in time to stop safely
- road users behind you may mistake your fog lights for brake lights and slow unnecessarily.

In foggy weather, you can't see as far as you can in good conditions, so always keep your speed down. Increase your distance from the vehicle in front in case it stops or slows suddenly.

HC r114, 226 RES s11, 12

Tip
Always allow more time for your journey in bad weather.

When riding on motorways in fog, reflective studs help you to see the road ahead and also help you to know which lane you're in.

- Red studs mark the left-hand edge of the carriageway.
- Amber studs mark the central reservation.

For more details, see section 9, Motorway riding.

HC r132 RES s7, 11

If you're parking on the road in foggy conditions, leave the parking lights switched on.

Very bad weather

In very bad weather, such as heavy snow or thick fog, don't travel unless your journey is essential. If you must travel, take great care and allow plenty of time.

Before you start your journey, make sure

- your lights are working
- your screen (if fitted) and visor are clean.

HC r228–235 RES s11, 12

When you're on the road, keep well back from the vehicle in front in case it stops suddenly. In icy conditions your stopping distance can be 10 times what it would be in dry conditions.

Tip
If the road looks wet and your tyres are making hardly any noise, you could be on black ice. Keep your speed down and use the highest gear possible to reduce the risk of skidding.

See this website for advice on riding in extreme weather conditions.

bikesafe.co.uk/advice-centre/winter-riding

Windy weather

Windy weather can affect all vehicles, but high-sided vehicles, cyclists, motorcyclists and cars towing caravans are likely to be the worst affected. A sudden gust may catch your motorcycle when you're

- passing a large vehicle on a dual carriageway or motorway
- riding on an exposed stretch of road
- passing gaps between buildings or hedges.

Look out for other vehicles that may also be affected by the wind and make allowances for them.

HC r232 RES s11, 12

Riding at night

When you're riding at night, you need to think about how clearly you can see and be seen, as well as how your lights might affect other road users.

Make sure that your headlights don't dazzle the vehicle you're following or any oncoming traffic. If you're dazzled by the headlights of an oncoming vehicle, slow down or stop if necessary.

HC r114–115 RES s13

Tip
If you meet other road users at night, including cyclists and pedestrians, dip your headlights so that you don't dazzle them.

When you overtake at night, you can't see a long way ahead and there may be bends in the road or other unseen hazards.

On a motorway, use

- dipped headlights, even if the road is well lit
- sidelights if you've broken down and are stopped on the hard shoulder. This will help other road users to see you.

RES s11, 12, 13

Keeping control of your motorcycle

For safety, before starting your engine, push the motorcycle forward to check that the rear wheel turns freely: this shows that the gear selector is in neutral. Check that the neutral light on your instrument panel is showing too.

Apply the front brake before you get on the motorcycle. If you're parked on a two-way road, you should get on from the left.

When you're astride your motorcycle, you should be able to put both feet on the ground comfortably, to support yourself and your machine. Never ride with the side stand in the down position – this can be dangerous, especially when cornering. Always fold the stand away safely before setting off.

Once you're moving, the normal riding position should be about central in the lane you're using. Try not to look down at the front wheel as this can affect your balance.

RES s6

You need to have full control of your motorcycle at all times. Riding with the clutch disengaged or in neutral for any length of time (called coasting) reduces your control of the motorcycle, especially steering and braking. This is particularly dangerous when you're travelling downhill, as your motorcycle will speed up when there's no **engine braking** to hold it back.

HC r122 RES s6, 8

engine braking
using the engine's resistance to help slow the vehicle

When you're riding up a steep hill, the engine has to work harder. If you close the throttle to reduce speed, you'll slow down sooner than usual. Changing down to a lower gear will help prevent the engine struggling as it delivers the power needed to climb the hill.

RES s8

On single-track roads, be aware of the limited space available. If you see a vehicle coming towards you, pull into (or opposite) a passing place.

HC r155

 See the Don't Risk It website for advice on riding on country roads.

dontriskit.info/country-roads

Always match your riding to the road and weather conditions. Your stopping distance will be affected by several factors, including

- your speed
- the condition of your tyres
- the road surface
- the weather.

HC r155 RES s8, 10

When riding normally, you should brake when the motorcycle is upright and moving in a straight line. Apply both brakes smoothly, the front brake just before the rear brake. If your motorcycle has linked brakes, check the motorcycle handbook for more details.

When stopping in an emergency, or on a wet road, there's an increased risk of skidding. Try to avoid braking so hard that you cause a skid, as it can be hard to get your motorcycle back under control once you've started skidding.

The main causes of a motorcycle skidding are

- changing direction suddenly or travelling too fast
- too much acceleration
- heavy or sharp braking
- any combination of the above.

If you don't have anti-lock brakes and your motorcycle begins to skid when you're braking on a wet road

- release the brake(s) causing the skid to allow the wheel(s) to turn
- re-apply the brakes, but avoid braking so hard that you skid again.

HC r119 RES s6, 8, 10

Traffic calming and road surfaces

Traffic calming is used to slow traffic and make the roads safer for vulnerable road users, especially pedestrians. One of the most common measures is road humps (sometimes called speed humps). Make sure that you stay within the speed limit and don't overtake other moving vehicles within traffic-calmed areas.

HC r153 RES s7

Rumble devices (raised markings across the road) may be used to warn you of a hazard, such as a roundabout, and to encourage you to reduce your speed.

KYTS p68, 75

In cities where trams operate, the areas used by the trams may have a different surface texture or colour, which may be edged with white line markings.

HC r300 KYTS p31

Tip

If it rains after a long, dry hot spell, the road surface can become unusually slippery. Loose chippings can also increase the risk of skidding, so slow down and be aware of the increased skid risk in these conditions.

HC r237 RES s12

Painted road markings, tar banding, tram rails and drain covers can all be very slippery in wet weather. Keep your motorcycle upright and avoid braking while riding over them. If this isn't possible, take great care as your tyres have very little grip on these surfaces.

Spilt diesel fuel is very slippery. It spills from overfilled fuel tanks and poorly fitting or missing filler caps. It's often found near filling stations, at roundabouts and on bends. If you see a rainbow pattern on the road surface, slow down in good time and avoid the area if possible.

HC r213, 306 RES s8, 12

Some motorcycles are fitted with a traction control system (TCS) that helps to prevent the rear wheel spinning while the motorcycle is accelerating. Accelerating on slippery surfaces increases the risk of this happening.

Meeting the standards

You must be able to

use the throttle smoothly to reach and keep to a suitable speed

change gear smoothly and in good time

coordinate
- steering
- leaning
- the use of the brakes
- the use of the throttle

steer the machine safely and responsibly in all road and traffic conditions.

You must know and understand

why it's best not to over-rev your engine when moving away and while stationary

the benefits of changing gear at the right time when going up and down hills

that different machines may have different numbers of gears with different ratios

how to change the direction of the machine by coordinating
- throttle
- lean
- steering input.

Notes

You can use this page to make your own notes or diagrams about the key points you need to remember.

Think about

- By how much must visibility be reduced before you can use fog lights?
- Why must you make sure that your fog lights are turned off when visibility improves again?
- In which weather conditions should you increase the distance between your motorcycle and the vehicle in front?
- Which road users are most likely to be affected by very windy weather?
- When can you use engine braking, and why is it a good idea?
- What are rumble devices used for?

Your notes

_____

_____

_____

_____

_____

_____

_____

_____

_____

_____

_____

_____

_____

_____

_____

_____

_____

_____

_____

_____

 # Things to discuss and practise with your trainer

These are just a few examples of what you could discuss and practise with your trainer. Read more about road conditions and motorcycle handling to come up with your own ideas.

Discuss with your trainer

- your stopping distances in different weather conditions
- how to use your front and back brakes in different situations and weather conditions
- what you should do if you get a sudden puncture.

Practise with your trainer

- positioning your motorcycle correctly in various situations, such as when turning right or left, and riding straight ahead
- going out at night to get used to riding with reduced visibility
- your gear selection and clutch control while riding downhill.

What should you do before starting a motorcycle engine?

☐ Check that the neutral lamp shows when the ignition is switched on

☐ Select first gear and apply the rear brake lightly

☐ Select first gear and apply the front brake firmly

☐ Check that your dipped headlights and tail light are on

Before starting the engine, make sure the motorcycle is in neutral. Do this by checking that the neutral warning light is lit when you switch on the ignition. If no neutral light is fitted, push the motorcycle forward to check that the rear wheel turns freely.

What should the motorcyclist do as they approach this junction?

Look out for road signs warning of side roads. A driver who's emerging may not be able to see a motorcyclist due to parked cars or heavy traffic. Ride defensively, slow down and be prepared to stop if necessary. Remember, no-one has priority at an unmarked crossroads.

☐ Stop, as the car has right of way

☐ Slow down and be ready to stop

☐ Dip their headlights and keep near the left-hand kerb

☐ Speed up to clear the junction without delay

What can motorcyclists do to improve their safety on the road?

☐ Anticipate the actions of others

☐ Stay just above the speed limit

☐ Keep positioned close to the kerb

☐ Remain well below the speed limit

Always ride defensively. This means looking and planning ahead, as well as anticipating the actions of other road users.

8.4 Mark one answer — RES s8, HC r119

What can cause a motorcycle to skid?

- ☐ Braking too gently
- ☐ Feathering the throttle
- ☐ Staying upright when cornering
- ☐ Braking too hard

To keep control of your motorcycle and prevent skidding, you should plan well ahead and avoid late, harsh braking. Try to avoid braking while changing direction, as the tyres may not have enough grip to cope with both together. Always consider how the road and weather conditions may affect your tyres' grip.

8.5 Mark one answer — RES s12

It's very cold and the road looks wet. What should you do if you can't hear any road noise as you ride?

- ☐ Continue riding at the same speed
- ☐ Ride slowly in as high a gear as possible
- ☐ Ride in as low a gear as possible
- ☐ Brake sharply to see if the road is slippery

Frozen rain on the road is called black ice. It can be hard to see, but it can be indicated by a lack of road noise and your steering may also feel very light. Reduce your speed and avoid harsh braking or steering. Riding in as high a gear as possible can help reduce the risk of wheelspin.

8.6 Mark one answer — RES s4, HC r83-84

When should you wear full protective clothing while riding a motorcycle?

- ☐ At all times
- ☐ Only on faster, open roads
- ☐ Just on long journeys
- ☐ Only during bad weather

Protective clothing is designed to protect you from the cold and wet. It also gives you some protection from injury, so it's important that you always wear protective clothing when you ride.

8.7 Mark one answer — RES s12

What should you do before you start a journey in foggy conditions?

- ☐ Make sure that you have a spare visor with you
- ☐ Make sure that you have a warm drink with you
- ☐ Check that your lights are working
- ☐ Check that the battery is fully charged

It's best to avoid riding in foggy weather. However, if you have to, there are some precautions you can take before setting off to help make your journey as safe as possible. These include checking that all your lights are clean and working, and that your visor is clean.

8.8 — Mark one answer — RES s8

Where's the best place to park your motorcycle?

☐ On soft tarmac
☐ On bumpy ground
☐ On grass
☐ On firm, level ground

Parking your motorcycle on soft ground might cause the stand to sink in, and the machine could fall over. The ground should be level, as well as firm, to keep the motorcycle stable. Use off-road parking or motorcycle parking areas when they're available.

8.9 — Mark one answer — RES s12

What should you do when you're riding in windy conditions?

☐ Stay close to large vehicles
☐ Keep your speed up
☐ Keep your speed down
☐ Stay close to the gutter

Strong winds can blow a motorcycle off course, and even across the road. In windy conditions, you need to slow down and avoid riding on exposed roads. You should also watch for gaps in buildings and hedges, where you may be affected by a sudden gust of wind.

8.10 — Mark one answer — RES s8

Where should you normally position your motorcycle while you're riding on the road?

☐ Close to the kerb
☐ In the centre of your lane
☐ On the right of your lane
☐ Near the centre of the road

When you're riding a motorcycle, it's very important to ride where other road users can see you. In normal weather, you should ride in the centre of your lane. This will help you avoid uneven road surfaces in the gutter, and allow others to overtake on the right if they wish.

8.11 — Mark one answer — RES s6

Your motorcycle is parked on a two-way road. How should you get on the machine?

☐ From the right and apply the rear brake
☐ From the left and leave the brakes alone
☐ From the left and apply the front brake
☐ From the right and leave the brakes alone

When you get onto a motorcycle, you should get on from the left side to avoid putting yourself in danger from passing traffic. You should also apply the front brake to prevent the motorcycle from rolling either forwards or backwards.

8.12   Mark one answer   RES s6

What will happen if you ride with your clutch lever pulled in for longer than is necessary?

☐ It will increase wear on the gearbox

☐ It will increase petrol consumption

☐ It will reduce your control of the motorcycle

☐ It will reduce the grip of the tyres

Riding with the clutch lever pulled in is known as coasting. If you coast, you lose the benefits of engine braking and you'll have reduced control of your motorcycle.

8.13   Mark one answer   RES s8

What should you do when you're approaching a road that has a surface of loose chippings?

☐ Ride normally

☐ Speed up

☐ Slow down

☐ Stop suddenly

The handling of your motorcycle will be greatly affected by the road surface. Look well ahead and be especially alert if the road looks uneven or you see a loose chippings warning sign. Slow down in good time, as braking harshly on a loose surface could easily cause you to skid. For the same reason, avoid making sudden changes of direction.

8.14   Mark one answer   RES s12, HC r237

How is the road surface affected when it rains after a long, dry, hot spell?

☐ It can become unusually slippery

☐ It can give better grip

☐ It can become covered in grit

☐ It can melt and break up

Oil and rubber can build up on the road during long spells of dry weather. When it rains, this can make the road surface very slippery.

What's most likely to cause a motorcycle to skid?

☐ Riding in wet weather

☐ Catching your foot on the ground

☐ Cornering too fast

☐ Riding in the winter

Riders cause skids when they push their tyres to the point that they can no longer grip the road. This happens when changing direction, braking and accelerating. The point at which tyres loose grip will vary with road, weather and tyre condition. Riding at a suitable speed for the conditions, planning, looking ahead for hazards and braking in good time will all help you to avoid skidding and losing control.

Your motorcycle doesn't have linked brakes. In an emergency, what should you do to stop quickly?

☐ Apply the rear brake only

☐ Apply the front brake only

☐ Apply the front brake just before the rear brake

☐ Apply the rear brake just before the front brake

You should plan ahead to avoid the need to stop suddenly, but if an emergency arises, you must be able to stop safely. Applying the front brake just before the rear brake will help you to stop safely and quickly.

What will happen if you look down at the front wheel while riding?

☐ It will make your steering lighter

☐ It will improve your balance

☐ You'll use less fuel

☐ You'll upset your balance

When riding, look ahead and around you. Don't look down at the front wheel, as this can severely upset your balance.

8.18 — Mark one answer — RES s6

In normal riding conditions, when should you brake?

☐ When the motorcycle is exceeding the speed limit

☐ When the motorcycle is being turned or ridden through a bend

☐ When the motorcycle is travelling below 20 mph

☐ When the motorcycle is upright and moving in a straight line

A motorcycle is most stable when it's upright and moving in a straight line. This is the best time to brake. With independent front and rear brakes, both brakes should be used, with the front brake being applied just before the rear brake.

8.19 — Mark one answer — RES s8, HC r126

What will affect the stopping distance of your motorcycle?

☐ The drive-chain adjustment

☐ The condition of the tyres

☐ The time of day

☐ The street lighting

Tyres are a major factor in the handling, stability and stopping distance of a motorcycle. Make sure they're in a safe and legal condition. The weather and road surface also play a part. Always anticipate well ahead and take account of the conditions when you're braking.

8.20 — Mark one answer — RES s11

You're on a motorway at night. When may you have your headlights switched off?

☐ When there are vehicles close in front of you

☐ When you're travelling below 50 mph

☐ When the motorway is lit

☐ When your motorcycle is broken down on the hard shoulder

Always use your headlights at night on a motorway, unless you've had to stop on the hard shoulder. If you have to use the hard shoulder, switch off your headlights but leave your parking lights on, so that your motorcycle can be seen by other road users.

8.21 — Mark one answer — RES s12

What should you do if you have to park on the road while visibility is reduced by fog?

☐ Leave parking lights on

☐ Leave no lights on

☐ Leave dipped headlights on

☐ Leave main-beam headlights on

If you have to park on the road in foggy weather, try to find a place to park off the road. If this isn't possible, leave your motorcycle facing in the same direction as the traffic and leave your parking lights on. It's important that your motorcycle can be seen by other road users.

Mark one answer RES s15

What should you do if you ride over broken glass and get a puncture?

☐ Close the throttle and roll to a stop

☐ Brake to a stop as quickly as possible

☐ Release your grip on the handlebars

☐ Steer from side to side to keep your balance

Your motorcycle will be very unstable if a tyre bursts. Try to keep a straight course and stop as gently as possible.

8.23 **Mark one answer** RES s8

How can you see spilt fuel on a wet road?

☐ By a rainbow-coloured pattern on the road surface

☐ By a series of skid marks on the road surface

☐ By a dull non-reflective road surface

☐ By a highly polished road surface

This rainbow-coloured pattern can be seen much more easily on a wet road. You should avoid riding over spilt fuel if possible. If you have to go over it, do so with extreme caution, knowing the surface will be slippery.

8.24 **Mark one answer** RES s8

Which type of road surface increases the risk of skidding for motorcyclists?

☐ Tar banding

☐ Dry tarmac

☐ Concrete

☐ Asphalt

When riding, it's important to look for

• potholes
• drain covers (especially when they're wet)
• tar banding
• oily and greasy surfaces
• road markings
• tram tracks
• wet mud and leaves.

Keen observation will give you more time to brake or change course if you need to avoid these slippery surfaces.

8.25 · Mark one answer · RES s12

You're riding on a wet road. How should you use the brakes in these conditions?

- ☐ Apply the rear brake well before the front brake
- ☐ Apply the front brake just before the rear brake
- ☐ Avoid using the front brake at all
- ☐ Avoid using the rear brake at all

On wet roads, you'll need to brake earlier and more smoothly than on dry roads. Always try to brake when the motorcycle is upright. This is particularly important in wet conditions.

8.26 · Mark one answer · RES s8

The road is wet and you're filtering past a line of queuing traffic. Why should you take particular care if you ride on painted road markings?

- ☐ You won't be seen in driver's mirrors
- ☐ Painted road markings can be slippery when they're wet
- ☐ You won't be able to see the road studs
- ☐ Painted road markings create more spray than normal road surface

When they're wet, painted road markings can be more slippery than the normal road surface. Other road-surface hazards that become slippery when they're wet include drain covers, leaves and mud. Take extra care when braking or cornering on these wet surfaces.

8.27 · Mark one answer · RES s8

Why should you be careful when riding over tram lines?

- ☐ Tram lines are always 'live'
- ☐ Trams have priority
- ☐ The steel rails will be raised above the road surface
- ☐ The steel rails can be slippery

The smooth steel surface can be slippery and dangerous for motorcyclists, especially when it's wet. Try to cross tram lines at right angles.

8.28 · Mark one answer · RES s8

You're riding a motorcycle that doesn't have anti-lock brakes (ABS). What should you do if you have to brake sharply and your motorcycle starts to skid?

- ☐ Continue braking and select a low gear
- ☐ Apply the brakes harder for better grip
- ☐ Select neutral and use the front brake only
- ☐ Release and reapply the brakes

If you skid as a result of braking harshly, you need to ease off the brakes to stop the skid. You should then reapply them progressively to stop.

8.29 Mark one answer   RES s8

What would make a rainbow-coloured pattern on a wet road surface?

☐ An uneven road surface

☐ A worn road surface

☐ Fuel spilt on the road

☐ Mud on the road

If fuel, especially diesel, is spilt on the road, it will make the surface very slippery. In wet weather, it can be seen as a rainbow-coloured pattern on the road.

8.30 Mark one answer   RES s5

What does a traction control system (TCS) help to prevent?

☐ Wheelspin when accelerating

☐ Skidding when braking too hard

☐ Uneven front tyre wear

☐ Uneven rear tyre wear

TCS helps to prevent the rear wheel from spinning, for example when accelerating on a slippery surface.

8.31 Mark one answer   RES s8

You're riding a motorcycle that doesn't have anti-lock brakes (ABS). What should you do if braking too hard has caused both wheels to skid?

☐ Release both brakes together

☐ Release the front brake, then the rear brake

☐ Release the front brake only

☐ Release the rear brake only

On a motorcycle that doesn't have ABS, braking too hard will cause a skid. Release the brakes immediately to allow the wheels to turn, then reapply them as firmly as the road surface and conditions will allow.

8.32 Mark one answer   RES s5

Your motorcycle doesn't have linked brakes. What should you do when braking normally to a stop?

☐ Apply only the front brake

☐ Apply only the rear brake

☐ Apply both brakes smoothly

☐ Apply either of the brakes gently

In normal riding, you should always use both brakes. Braking when the motorcycle is upright and travelling in a straight line helps you to keep control. If your motorcycle has linked brakes, refer to the vehicle handbook.

8.33 | Mark one answer | RES s6

You're sitting on a stationary motorcycle. What should you be able to do when you're checking your riding position?

☐ Just touch the ground with your toes

☐ Place both feet on the ground

☐ Operate the centre stand

☐ Adjust your mirrors by stretching

When sitting astride a stationary motorcycle, you should be able to place both feet on the ground. This should enable you to keep your balance while using one foot to operate the foot controls.

8.34 | Mark one answer | RES s12, HC r237

It's been raining after a long dry spell. How will the road surface be affected?

☐ It will be rough

☐ It will be flooded

☐ It will be sticky

☐ It will be slippery

During a long spell of hot, dry weather, the road surface will become coated with rubber and dust. When it rains, the road surface will be unusually slippery. Take extra care, particularly at junctions, bends and roundabouts, and allow double the usual stopping distance.

8.35 | Mark one answer | RES s6

Riding with the side stand down could cause you to crash. When is this most likely to happen?

☐ When you're going uphill

☐ When you're accelerating

☐ When you're braking

☐ When you're cornering

Cornering with the side stand down could lead to a serious crash. Many motorcycles have a device that stops the engine if you try to ride off with the side stand down, but don't rely on this.

8.36 | Mark one answer | RES s8, HC r143

When may you overtake another vehicle on their left?

☐ When you're in a one-way street

☐ When approaching a motorway slip road where you'll be turning off

☐ When the vehicle in front is signalling to turn left

☐ When a slower vehicle is travelling in the right-hand lane of a dual carriageway

You may pass slower vehicles on their left while travelling along a one-way street. Be aware of drivers who may need to change lanes and may not expect faster traffic passing on their left.

You're travelling in very heavy rain. How is this likely to affect your overall stopping distance?

☐ It will be doubled

☐ It will be halved

☐ It will be ten times greater

☐ It will be no different

The road will be very wet and spray from other vehicles will reduce your visibility. Tyre grip will also be reduced, increasing your stopping distance. You should at least double your separation distance to make sure you can stop safely in the space you've allowed.

What should you do when you're overtaking at night?

☐ Wait until a bend so that you can see oncoming headlights

☐ Sound your horn twice before moving out

☐ Go past slowly so that you can react to unseen hazards

☐ Beware of bends in the road ahead

Don't overtake if there's a possibility of a road junction, bend or brow of a bridge or hill ahead. There are many hazards that are difficult to see in the dark. Only overtake if you're certain that the road ahead is clear. Don't take a chance.

When may you wait in a box junction?

☐ When you're stationary in a queue of traffic

☐ When approaching a pelican crossing

☐ When approaching a zebra crossing

☐ When oncoming traffic prevents you turning right

The purpose of a box junction is to keep the junction clear by preventing vehicles from stopping in the path of crossing traffic.

You mustn't enter a box junction unless your exit is clear. However, you may enter the box and wait if you want to turn right and are only prevented from doing so by oncoming traffic.

8.40 — Mark one answer — HC p109, KYTS p72

Which plate may appear with this road sign?

| ☐ Humps for ½ mile | ☐ Hump Bridge |
| ☐ Low Bridge | ☐ Soft Verge |

Road humps are used to slow down traffic. They're found in places where there are often pedestrians, such as

- shopping areas
- near schools
- residential areas.

Watch out for people close to the kerb or crossing the road.

8.41 — Mark one answer — RES s7, HC r153

What's the reason for traffic-calming measures?

- ☐ To stop road rage
- ☐ To make overtaking easier
- ☐ To slow traffic down
- ☐ To make parking easier

Traffic-calming measures make the roads safer for vulnerable road users, such as cyclists, pedestrians and children. These can be designed as chicanes, road humps or other obstacles that encourage drivers and riders to slow down.

8.42 — Mark one answer — RES s11, HC r132

What colour are the reflective studs along the left-hand edge of the motorway?

- ☐ Green
- ☐ Amber
- ☐ Red
- ☐ White

Reflective studs are used to help you in poor visibility. Different colours are used so that you'll know which lane you're in. These are

- red on the left-hand edge of the carriageway
- white between lanes
- amber on the right-hand edge of the carriageway
- green between the carriageway and slip roads.

What's a rumble device designed to do?

☐ Give directions

☐ Prevent cattle escaping

☐ Alert you to low tyre pressure

☐ Alert you to a hazard

A rumble device consists of raised markings or strips, designed to give drivers an audible, visual and tactile warning. These devices are used in various locations, including in the line separating the hard shoulder and the left-hand lane on the motorway and on the approach to some hazards, to alert drivers to the need to slow down.

What should you do if you have to make a journey in foggy conditions?

☐ Follow other vehicles' tail lights closely

☐ Avoid using dipped headlights

☐ Leave plenty of time for your journey

☐ Keep two seconds behind the vehicle ahead

If you're planning to make a journey when it's foggy, listen to the weather reports. If visibility is very poor, avoid making unnecessary journeys. If you do travel, leave plenty of time – and if someone is waiting for you to arrive, let them know that your journey will take longer than normal. This will also take off any pressure you may feel to rush.

What must you do when you're overtaking a car at night?

☐ Flash your headlights before overtaking

☐ Select a higher gear

☐ Switch your headlights to main beam before overtaking

☐ Make sure you don't dazzle other road users

To prevent your headlights from dazzling the driver of the car in front, wait until you've passed them before switching to main beam.

8.46 — Mark one answer — HC r153

You're travelling on a road that has road humps. What should you do when the driver in front is travelling more slowly than you?

Be patient and stay behind the car in front. You shouldn't normally overtake other vehicles in areas subject to traffic calming. If you overtake here, you may easily exceed the speed limit, defeating the purpose of the traffic-calming measures.

☐ Sound your horn
☐ Overtake as soon as you can
☐ Flash your headlights
☐ Slow down and stay behind

8.47 — Mark one answer — KYTS p68

What's the purpose of the yellow lines painted across the road?

These lines may be painted on the road on the approach to a roundabout, a village or a particular hazard. The lines are raised and painted yellow, and their purpose is to make you aware of your speed. Reduce your speed in good time so that you avoid having to brake harshly over the last few metres before reaching the junction.

☐ To show a safe distance between vehicles
☐ To keep the area clear of traffic
☐ To make you aware of your speed
☐ To warn you to change direction

8.48 — Mark one answer — RES s10, HC r155

What should you do when you meet an oncoming vehicle on a single-track road?

☐ Reverse back to the main road
☐ Carry out an emergency stop
☐ Stop at a passing place
☐ Switch on your hazard warning lights

Take care when using single-track roads. It can be difficult to see around bends, because of hedges or fences, so expect to meet oncoming vehicles. Drive carefully and be ready to pull into or stop opposite a passing place, where you can pass each other safely.

The road is wet. Why would a motorcyclist steer around drain covers while they were cornering?

☐ To avoid puncturing the tyres on the edge of the drain covers

☐ To prevent the motorcycle sliding on the metal drain covers

☐ To help judge the bend using the drain covers as marker points

☐ To avoid splashing pedestrians on the pavement

Other drivers or riders may have to change course due to the size or characteristics of their vehicle. Understanding this will help you to anticipate their actions. Motorcyclists and cyclists will be checking the road ahead for uneven or slippery surfaces, especially in wet weather. They may need to move across their lane to avoid surface hazards such as potholes and drain covers.

Why should you test your brakes after this hazard?

☐ You'll be on a slippery road

☐ Your brakes will be wet

☐ You'll be going down a long hill

☐ You'll have just crossed a long bridge

A ford is a crossing over a stream that's shallow enough to drive or ride through. After you've gone through a ford or deep puddle, your brakes will be wet and they won't work as well as usual. To dry them out, apply a light brake pressure while moving slowly. Don't travel at normal speeds until you're sure your brakes are working properly again.

8.51   Mark one answer   **RES s12, HC r234**

Why should you reduce your speed when you're driving or riding in fog?

☐ The brakes don't work as well

☐ You'll be dazzled by other headlights

☐ The engine will take longer to warm up

☐ It's more difficult to see what's ahead

You won't be able to see as far ahead in fog as you can on a clear day. You'll need to reduce your speed so that, if a hazard looms out of the fog, you have the time and space to take avoiding action.

Travelling in fog is hazardous. If you can, try to delay your journey until it has cleared.

Case study practice – 8 Road conditions and motorcycle handling

You're carrying a friend on the back of your motorcycle.

You buy fuel at the service station, then make various checks, including your tyre pressures.

You want to turn left when you leave the forecourt. There are parked cars obscuring your view.

It begins to snow just before you reach your destination.

8.1 How will your friend affect your journey?

Mark **one** answer

☐ The extra weight can affect your balance

☐ Your stopping distance will be shorter

☐ It will be easier for you to accelerate

☐ They can help with observation

RES s14

8.2 What should you ask your friend to do during the journey?

Mark **one** answer

☐ Lean to the side in order to see ahead

☐ Lean with you when going round bends

☐ Look behind and then signal for you

☐ Keep upright when going round bends

RES s14

8.3 Other than tyre pressures, what might need adjusting under these circumstances?

Mark **one** answer

- ☐ Brakes
- ☐ Headlights
- ☐ Handlebars
- ☐ Seating

RES s14

8.4 What should you do as you leave the service-station forecourt?

Mark **one** answer

- ☐ Stop and wait until some of the parked cars move away
- ☐ Keep moving and merge with the traffic
- ☐ Stop and make your passenger signal to oncoming traffic
- ☐ Edge forward slowly until you can see clearly

RES s9 **HC r170**

8.5 Why would you choose to leave a larger gap towards the end of your journey?

Mark **one** answer

- ☐ So your passenger can see more clearly
- ☐ To keep away from exhaust fumes
- ☐ Your passenger told you to keep further back
- ☐ You'll need more room in which to stop safely

RES s14

Section nine

⊞ Motorway riding

In this section, you'll learn about

- how to ride safely on motorways
- the speed limits that apply on motorways and how they're used to avoid congestion
- the markings used on motorway lanes
- what to do if your motorcycle breaks down on the motorway.

Motorway riding

Motorways are designed to help traffic travel at constant, higher speeds than on single carriageways. Due to the traffic's speed, situations on motorways can change more quickly than on other roads, so you need to be especially alert at all times.

Check your motorcycle thoroughly before starting a long motorway journey. Riding at high speeds for long periods of time may increase the risk of a breakdown. See section 3, Safety and your motorcycle, for more information about what to check.

RES s11

Tip

Motorcyclists with provisional entitlement may not ride on the motorway.

HC r253

Remember, to ride on a motorway, your motorcycle **MUST** have an engine capacity of 50 cc or more.

Pedestrians and horse riders can't use a motorway. The following vehicles can't be used on a motorway

- bicycles
- motorcycles under 50 cc
- powered wheelchairs/mobility scooters
- agricultural vehicles
- some slow-moving vehicles.

HC r253

Riding on the motorway

When you join the motorway

- use the slip road to adjust your speed to match the traffic already on the motorway
- give way to traffic already on the motorway.

HC r259 RES s11

All traffic, whatever its speed, should normally use the left-hand lane of the motorway. Use the middle and right-hand lanes only for overtaking other vehicles and return to the left lane when you've finished overtaking.

HC r264, 267 RES s11

You should normally only overtake on the right. However, you may overtake on the left if traffic is moving slowly in queues and the queue on your right is moving more slowly than the one you're in.

HC r268 RES s11

Where the motorway goes uphill steeply, there may be a separate lane for slow-moving vehicles. This helps the faster-moving traffic to flow more easily.

HC r139 RES s11

If you're travelling in the left-hand lane and traffic is joining from a slip road, move to another lane if you're able to do so safely. This helps the flow of traffic joining the motorway, especially at peak times.

RES s11

Take care when filtering through queuing traffic as a driver may change lane into your path.

Countdown markers on the left-hand verge show that you're approaching the next exit. If you want to leave the motorway, try to get into the left-hand lane in good time. If you accidentally go past the exit you wanted, carry on to the next one. Never try to stop and go back.

HC r272 RES s11

Speed limits

The national speed limit for cars and motorcycles on a motorway is 70 mph (112 km/h). The same limit applies to all lanes. Obey any signs showing a lower speed limit.

HC r261, p40 RES s11

A vehicle towing a trailer

- is restricted to a lower speed limit of 60 mph (96 km/h)
- isn't allowed to travel in the right-hand lane of a motorway with three or more lanes, unless there are lane closures
- in Northern Ireland shouldn't use the right-hand lane of a three-lane motorway.

Tip
You can use your hazard lights to warn traffic behind you that the traffic ahead is slowing down or stopping suddenly. Switch them off as soon as following traffic has reacted to your signal.

When you're approaching roadworks, watch for lower speed limits, especially if there's a contraflow system. You should

- obey all speed limits
- keep a safe distance from the vehicle ahead.

HC r289–290 RES s11

See section 4, Safety margins, for more information about contraflow systems.

Reducing congestion

Active traffic management (ATM), also known as 'smart motorways', tries to reduce congestion and make journey times more reliable. Where this is in use, **mandatory speed limit** signs will show on the gantries. The speed limit helps to keep the traffic speed constant so that traffic is less likely to bunch up and journey times can be improved.

RES s18

mandatory speed limit
the maximum speed at which you may travel and will be shown inside a red circle

In ATM areas, the hard shoulder is sometimes used as a normal traffic lane. You'll know when you can use this because a speed-limit sign will be shown above all lanes, including the hard shoulder. A red cross showing above the hard shoulder means that you shouldn't travel in this lane and it should be used only in an emergency or breakdown.

Emergency refuge areas have been built in these areas for use in cases of emergency or breakdown.

Find out more about ATM here.

www.gov.uk/guidance/how-to-drive-on-a-smart-motorway

Traffic officers operate in England and Wales, covering motorways and some 'A' class roads. They

- can stop and direct anyone on a motorway or an 'A' road
- respond to calls made on roadside emergency telephones.

HC r105, 108 RES s18

Lane markings

Reflective studs help you to see where you are on the carriageway, especially at night or in fog. Different colours are used in different places.

HC r132 RES s11

green – between the carriageway and slip roads

white – between lanes

amber – between the edge of the carriageway and the central reservation

red – between the hard shoulder and carriageway

fluorescent green/yellow – at contraflow systems and roadworks

Stopping and breakdowns

Motorways are designed to keep traffic moving, so you mustn't stop on the motorway unless you have to.

Only stop on the motorway

- if flashing red lights show above every lane
- when told to do so by the police, Driver and Vehicle Standards Agency (DVSA) officers or traffic officers
- in a traffic jam
- in an emergency or breakdown.

Move over if signals on the overhead gantries advise you to do so.

HC r258, 270 RES s11 KYTS p90

Should you need to stop for any other reason, such as to have a rest, make a phone call or look at a map, either leave at the next exit or go to a service area.

HC r270 RES s11

265

If your motorcycle breaks down or a tyre has a puncture, try to get onto the hard shoulder and call for help. If you can, use one of the emergency telephones. These are

- normally at one-mile intervals. Marker posts at 100-metre intervals point you in the direction of the nearest phone
- connected directly to a control centre, where the operator will deal with your call and direct the appropriate services to help you.

HC r275 RES s11, 16

When you're using an emergency phone, stand facing the oncoming traffic so that you can see any hazards approaching – for example, the draught from a large vehicle driving past could take you by surprise.

If you decide to use your mobile phone

- make a note of your location (the number on the nearest marker post) before you make the call
- give this information to the emergency services.

HC r275 RES s11, 16

While your motorcycle is on the hard shoulder

- switch on the hazard lights, if fitted
- switch on the parking lights at night or if visibility is poor.

RES s11

When you're ready to return to the carriageway, ride along the hard shoulder to gain speed before rejoining the main carriageway by moving into a safe gap in the traffic.

HC r276 RES s16

Meeting the standards

You must be able to

join a motorway or dual carriageway safely and responsibly from the left or the right

allow for other road users joining or leaving the motorway

change lanes safely and responsibly.

You must know and understand

that you mustn't stop on a motorway except in an emergency

that you mustn't

- pick anybody up on a motorway
- set anybody down on a motorway
- walk on a motorway, except in an emergency

the need to look well ahead for other road users joining or leaving the motorway or for queuing traffic

that some stretches of motorway may have

- local, active traffic management (sometimes called smart motorways)
- control systems installed, which will change speed limits and the direction of flow in particular lanes.

You must obey the instructions given by these systems.

Notes

You can use this page to make your own notes or diagrams about the key points you need to remember.

Think about

- At what speed should you be riding when you join the motorway?
- What should you do if you miss the exit that you want to take off the motorway?
- What information do the marker posts give you?
- What should you do if your motorcycle breaks down on the motorway?

Your notes

_____
_____
_____
_____
_____
_____
_____
_____
_____

Things to discuss and practise with your trainer

These are just a few examples of what you could discuss and practise with your trainer. Read more about motorway riding to come up with your own ideas.

Discuss with your trainer

- how you should join the motorway and what to look out for as you do so
- the different national speed limits for various vehicles on the motorway, and in which lanes these vehicles may travel
- what you should do if you break down on the motorway
- what ATM stands for and its purpose on the motorway.

Practise with your trainer

Until you hold a full motorcycle licence, you won't be able to ride on the motorway, so practising your riding there won't be possible. Instead, practise with your trainer

- on a dual carriageway, some of the techniques of riding on the motorway; for example, joining from a slip road, lane discipline and riding at higher speeds
- identifying motorway signs, signals and road markings from _Know Your Traffic Signs_ and _The Official Highway Code_.

Mark one answer RES s11, HC r270

When may you stop on the hard shoulder of a motorway?

☐ Only in an emergency

☐ If you feel tired and need to rest

☐ If you've gone past your exit

☐ To answer your mobile phone

You mustn't stop on the hard shoulder, except in an emergency. If you're on a smart motorway, and the hard shoulder is in use as a running lane, try and reach an emergency refuge area or take the next exit. Never use the hard shoulder to have a rest or a picnic, answer a mobile phone or check a road map. Also, you mustn't travel back along the hard shoulder if you've gone past your exit.

Mark one answer RES s11, HC r272

You're riding on the motorway. Where should you position your motorcycle well before you reach your exit slip-road?

☐ In the middle lane

☐ In the left-hand lane

☐ On the hard shoulder

☐ In any lane

You'll see the first advance direction sign one mile from a motorway exit. If you're travelling at 60 mph, you'll only have about 50 seconds before you reach the countdown markers. There'll be another sign at the half-mile point. Move to the left-hand lane in good time. Don't cut across traffic at the last moment and don't risk missing your exit.

Mark one answer RES s11

What should you do if you're joining a motorway from a slip road?

☐ Adjust your speed to match the speed of the traffic on the motorway

☐ Accelerate as quickly as you can and ride straight out

☐ Ride onto the hard shoulder until a gap appears

☐ Expect drivers on the motorway to give way to you

Give way to vehicles that are already on the motorway, and join the left-hand lane when there's a suitable gap in the traffic. Don't expect traffic on the motorway to give way to you, but try to avoid stopping at the end of the slip road.

9.4   Mark one answer   RES s11, HC r253

What's the minimum engine size your motorcycle must have, if you want to ride it on the motorway?

☐ 50 cc
☐ 125 cc
☐ 150 cc
☐ 250 cc

Riders of motorcycles with an engine smaller than 50 cc aren't allowed to use motorways, due to their restricted speed. They may cause a hazard – both for the rider and for drivers of other vehicles.

9.5   Mark one answer   RES s11, HC r264

You're riding at 70 mph on a three-lane motorway. Which lane should you use if there's no traffic ahead?

☐ Any lane
☐ The middle lane
☐ The right-hand lane
☐ The left-hand lane

If you're not overtaking, use the left-hand lane regardless of the speed at which you're travelling.

9.6   NI EXEMPT   Mark one answer   RES s11, HC p40

You're riding on a motorway. Unless signs show otherwise, what's the national speed limit?

☐ 50 mph
☐ 60 mph
☐ 70 mph
☐ 80 mph

The national speed limit of 70 mph applies to cars and motorcycles on the motorway, unless they're towing a trailer. On smart motorways, this speed limit can be reduced and overhead signs will show the new limit in force.

9.7   Mark one answer   RES s11

Why is it particularly important to carry out a check of your motorcycle before making a long motorway journey?

☐ You'll have to do more harsh braking on motorways
☐ Motorway service stations don't deal with breakdowns
☐ The road surface will wear down the tyres faster
☐ Continuous high speeds increase the risk of your motorcycle breaking down

Before starting a motorway journey, make sure your motorcycle can cope with the demands of high-speed riding. Things you need to check include oil, water, tyres and fuel. When you're travelling a long way, it's a good idea to plan rest stops in advance.

271

Mark one answer RES s11, HC r259

You're joining a motorway from a slip road. How should you deal with traffic already on the motorway?

☐ Carry on along the hard shoulder until you see a safe gap

☐ Stop at the end of the slip road and look for a safe gap

☐ Use the slip road to accelerate until you're moving much faster than the motorway traffic

☐ Match your speed to traffic in the left-hand lane and filter into a safe gap

You should give way to traffic already on the motorway. Where possible, traffic may move over to let you in, but don't force your way into the traffic stream. Traffic could be travelling at high speed, so try to match your speed to filter in without affecting the traffic flow.

9.9 Mark one answer HC r261, p40

What's the national speed limit on motorways for cars and motorcycles?

☐ 30 mph

☐ 50 mph

☐ 60 mph

☐ 70 mph

Travelling at the national speed limit doesn't allow you to hog the right-hand lane. Always use the left-hand lane whenever possible. When leaving a motorway, get into the left-hand lane well before your exit. Reduce your speed on the slip road and look out for sharp bends or curves and traffic queuing at roundabouts.

9.10 Mark one answer RES s11

Which vehicles should use the left-hand lane on a three-lane motorway?

☐ Any vehicle that isn't overtaking

☐ Large vehicles only

☐ Emergency vehicles only

☐ Slow vehicles only

On a motorway, all traffic should use the left-hand lane unless overtaking. When overtaking a number of slower vehicles, move back to the left-hand lane when you're safely past. Check your mirrors frequently and don't stay in the middle or right-hand lane if the left-hand lane is free.

9.11 — Mark one answer — RES s11

Which vehicles aren't allowed to use the right-hand lane of a three-lane motorway?

☐ Small delivery vans

☐ Motorcycles

☐ Vehicles towing a trailer

☐ Motorcycle and sidecar outfits

On the motorway, any vehicle towing a trailer is restricted to 60 mph. It isn't allowed in the right-hand lane, as it might hold up faster-moving traffic that wishes to overtake in that lane.

9.12 — Mark one answer — RES s11, HC r275

Your vehicle breaks down on a motorway and you need to call for help. Why might it be better to use an emergency roadside telephone rather than a mobile phone?

☐ It connects you to a local garage

☐ Using a mobile phone will distract other drivers

☐ It allows easy location by the emergency services

☐ Mobile phones don't work on motorways

On a motorway, it's best to use a roadside emergency telephone so that the emergency services are able to find you easily. The location of the nearest telephone is shown by an arrow on marker posts at the edge of the hard shoulder. If you use a mobile, find out the number on the nearest marker post before you call. This number will let the operator know where you are and in which direction you're travelling.

9.13 — Mark one answer — RES s11, HC r276

Your vehicle broke down on the hard shoulder of a motorway, but has now been repaired. How should you rejoin the main carriageway?

☐ Move out onto the carriageway, then build up your speed

☐ Move out onto the carriageway using your hazard warning lights

☐ Gain speed on the hard shoulder before moving out onto the carriageway

☐ Wait on the hard shoulder until someone flashes their headlights at you

Signal your intention and build up sufficient speed on the hard shoulder so that you can filter into a safe gap in the traffic. Don't push your way into a small gap or cause other traffic to alter speed or direction.

You're travelling along a motorway. Where would you find a crawler or climbing lane?

Large, slow-moving vehicles can hinder the progress of other traffic. On a steep gradient, an extra crawler lane may be provided for slow-moving vehicles to allow faster-moving traffic to flow more easily.

☐ On a steep gradient

☐ Before a service area

☐ Before a junction

☐ Along the hard shoulder

What do these motorway signs mean?

The exit from a motorway is indicated by countdown markers. These are positioned 90 metres (100 yards) apart, the first being 270 metres (300 yards) from the start of the slip road. Move into the left-hand lane well before you reach the start of the slip road.

☐ They're countdown markers to a bridge

☐ They're distance markers to the next telephone

☐ They're countdown markers to the next exit

☐ They warn of a police control ahead

9.16   Mark one answer   RES s7, HC r132

Where are amber reflective studs found on a motorway?

☐ Between the hard shoulder and the carriageway

☐ Between the acceleration lane and the carriageway

☐ Between the central reservation and the carriageway

☐ Between each pair of lanes

On motorways, reflective studs of various colours are fixed in the road between the lanes. These help you to identify which lane you're in when it's dark or in poor visibility. Amber-coloured studs are found on the right-hand edge of the main carriageway, next to the central reservation.

9.17   Mark one answer   RES s7, HC r132

What colour are the reflective studs between the lanes on a motorway?

☐ Green

☐ Amber

☐ White

☐ Red

White studs are found between the lanes on motorways. They reflect back the light from your headlights. This is especially useful in bad weather, when visibility is restricted.

9.18   Mark one answer   RES s7, HC r132

What colour are the reflective studs between a motorway and a slip road?

☐ Amber

☐ White

☐ Green

☐ Red

The studs between the carriageway and the hard shoulder are normally red. These change to green where there's a slip road, helping you to identify slip roads when visibility is poor or when it's dark.

9.19   Mark one answer   RES s11, HC r275

Your vehicle has broken down on a motorway. In which direction should you walk to find the nearest emergency telephone?

☐ With the traffic flow

☐ Facing oncoming traffic

☐ In the direction shown on the marker posts

☐ In the direction of the nearest exit

Along the hard shoulder there are marker posts at 100-metre intervals. These will direct you to the nearest emergency telephone.

9.20 — Mark one answer — RES s11, HC r259

Why is it important to make full use of the slip road as you join a motorway?

☐ Because there's space available to turn round if you need to

☐ To allow you direct access to the overtaking lanes

☐ To allow you to fit safely into the traffic flow in the left-hand lane

☐ Because you can continue on the hard shoulder

Try to join the motorway without affecting the progress of the traffic in the left-hand lane and always give way to traffic already on the motorway. At busy times, you may have to slow down to merge into slow-moving traffic.

9.21 — Mark one answer — RES s11, HC r275

How should you position yourself when you use the emergency telephone on a motorway?

☐ Stay close to the carriageway

☐ Face the oncoming traffic

☐ Keep your back to the traffic

☐ Stand on the hard shoulder

Traffic is passing you at speed. If the draught from a large lorry catches you by surprise, it could blow you off balance and even onto the carriageway. By facing the oncoming traffic, you can see approaching lorries and so be prepared for their draught. You'll also be in a position to see any other hazards approaching.

9.22 — Mark one answer — RES s11, HC r132

What colour are the reflective studs between the hard shoulder and the left-hand lane of a motorway?

☐ Green

☐ Red

☐ White

☐ Amber

Red studs are placed between the edge of the carriageway and the hard shoulder. Where slip roads leave or join the motorway, the studs are green.

9.23 — Mark one answer — RES s11, HC r264

On a three-lane motorway, which lane should you use if there's no traffic ahead?

☐ Left

☐ Right

☐ Centre

☐ Either the right or centre

On a three-lane motorway, you should travel in the left-hand lane unless you're overtaking. This applies regardless of the speed at which you're travelling.

9.24 — Mark one answer — RES s11, HC r290

What should you do when going through a contraflow system on a motorway?

☐ Use dipped headlights

☐ Keep a good distance from the vehicle ahead

☐ Switch lanes to keep the traffic flowing

☐ Stay close to the vehicle ahead to reduce queues

At roadworks, and especially where a contraflow system is operating, a speed restriction is likely to be in place. Keep to the lower speed limit and don't

- switch lanes
- get too close to the vehicle in front of you.

Be aware that there will be no permanent barrier between you and the oncoming traffic.

9.25 — Mark one answer — RES s11, HC r132

You're on a three-lane motorway. Which lane are you in if there are red reflective studs on your left and white ones to your right?

☐ In the right-hand lane

☐ In the middle lane

☐ On the hard shoulder

☐ In the left-hand lane

The colours of the reflective studs on the motorway and their locations are

- red – between the hard shoulder and the carriageway
- white – between lanes
- amber – between the carriageway and the central reservation
- green – along slip-road exits and entrances
- bright green/yellow – at roadworks and contraflow systems.

9.26

RES s11, HC r288

What should you do when you're approaching roadworks on a motorway?

☐ Speed up to clear the area quickly

☐ Always use the hard shoulder

☐ Obey the speed limit

☐ Stay very close to the vehicle in front

Be aware of reduced speed limits at roadworks. Speed limits shown inside a red circle are mandatory and cameras are often used to enforce the reduced limit. Slow down in good time and keep your distance from the vehicle in front.

9.27

HC r253

Which vehicles are prohibited from using the motorway?

☐ Powered mobility scooters

☐ Motorcycles over 50 cc

☐ Double-deck buses

☐ Cars with automatic transmission

Motorways mustn't be used by pedestrians, cyclists, motorcycles under 50 cc, certain slow-moving vehicles without permission, and powered wheelchairs/mobility scooters.

9.28

HC r254

What should you do while you're driving or riding along a motorway?

☐ Look much further ahead than you would on other roads

☐ Travel much faster than you would on other roads

☐ Maintain a shorter separation distance than you would on other roads

☐ Concentrate more than you would on other roads

Traffic on motorways usually travels faster than on other roads. You need to be looking further ahead to give yourself more time to react to any hazard that may develop.

9.29

RES s11, HC r264

What should you do immediately after joining a motorway?

☐ Try to overtake

☐ Re-adjust your mirrors

☐ Position your vehicle in the centre lane

☐ Stay in the left-hand lane

When you've just joined a motorway, stay in the left-hand lane long enough to get used to the higher speeds of motorway traffic before considering overtaking.

9.30
Mark one answer   RES s11, HC r265

When would you use the right-hand lane on a three-lane motorway?

☐ When you're turning right

☐ When you're overtaking

☐ When you're travelling above the speed limit

☐ When you're trying to save fuel

The right-hand lane of the motorway is for overtaking. Sometimes you may be directed into a right-hand lane as a result of roadworks or a traffic incident. This will be indicated by signs or officers directing the traffic.

9.31
Mark one answer   RES s11, HC r269, 270

You're on a motorway that isn't subject to smart motorway regulations. When should you use the hard shoulder?

☐ When you're stopping in an emergency

☐ When you're leaving the motorway

☐ When you're stopping for a rest

☐ When you're joining the motorway

Don't use the hard shoulder for stopping unless it's an emergency. If you want to stop for any other reason, go to the next exit or service area.

9.32
Mark one answer   HC p102

You're in the right-hand lane of a three-lane motorway. What do these overhead signs mean?

You must obey these signs even if there appear to be no problems ahead. There could be queuing traffic or another hazard that you can't see yet.

☐ Move to the left and reduce your speed to 50 mph

☐ There are roadworks 50 metres (55 yards) ahead

☐ Use the hard shoulder until you've passed the hazard

☐ Leave the motorway at the next exit

9.33   Mark one answer   RES s11, HC r270

When are you allowed to stop on a motorway?

☐ When you need to walk and get fresh air

☐ When you wish to pick up hitchhikers

☐ When you're signalled to do so by traffic signals

☐ When you need to use a mobile telephone

You must stop if overhead gantry signs show a red cross above every lane on the motorway. If any of the other lanes doesn't show a red cross, you may move into that lane and continue if it's safe to do so.

9.34   Mark one answer   RES s11

You're travelling in the left-hand lane of a three-lane motorway. How should you react to traffic joining from a slip road?

☐ Increase your speed to ensure they join behind you

☐ Adjust your speed or change lane if you can do so safely

☐ Maintain a steady speed

☐ Switch on your hazard warning lights

Plan well ahead when approaching a slip road. If you see traffic joining the motorway, be prepared to adjust your speed or move to another lane if it's safe to do so. This can help the flow of traffic joining the motorway, especially at peak times.

9.35   Mark one answer   RES s11, HC r264

How should you use the lanes on a motorway?

☐ Use the lane that has the least traffic

☐ Keep to the left-hand lane unless you're overtaking

☐ Overtake using the lane that's clearest

☐ Stay in one lane until you reach your exit

You should normally travel in the left-hand lane unless you're overtaking a slower-moving vehicle. When you've finished overtaking, move back into the left-hand lane, but don't cut across in front of the vehicle that you've overtaken.

9.36   Mark one answer   RES s11, HC r268

You're travelling along a motorway. When are you allowed to overtake on the left?

☐ When you can see well ahead that the hard shoulder is clear

☐ When the traffic in the right-hand lane is signalling right

☐ When you warn drivers behind by signalling left

☐ When in queues and traffic to your right is moving more slowly than you are

Never overtake on the left, unless the traffic is moving in queues and the queue on your right is moving more slowly than the one you're in.

9.37 — Mark one answer — RES s18

When would you use an emergency refuge area on a smart motorway?

☐ In cases of emergency or breakdown

☐ If you think you'll be involved in a road rage incident

☐ To stop and check where you are

☐ To make a private phone call

On smart motorways, emergency refuge areas are built at the side of the hard shoulder. If you break down, try to get your vehicle into the refuge, where there's an emergency telephone. The phone connects directly to a control centre. Remember to take care when rejoining the motorway, especially if the hard shoulder is being used as a running lane.

9.38 — Mark one answer — RES s18, HC r108

Traffic officers operate on motorways and some primary routes in England and Wales. What are they authorised to do?

☐ Stop and arrest drivers who break the law

☐ Repair broken-down vehicles on the motorway

☐ Issue fixed penalty notices

☐ Stop and direct anyone on a motorway

Traffic officers don't have enforcement powers but are able to stop and direct people on motorways and some 'A' class roads. They operate in England and Wales and work in partnership with the police at incidents, providing a highly trained and visible service. They're recognised by an orange-and-yellow jacket and their vehicle has yellow-and-black markings.

You're on a smart motorway. What does it mean when a red cross is displayed above the hard shoulder?

Some motorways have been redesigned as smart motorways. At certain times, the hard shoulder will be open as a running lane. However, a red cross above the hard shoulder shows that it isn't open as a running lane and should only be used for emergencies and breakdowns.

- ☐ Pull up in this lane to answer your mobile phone
- ☐ Use this lane as a running lane
- ☐ This lane can be used if you need a rest
- ☐ You shouldn't travel in this lane

You're on a smart motorway. What does it mean when a mandatory speed limit is displayed above the hard shoulder?

A mandatory speed-limit sign above the hard shoulder shows that this part of the road can be used as a running lane between junctions. You must stay within the speed limit. Look out for vehicles that may have broken down and could be blocking the hard shoulder.

- ☐ You shouldn't travel in this lane
- ☐ The hard shoulder can be used as a running lane
- ☐ You can park on the hard shoulder if you feel tired
- ☐ You can pull up in this lane to answer a mobile phone

9.41 — Mark one answer — RES s18, HC r269

How do smart motorways prevent traffic bunching?

☐ By using higher speed limits

☐ By using advisory speed limits

☐ By using minimum speed limits

☐ By using variable speed limits

When a smart motorway is operating, you must follow the mandatory signs on the gantries above each lane, including the hard shoulder. Variable speed limits help keep the traffic moving and also help to prevent bunching.

9.42 — Mark one answer — RES s18, HC r261

What helps to reduce traffic bunching on a motorway?

☐ Variable speed limits

☐ Contraflow systems

☐ National speed limits

☐ Lane closures

Congestion can be reduced by keeping traffic at a constant speed. At busy times, maximum speed limits are displayed on overhead gantries. These can be varied quickly, depending on the amount of traffic. By keeping to a constant speed on busy sections of motorway, overall journey times are normally improved.

9.43 — Mark one answer — RES s11, HC r270

When may you stop on a motorway?

☐ If you have to read a map

☐ When you're tired and need a rest

☐ If your mobile phone rings

☐ In an emergency or breakdown

You shouldn't normally stop on a motorway, but there may be occasions when you need to do so. If your vehicle breaks down or there's an emergency, stop on the hard shoulder and use the emergency telephones to call for assistance.

9.44 — Mark one answer — HC r261, p40

What's the national speed limit for a car or motorcycle on a motorway?

☐ 50 mph

☐ 60 mph

☐ 70 mph

☐ 80 mph

The national speed limit for a car or motorcycle on a motorway is 70 mph. Lower speed limits may be in force; for example, at roadworks. Variable speed limits also operate in some areas when the motorway is very busy. Cars or motorcycles towing trailers are subject to a lower speed limit.

283

Mark one answer

RES s11 , HC r275

You stop on the hard shoulder of a motorway and use the emergency telephone. Where's the best place to wait for help to arrive?

☐ Next to the phone

☐ Well away from the carriageway

☐ With your vehicle

☐ On the hard shoulder

When you're on the hard shoulder, you're at risk of being injured by motorway traffic. The safest place to wait is away from the carriageway, but near enough to see the emergency services arriving.

Mark one answer

RES s11, HC r270

You're on a motorway. What must you do if there's a red cross showing above every lane?

A red cross signal above all lanes mean you must stop and wait. Don't change lanes and don't try to continue any further along the motorway.

☐ Pull onto the hard shoulder

☐ Slow down and watch for further signals

☐ Leave at the next exit

☐ Stop and wait

9.47 — Mark one answer — RES s18, HC r269

You're on a smart motorway. What does it mean if a red cross is showing above the hard shoulder and mandatory speed limits above all other lanes?

A red cross above the hard shoulder shows that it's closed as a running lane and should only be used for emergencies or breakdowns. On a smart motorway, the hard shoulder may be used as a running lane at busy times. This will be shown by a mandatory speed limit on the gantry above the hard shoulder.

- ☐ The hard shoulder can be used as a rest area if you feel tired
- ☐ The hard shoulder is for emergency or breakdown use only
- ☐ The hard shoulder can be used as a normal running lane
- ☐ The hard shoulder has a speed limit of 50 mph

9.48 — Mark one answer — RES s18, HC r269

On a smart motorway, what does this sign mean?

You must obey mandatory speed-limit signs above motorway lanes, including the hard shoulder. In this case, you can use the hard shoulder as a running lane but you should look for any vehicles that may have broken down and may be blocking the hard shoulder.

- ☐ Use any lane except the hard shoulder
- ☐ Use the hard shoulder only
- ☐ Use the three right-hand lanes only
- ☐ Use all the lanes, including the hard shoulder

Mark one answer

Where should you stop to rest if you feel tired while you're travelling along a motorway?

☐ On the hard shoulder

☐ At the nearest service area

☐ On a slip road

☐ On the central reservation

If you feel tired, stop at the nearest service area. If that's too far away, leave the motorway at the next exit and find a safe place to stop. You mustn't stop on the carriageway or hard shoulder of a motorway except in an emergency, when in a traffic queue, or when signalled to do so by a police officer, a traffic officer or traffic signals. Plan your journey so that you have regular rest stops.

Case study practice – 9 Motorway riding

It's raining. You're riding your motorcycle and newly fitted sidecar.

On the motorway, you ride in the left-hand lane. You see flashing amber lights on the central reservation, with a sign showing '50'.

Later, you need to exit at the next junction, so you watch for countdown markers.

You then reach the marker showing three bars.

9.1 What would be affected by the new addition to your motorcycle?

Mark **one** answer

- ☐ Steering and braking
- ☐ Your speed limits
- ☐ Vehicle tax
- ☐ Fuel type and exhaust

RES s14

9.2 Why would you take this position on the motorway?

Mark **one** answer

- ☐ It's the only lane which is empty of other traffic
- ☐ You're not allowed in the other two lanes
- ☐ All traffic should do so unless they're overtaking
- ☐ You're only licensed to use this lane

RES s11 HC r264

9.3 What gap should you leave between your motorcycle and the vehicle in front?

Mark **one** answer

- ☐ One second
- ☐ Two seconds
- ☐ Four seconds
- ☐ Ten seconds

HC r126

9.4 What's meant by the sign and the lights?

Mark **one** answer

- ☐ Temporary minimum speed advised
- ☐ Temporary maximum distance advised
- ☐ Temporary maximum speed advised
- ☐ Temporary minimum distance advised

RES s11

9.5 At the marker, how far are you from the exit you need?

Mark **one** answer

- ☐ 400 yards
- ☐ 300 yards
- ☐ 200 yards
- ☐ 100 yards

RES s11 **HC p112**

Section ten

⟨r⟩ Rules of the road

In this section, you'll learn about

- the speed limits that you need to obey
- how to use junctions and lanes safely
- rules about overtaking
- riding over pedestrian crossings and level crossings
- where you can stop and park safely and legally.

Rules of the road

It's important that everyone knows and follows the rules of the road. Some are legal requirements and some are recommended best practice, but they all help to make the roads safer.

Speed limits

You **MUST NOT** ride faster than the speed limit for the road you're on or your vehicle type. Where no other limit is shown, the national speed limit for cars and motorcycles is

- 60 mph (96 km/h) on a single carriageway road
- 70 mph (112 km/h) on a dual carriageway or motorway.

There are lower speed limits for these vehicles when towing a trailer or caravan

- 50 mph (80 km/h) on a single carriageway road
- 60 mph (96 km/h) on a dual carriageway or motorway.

HC r124, p40

Where there are street lights, there's normally a 30 mph (48 km/h) speed limit for all vehicles unless signs show otherwise.

HC r124, p40

On some roads you may see a sign showing a minimum speed limit. You should travel above the limit shown on the sign unless it's not safe to do so.

HC p107

Do you sometimes go over the speed limit? Ask your trainer to help you identify correct speed limits. Talk to them about how to keep to a speed that's appropriate for the riding conditions. Remember, the speed limit is the absolute maximum. It doesn't mean that it's safe to ride at that speed whatever the conditions. Riding at speeds too fast for the road and traffic conditions is dangerous.

Speed limits

Type of vehicle	Built-up areas* mph (km/h)	Single carriage-ways mph (km/h)	Dual carriage-ways mph (km/h)	Motorways mph (km/h)
Cars and motorcycles (including car-derived vans up to 2 tonnes maximum laden weight)	30 (48)	60 (96)	70 (112)	70 (112)
Cars towing caravans or trailers (including car-derived vans and motorcycles)	30 (48)	50 (80)	60 (96)	60 (96)
Buses, coaches and minibuses (not exceeding 12 metres in overall length)	30 (48)	50 (80)	60 (96)	70 (112)
Goods vehicles (not exceeding 7.5 tonnes maximum laden weight)	30 (48)	50 (80)	60 (96)	70† (112)
Goods vehicles (exceeding 7.5 tonnes maximum laden weight) in England and Wales	30 (48)	50 (80)	60 (96)	60 (96)
Goods vehicles (exceeding 7.5 tonnes maximum laden weight) in Scotland	30 (48)	40 (64)	50 (80)	60 (96)

*The 30 mph limit usually applies to all traffic on all roads with street lighting unless signs show otherwise.
†60 mph (96 km/h) if articulated or towing a trailer.

Be aware that large vehicles may have speed limiters – buses and coaches are restricted to 62 mph and large goods vehicles to 56 mph.

Always ride with care and take account of the road and weather conditions. If you're riding along a street where cars are parked, keep your speed down and beware of

pedestrians (especially children) stepping out from behind parked vehicles

vehicles pulling out

drivers' doors opening.

HC r152 RES s10

At roadworks, there may be temporary speed limits to slow traffic down. These are mandatory speed limits and may be enforced by cameras.

HC r288 KYTS p90

The Think! road safety website has more advice on speed and speed limits.

http://think.gov.uk/road-safety-laws/#speed

Safety at roundabouts and junctions takes good judgement and excellent control of your motorcycle. If you're finding this a challenge, chat to your trainer about the barriers you're facing. Ask them to help you practice by choosing quiet junctions and roundabouts. Remember: waiting for a safe gap is no reflection on your riding skills. It may take some time to judge the speed of the traffic, but this is a critical part of knowing when it's safe to go.

Lanes and junctions

Some roads have lanes reserved for specific vehicles, such as cycles, buses, trams or, in some places, motorcycles. These are marked by signs and road markings, and should be used only by those vehicles during the lanes' hours of operation, unless signs indicate otherwise.

HC r141

Never ride or park in a cycle lane marked by a solid white line during its hours of operation. Don't ride or park in a cycle lane marked by a broken line unless it's unavoidable.

HC r140–141 KYTS p32–36

You should only ride over a footpath when it's necessary in order to reach a property.

HC r145

On a dual carriageway, the right-hand lane is only for turning right or overtaking. The same rule applies to three-lane dual carriageways.

Tip

If you want to turn right onto a dual carriageway that has a central reservation that's too narrow to fit the length of your vehicle, wait until the road is clear in both directions before you emerge. If you emerge into the central reservation but your vehicle is too long, it could obstruct traffic coming from your right.

HC r173 RES s9

Always be careful at junctions. As you approach a junction, move into the correct position in plenty of time.

When you're turning left, keep well to the left as you approach the junction. In slow-moving traffic, remember to check for cyclists to your left before you turn.

HC r181–183 RES s9

If you're on a busy road and you find you're travelling in the wrong direction, or you're in the wrong lane at a busy junction, keep going until you can find somewhere safe, such as a quiet side road, where you can turn around.

HC r200 RES s6, 9

A box junction is marked by yellow hatched lines, and should be kept clear. Only enter it if your exit road is clear – otherwise, wait on your side of the junction. You can, however, wait in the box if you want to turn right and are waiting for a gap in the oncoming traffic before you can turn.

HC r174 RES s7, 9

Tip

If something is blocking your side of the road, such as a parked car, you should give way to oncoming traffic if there isn't room for you both to continue safely.

RES s8

Crossroads

If you're turning right at a crossroads when an oncoming road user is also turning right, it's normally safer to keep the other vehicle to your right and turn behind it. If you have to pass in front of the other vehicle, take extra care as your view may be blocked.

HC r181

At crossroads where there aren't any signs or markings, no-one has priority. Check very carefully in all directions before you proceed.

HC r146 RES s9

Roundabouts

Roundabouts are designed to help traffic flow smoothly. Follow signs and road markings as you approach and ride around them. Normally, if you're going straight ahead

- don't signal as you approach
- signal left just after you pass the exit before the one you want.

HC r185–186 RES s9

Some vehicles may not follow the normal rules.

- Cyclists and horse riders may stay in the left-hand lane even if they're turning right.
- Long vehicles may take up a different position to stop the rear of the vehicle hitting the kerb.

HC r187

Overtaking

Overtaking can be dangerous. Ask yourself if you really need to do it, and never overtake if you're in any doubt as to whether it's safe.

HC r163 RES s8

You should normally overtake other vehicles on the right, but in a one-way street you can pass slower traffic on the left. Take extra care if you're overtaking on a dual carriageway, as the right-hand lane can also be used by traffic turning right.

HC r137–138 RES s8

Tip
At night, if a vehicle overtakes you, dip your headlights as soon as it passes you, otherwise your lights could dazzle the other driver.

HC r115

Pedestrian crossings

If someone is standing on the pavement waiting to cross at a zebra crossing, stop and let them cross if it's safe to do so.

Pelican crossings are controlled by traffic lights. When the red light changes to flashing amber, wait for any pedestrians to finish crossing before you move off.

On toucan crossings, cyclists are allowed to cycle across at the same time as pedestrians.

HC r195–199 RES s8 KYTS p124

For more information on pedestrian crossings, see section 6, Vulnerable road users.

Level crossings

A level crossing is where a railway line crosses the road.

It may have countdown markers to warn you if the crossing is hidden, such as around a bend.

Controlled crossings have traffic-light signals with twin flashing red lights, plus a warning alarm for pedestrians.

Crossings may or may not have barriers.

If this happens ...	you should do this
The warning lights come on as you're approaching the crossing.	Stop. You **MUST** obey the red lights, by law.
You're already on the crossing when the warning lights come on or a bell rings.	Keep going and clear the crossing.
You're waiting at a level crossing and a train has passed but the red lights keep flashing.	You **MUST** wait: there may be another train coming.

HC r293, p109 RES s7 KYTS p26–29

Some types of level crossing don't have lights. These include crossings with user-operated gates or barriers, and open crossings. Be careful at all level crossings, and take particular care when crossing rails – they may be slippery, particularly in wet weather.

HC r295–299 RES s8

 See the Network Rail guide to using level crossings safely.

networkrail.co.uk/running-the-railway/
looking-after-the-railway/level-crossings

Stopping and parking

Always think carefully about where you stop and park your motorcycle, to make sure it's safe and legal.

At night, the safest place to park your motorcycle is in your garage, if you have one. If you're away from home, try to find a secure car park, or park in a well-lit area.

HC r239, p131 RES s8

If you have to park on a road at night, you **MUST** leave your parking lights on if the speed limit on that road is over 30 mph (48 km/h). You should normally park on the left-hand side of the road so that other road users can see your reflectors, but in a one-way street you can park on either side.

HC r248–250 RES s13

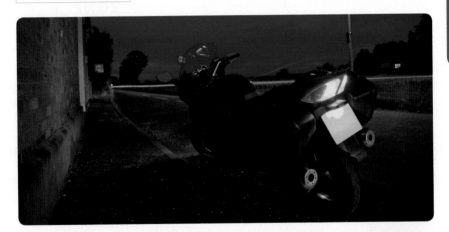

You **MUST NOT** stop on a **clearway**. On an urban clearway, you may stop, but only to drop off and pick up passengers. On a road marked with double white lines (even where one of the lines is broken), you may stop, but only to drop off and pick up passengers or to load/unload goods.

HC r240 RES s7

clearway
a stretch of road or street where stopping isn't allowed

Don't park where you would cause a danger or get in the way of other road users, such as

- on or near the brow of a hill
- at a bus stop
- opposite a traffic island
- in front of someone else's drive
- near a school entrance
- opposite or within 10 metres (32 feet) of a junction (in Northern Ireland, within 15 metres or 48 feet of a junction), unless there's an authorised parking space.

HC r242–243

You also need to make sure that you don't cause an obstruction by stopping or parking where there are restrictions shown by signs and yellow lines. In a controlled parking zone, you'll have to pay to park. Make sure you park within marked bays on the days and times shown on the zone entry signs.

HC r238, 245 RES s7 KYTS p39–50

Tip
By law, you **MUST** stop

- if you're involved in a road traffic incident
- at a red traffic light
- when signalled to do so by a police officer, traffic warden, Driver and Vehicle Standards Agency (DVSA) officer, traffic officer or school crossing patrol.

HC r105, 109, 286

Meeting the standards

You must be able to

apply a safe, systematic procedure to safely and responsibly negotiate

- junctions
- roundabouts
- crossings

turn left and right and go ahead safely and responsibly

emerge safely and responsibly into streams of traffic

cross the path of traffic safely when turning right.

You must know and understand

the rules that apply to particular junctions and roundabouts; for example, priority rules

the rules about

- merging into a stream of traffic
- crossing the path of an approaching stream of traffic
- all types of pedestrian crossing
- train and tram crossings

how to work out the speed limit where you can't see speed-limit signs.

Notes

You can use this page to make your own notes or diagrams about the key points you need to remember.

Think about

- Where might you see a minimum-speed-limit sign?
- When can you ride in a bus lane?
- What's a box junction? What mustn't you do at one of these junctions?
- Where could you park your motorcycle when you're away from home?
- What should you do if you've just ridden onto a level crossing and the warning lights start flashing?
- How close to a junction are you allowed to park?

Your notes

_____

_____

_____

_____

_____

_____

_____

_____

_____

 ## Things to discuss and practise with your trainer

These are just a few examples of what you could discuss and practise with your trainer. Read more about rules of the road to come up with your own ideas.

Discuss with your trainer

- what the 'national speed limit applies' sign looks like. What does this mean in mph on different roads and for different vehicles?
- what the speed limit will usually be if there are street lights along the road
- what the different lanes are used for on
  - a two-lane dual carriageway
  - a three-lane dual carriageway
  - a motorway.

Practise with your trainer

- negotiating roundabouts with several lanes on approach
- riding in areas with changing speed limits
- entering, exiting and overtaking on busy dual carriageways.

10.1 Mark one answer RES s8, 9

You're riding slowly in a town centre. Why should you glance over your left shoulder before turning left?

☐ To check for cyclists
☐ To help keep your balance
☐ To look for traffic signs
☐ To check for potholes

When riding slowly, you must remember to look out for cyclists - they can travel quickly and fit through surprisingly narrow spaces. Before you turn left in slow-moving traffic, it's important to check that a cyclist isn't trying to filter past on your left.

10.2 Mark one answer RES s7, HC r140, 300

Which lane must not be used by a motorcyclist?

☐ Crawler lane
☐ Overtaking lane
☐ Acceleration lane
☐ Tram lane

Always plan ahead and be aware of lanes and areas designated for specific road users only. The restrictions are sometimes in force only at certain times of day, and signs will show when they apply. In some towns, motorcycles are permitted to use bus lanes – check the signs carefully.

10.3 Mark one answer HC p112, KYTS p46

What does this sign mean?

In some towns and cities there are special areas reserved for parking motorcycles. Look out for these signs.

☐ No parking for solo motorcycles
☐ Parking for solo motorcycles
☐ Passing place for motorcycles
☐ Police motorcycles only

10.4 — Mark one answer — RES s8

You're riding on a busy dual carriageway. What should you do before you change lanes?

☐ Rely totally on your mirrors

☐ Always increase your speed

☐ Signal so that others will give way

☐ Use mirrors and shoulder checks

Before changing direction, as well as using your mirrors, you may need to take a quick sideways glance to check for vehicles in your blind spots. These are the areas behind and to the side of you that aren't covered by your mirrors.

10.5 — Mark one answer — RES s8, HC r241

You're looking for somewhere to park your motorcycle. What should you do if the area is full, except for spaces marked 'disabled use'?

☐ Use these one of these spaces because elsewhere is full

☐ Park in one of these spaces but stay with your motorcycle

☐ Use one of the spaces as long as one is kept free

☐ Wait for a regular parking space to become free

It's illegal to park in a space reserved for disabled users unless you're permitted to do so. These spaces are provided for people with limited mobility, who may need extra space to get into and out of their vehicle.

10.6 — Mark one answer — RES s10, HC r155-156

You're on a narrow road with passing places. What should you do if a car is coming towards you?

If you meet another vehicle on a narrow road and the passing place is on your left, pull into it. If the passing place is on your right, wait opposite it.

☐ Pull into a passing place on your right

☐ Force the other driver to reverse

☐ Turn round and ride back to the main road

☐ Pull into a passing place on your left

You're turning right at this crossroads. The oncoming driver is also turning right. Why is it safer to turn behind the car?

When turning right at this crossroads, keeping the oncoming car to your right will give you a clear view of the road ahead.

☐ So you can see approaching traffic

☐ So you can keep close to the kerb

☐ So you can keep clear of following traffic

☐ So you can make oncoming vehicles stop

What should you do when you're filtering through slow-moving or stationary traffic?

☐ Watch for vehicles emerging from side roads

☐ Continually use your horn as a warning

☐ Stand up on the footrests for a good view ahead

☐ Ride with your hazard warning lights on

Other road users may not expect or look for motorcycles filtering through slow-moving or stationary traffic. Your view will be reduced by the vehicles around you. Watch out for pedestrians walking between the vehicles, vehicles changing direction and vehicles turning into or out of side roads.

You're riding towards roadworks where temporary traffic lights are on red. What should you do if the road ahead is clear?

☐ Ride on with extreme caution

☐ Ride on at normal speed

☐ Carry on if approaching cars have stopped

☐ Wait for the green light

You must obey all traffic signs and signals. Just because the lights are temporary, it doesn't mean that you can disregard them.

10.10 — Mark one answer — RES s19

What should you fit to your motorcycle if you're going abroad and you'll be riding on the right-hand side of the road?

☐ Twin headlights
☐ Headlight deflectors
☐ Tinted yellow brake lights
☐ Tinted red indicator lenses

When abroad and riding on the right, deflectors are usually required to prevent your headlights from dazzling approaching drivers.

10.11 — Mark one answer — RES s14

What's the minimum engine size required to tow a trailer with your motorcycle?

☐ 50 cc
☐ 125 cc
☐ 525 cc
☐ 1000 cc

Towing a trailer requires special care. You must obey the restrictions that apply when towing – including the 125 cc minimum size of your motorcycle engine and the reduced national speed limits. Don't forget the trailer is there, especially when negotiating bends and junctions.

10.12 — Mark one answer — HC r124, p40

What's the national speed limit on a single carriageway?

☐ 40 mph
☐ 50 mph
☐ 60 mph
☐ 70 mph

You don't have to ride at the speed limit. Use your own judgement and ride at a speed that suits the prevailing road, weather and traffic conditions.

10.13 — Mark one answer — HC r105, 109, 286

When must you stop your motorcycle?

☐ At a clear pelican crossing when the amber light is flashing
☐ At an empty zebra crossing
☐ When signalled to do so by a police officer
☐ At a junction with double broken white lines

Don't stop or hold up traffic unnecessarily. However, there are occasions when you must stop by law. These include

• when signalled to do so by a school crossing patrol, police officer or traffic officer
• at a red traffic light
• at a junction with a 'stop' sign.

307

What's the meaning of this sign?

This sign doesn't tell you the speed limit in figures. You should know the speed limit for the type of road that you're on and the type of vehicle that you're driving. Study your copy of The Highway Code.

☐ Local speed limit applies

☐ No waiting on the carriageway

☐ National speed limit applies

☐ No entry for vehicles

What's the national speed limit for cars and motorcycles on a dual carriageway?

☐ 30 mph

☐ 50 mph

☐ 60 mph

☐ 70 mph

Make sure that you know the speed limit for the road that you're on. The speed limit on a dual carriageway or motorway is 70 mph for cars and motorcycles, unless signs indicate otherwise. The speed limits for different types of vehicle are listed in The Highway Code.

There are no speed-limit signs on the road. How is a 30 mph limit generally indicated?

☐ By hazard warning lines

☐ By street lighting

☐ By pedestrian islands

☐ By double or single yellow lines

There's a 30 mph speed limit where there are street lights unless signs show another limit.

10.17   Mark one answer   HC r124

What will the speed limit usually be where you can see street lights but no speed-limit signs?

☐ 30 mph

☐ 40 mph

☐ 50 mph

☐ 60 mph

The presence of street lights generally indicates that there's a 30 mph speed limit, unless signs tell you otherwise.

10.18   Mark one answer   KYTS p21

What does this sign mean?

The red slash through the sign indicates that the restriction has ended. In this case, the restriction was a minimum speed limit of 30 mph.

☐ Minimum speed 30 mph

☐ End of maximum speed

☐ End of minimum speed

☐ Maximum speed 30 mph

10.19   Mark one answer   RES s8, HC r163

What should you do if you want to overtake a tractor but aren't sure that it's safe?

☐ Follow another vehicle as it overtakes the tractor

☐ Sound your horn to make the tractor driver pull over

☐ Speed past, flashing your lights at oncoming traffic

☐ Stay behind it if you're in any doubt

Following a tractor can be frustrating, but never overtake if you're unsure whether it's safe. Ask yourself: 'Can I see far enough down the road to ensure that I can complete the manoeuvre safely?' It's better to be delayed for a minute or two than to take a chance that may cause a collision.

Which vehicle is most likely to take an unusual course at a roundabout?

☐ Estate car

☐ Milk float

☐ Delivery van

☐ Long vehicle

Long vehicles might have to take a slightly different position when approaching the roundabout or going around it. This is to stop the rear of the vehicle cutting in and mounting the kerb.

When may you stop on a clearway?

☐ Never

☐ When it's busy

☐ In the rush hour

☐ During daylight hours

Clearways are in place so that traffic can flow without the obstruction of parked vehicles. Just one parked vehicle can cause an obstruction for all other traffic. You mustn't stop where a clearway is in force, not even to pick up or set down passengers.

What's the meaning of this sign?

☐ No entry

☐ Waiting restrictions

☐ National speed limit

☐ School crossing patrol

This sign indicates that there are waiting restrictions. It's normally accompanied by details of when the restrictions are in force.

Details of most signs in common use are shown in The Highway Code. For more comprehensive coverage, see Know Your Traffic Signs.

10.23 — Mark one answer — RES s13

You're looking for somewhere to park at night. When may you park on the right-hand side of the road?

- ☐ When you're in a one-way street
- ☐ When you have your sidelights on
- ☐ When you're more than 10 metres (32 feet) from a junction
- ☐ When you're under a lamppost

Red rear reflectors show up when headlights shine on them. These are useful when you're parked at night, but they'll only reflect if you park in the same direction as the traffic flow. Normally you should park on the left, but in a one-way street you may also park on the right-hand side of the road.

10.24 — Mark one answer — RES s8, HC r137-138

When should you use the right-hand lane of a three-lane dual carriageway?

- ☐ When you're overtaking only
- ☐ When you're overtaking or turning right
- ☐ When you're using cruise control
- ☐ When you're turning right only

You should normally use the left-hand lane on any dual carriageway unless you're overtaking or turning right.

When overtaking on a dual carriageway, look for vehicles ahead that are turning right. They may be slowing or stopped. You need to see them in good time so that you can take appropriate action.

10.25 — Mark one answer — RES s8

You're approaching a busy junction. What should you do when, at the last moment, you realise you're in the wrong lane?

- ☐ Continue in that lane
- ☐ Force your way into the lane you need
- ☐ Stop until the area has cleared
- ☐ Use arm signals to help you change lane

There are times when road markings are obscured by queuing traffic, or you're unsure which lane to use. If, at the last moment, you find you're in the wrong lane, don't cut across or bully other drivers to let you in. Follow the lane you're in and find somewhere safe to turn around and rejoin your route.

10.26 — Mark one answer — RES s8, HC r143

Where may you overtake on a one-way street?

- ☐ Only on the left-hand side
- ☐ Overtaking isn't allowed
- ☐ Only on the right-hand side
- ☐ On either the right or the left

You can overtake other traffic on either side when travelling in a one-way street. Make full use of your mirrors and ensure it's clear all around before you attempt to overtake. Look for signs and road markings, and use the most suitable lane for your destination.

What signal should you give when you're going straight ahead at a roundabout?

☐ Signal left before leaving the roundabout

☐ Don't signal at any time

☐ Signal right when you're approaching the roundabout

☐ Signal left when you're approaching the roundabout

When going straight ahead at a roundabout, don't signal as you approach it. Signal left just after passing the exit before the one you wish to take.

Which vehicle might have to take a different course from normal at a roundabout?

☐ Sports car

☐ Van

☐ Estate car

☐ Long vehicle

A long vehicle may have to straddle lanes either on or approaching a roundabout so that the rear wheels don't mount the kerb.

If you're following a long vehicle, stay well back and give it plenty of room.

When may you enter a box junction?

☐ When there are fewer than two vehicles ahead

☐ When signalled by another road user

☐ When your exit road is clear

☐ When traffic signs direct you

Yellow box junctions are marked on the road to prevent the road becoming blocked. Don't enter the box unless your exit road is clear. You may wait in the box if you want to turn right and your exit road is clear but oncoming traffic or other vehicles waiting to turn right are preventing you from making the turn.

10.30   Mark one answer   RES s7, HC r174

When may you stop and wait in a box junction?

The purpose of yellow box markings is to keep junctions clear of queuing traffic. You may only wait in the marked area when you're turning right and your exit lane is clear but you can't complete the turn because of oncoming traffic or other traffic waiting to turn right.

- ☐ When oncoming traffic prevents you from turning right
- ☐ When you're in a queue of traffic turning left
- ☐ When you're in a queue of traffic going ahead
- ☐ When you're on a roundabout

10.31   Mark one answer   HC r105–109

Who is authorised to signal you to stop?

- ☐ A motorcyclist
- ☐ A pedestrian
- ☐ A police officer
- ☐ A bus driver

You must obey signals to stop given by police and traffic officers, traffic wardens and school crossing patrols. Failure to do so is an offence and could lead to prosecution.

10.32   Mark one answer   RES s8, HC r195

What should you do if you see a pedestrian waiting at a zebra crossing?

- ☐ Go on quickly before they step onto the crossing
- ☐ Stop before you reach the zigzag lines and let them cross
- ☐ Be ready to slow down or stop to let them cross
- ☐ Ignore them as they're still on the pavement

By standing on the pavement, the pedestrian is showing an intention to cross. By looking well ahead, you'll give yourself time to see the pedestrian, check your mirrors and respond safely.

Which road users benefit from toucan crossings?

☐ Car drivers and motorcyclists

☐ Cyclists and pedestrians

☐ Bus and lorry drivers

☐ Tram and train drivers

Toucan crossings are similar to pelican crossings but there's no flashing amber phase. Cyclists share the crossing with pedestrians and are allowed to cycle across when the green cycle symbol is shown.

You're waiting at a pelican crossing. What does it mean when the red light changes to flashing amber?

☐ Give way to pedestrians on the crossing

☐ Move off immediately without any hesitation

☐ Wait for the green light before moving off

☐ Get ready and go when the continuous amber light shows

This light allows pedestrians already on the crossing to get to the other side in their own time, without being rushed. Don't rev your engine or start to move off while they're still crossing.

You see these double white lines along the centre of the road. When may you park on the left?

You mustn't park or stop on a road marked with double white lines (even where one of the lines is broken) except to pick up or set down passengers.

☐ If the line nearest to you is broken

☐ When there are no yellow lines

☐ To pick up or set down passengers

☐ During daylight hours only

10.36 — Mark one answer — HC r181

You're turning right at a crossroads. An oncoming driver is also turning right. What's the advantage of turning behind the oncoming vehicle?

- ☐ You'll have a clearer view of any approaching traffic
- ☐ You'll use less fuel because you can stay in a higher gear
- ☐ You'll have more time to turn
- ☐ You'll be able to turn without stopping

When turning right at a crossroads where oncoming traffic is also turning right, it's generally safer to turn behind the approaching vehicle. This allows you a clear view of approaching traffic and is called 'turning offside to offside'. However, some junctions, usually controlled by traffic-light filters – are marked for vehicles to turn nearside to nearside.

10.37 — Mark one answer — RES s10, HC r152

You're travelling along a residential street. There are parked vehicles on the left-hand side. Why should you keep your speed down?

- ☐ So that oncoming traffic can see you more clearly
- ☐ You may set off car alarms
- ☐ There may be delivery lorries on the street
- ☐ Children may run out from between the vehicles

Travel slowly and carefully near parked vehicles. Beware of

- vehicles pulling out, especially bicycles and motorcycles
- pedestrians, especially children, who may run out from between cars
- drivers opening their doors.

10.38 — Mark one answer — RES s7

What should you do when there's an obstruction on your side of the road?

- ☐ Carry on, as you have priority
- ☐ Give way to oncoming traffic
- ☐ Wave oncoming vehicles through
- ☐ Accelerate to get past first

Take care if you have to pass an obstruction, such as a parked vehicle, on your side of the road. Give way to oncoming traffic if there isn't enough room for you both to continue safely.

10.39 — Mark one answer — HC r137

When would you use the right-hand lane of a two-lane dual carriageway?

- ☐ When you're turning right or overtaking
- ☐ When you're passing a side road on the left
- ☐ When you're staying at the minimum allowed speed
- ☐ When you're travelling at a constant high speed

Normally you should travel in the left-hand lane and only use the right-hand lane for overtaking or turning right. Move back into the left lane as soon as it's safe but don't cut in across the path of the vehicle you've just passed.

10.40   Mark one answer   RES s9, HC r146

Who has priority at an unmarked crossroads?

☐ The larger vehicle

☐ No-one has priority

☐ The faster vehicle

☐ The smaller vehicle

Practise good observation in all directions before you emerge or make a turn. Proceed only when you're sure it's safe to do so.

10.41   NI EXEMPT   Mark one answer   HC r243

What's the nearest you may park to a junction?

☐ 10 metres (32 feet)

☐ 12 metres (39 feet)

☐ 15 metres (49 feet)

☐ 20 metres (66 feet)

Don't park within 10 metres (32 feet) of a junction (unless in an authorised parking place). This is to allow drivers emerging from, or turning into, the junction a clear view of the road they're joining. It also allows them to see hazards such as pedestrians or cyclists at the junction.

10.42   Mark one answer   HC r239

You're looking for somewhere to safely park your vehicle. Where would you choose to park?

☐ At or near a bus stop

☐ In a designated parking space

☐ Near the brow of a hill

☐ On the approach to a level crossing

It may be tempting to park where you shouldn't while you run a quick errand. Careless parking is a selfish act and could endanger other road users.

10.43   Mark one answer   RES s7, HC r293, KYTS p27

You're waiting at a level crossing. What must you do if a train passes but the lights keep flashing?

☐ Carry on waiting

☐ Phone the signal operator

☐ Edge over the stop line and look for trains

☐ Park and investigate

If the lights at a level crossing keep flashing after a train has passed, you should continue to wait, because another train might be coming. Time seems to pass slowly when you're held up in a queue. Be patient and wait until the lights stop flashing.

10.44 Mark one answer HC p107

What does this sign mean?

This sign shows that you're leaving a controlled parking zone and those restrictions no longer apply.

☐ No through road
☐ End of traffic-calming zone
☐ Free-parking zone ends
☐ End of controlled parking zone

10.45 Mark one answer HC r288, KYTS p139

What must you do if you come across roadworks that have a temporary speed limit displayed?

☐ Obey the speed limit
☐ Obey the limit, but only during rush hour
☐ Ignore the displayed limit
☐ Use your own judgement; the limit is only advisory

Where there are extra hazards, such as at roadworks, it's often necessary to slow traffic by imposing a lower speed limit. These speed limits aren't advisory; they must be obeyed.

10.46 Mark one answer HC r115

You're in a built-up area at night and the road is well lit. Why should you use dipped headlights?

☐ So that you can see further along the road
☐ So that you can go at a much faster speed
☐ So that you can switch to main beam quickly
☐ So that you can be easily seen by others

You may be difficult to see when you're travelling at night, even on a well-lit road. If you use dipped headlights rather than sidelights, other road users should be able to see you more easily.

Mark one answer **RES s9, HC r173**

You're turning right onto a dual carriageway. What should you do if the central reservation is too narrow to contain your vehicle?

☐ Proceed to the central reservation and wait

☐ Wait until the road is clear in both directions

☐ Stop in the first lane so that other vehicles give way

☐ Emerge slightly to show your intentions

When the central reservation is narrow, it may not be able to contain your vehicle. In this case, you should treat a dual carriageway as one road. Wait until the road is clear in both directions before emerging to turn right. If you try to treat it as two separate roads and wait in the middle, your vehicle will stick out and cause an obstruction that may lead to a collision.

10.48 **Mark one answer** **HC p40**

What's the national speed limit on a single carriageway road for cars and motorcycles?

☐ 30 mph

☐ 50 mph

☐ 60 mph

☐ 70 mph

Exceeding the speed limit is dangerous and can result in you receiving penalty points on your licence. It isn't worth it. You should know the speed limit for the road that you're on by observing the road signs. Different speed limits apply if you're towing a trailer.

10.49 **Mark one answer** **RES s13, HC r249**

What should you do when you park at night on a road that has a 40 mph speed limit?

☐ Park facing the traffic

☐ Leave parking lights switched on

☐ Leave dipped headlights switched on

☐ Park near a street light

You must use parking lights when parking at night on a road or in a lay-by on a road with a speed limit greater than 30 mph. You must also park in the direction of the traffic flow and not close to a junction.

10.50   Mark one answer   KYTS p27

Where will you see these red and white markers?

☐ Approaching the end of a motorway

☐ Approaching a concealed level crossing

☐ Approaching a concealed speed-limit sign

☐ Approaching the end of a dual carriageway

If there's a bend just before a level crossing, you may not be able to see the level-crossing barriers or waiting traffic. These signs give you an early warning that you may find these hazards just around the bend.

10.51   Mark one answer   RES s18, HC r108

You're travelling on a motorway in England. When must you stop your vehicle?

☐ When signalled to stop by a roadworks supervisor

☐ When signalled to stop by a traffic officer

☐ When signalled to stop by a pedestrian on the hard shoulder

☐ When signalled to stop by a driver who has broken down

You'll find traffic officers on motorways and some primary routes in England and Wales. They work in partnership with the police, helping to keep traffic moving and helping to make your journey as safe as possible. It's an offence not to comply with the directions given by a traffic officer.

10.52   Mark one answer   RES s9, HC r186

How should you signal if you're going straight ahead at a roundabout?

☐ Signal right on the approach and then left to leave the roundabout

☐ Signal left after you leave the roundabout and enter the new road

☐ Signal right on the approach to the roundabout and keep the signal on

☐ Signal left just after you pass the exit before the one you're going to take

To go straight ahead at a roundabout, you should normally approach in the left-hand lane, but check the road markings. At some roundabouts, the left lane on approach is marked 'left turn only', so make sure you use the correct lane to go ahead. You won't normally need to signal as you approach, but signal before you leave the roundabout, as other road users need to know your intentions.

Case study practice – 10 Rules of the road

You're riding your motorcycle in a residential area.

At a signed mini-roundabout, you turn right.

Later, you come to roadworks. There are temporary traffic lights showing red, but no oncoming traffic.

Once past, you turn right into a residential street containing road humps. You see a sign showing red-and-black arrows, asking road users to give way to oncoming traffic.

10.1 What colour is the roundabout sign?

Mark **one** answer

☐ Blue and white

☐ Red and white

☐ Green and white

☐ Black and white

HC p107 KYTS p19, 69

10.2 What should you do at the traffic lights?

Mark **one** answer

☐ Ride past the lights quickly as there's no oncoming traffic

☐ Stop and wait until the green light shows

☐ Get off and wheel your motorcycle through the roadworks

☐ Call the helpline because the lights must be faulty

HC p109

10.3 What should you do before making the turn?

Mark **one** answer

☐ Check that your hazard warning lights are working

☐ Turn and look back over your left shoulder

☐ Position yourself by the left-hand kerb

☐ Take a look over your right shoulder

RES s8, 9

10.4 What are the features in the residential street for?

Mark **one** answer

☐ To increase reaction time

☐ To monitor tyre pressure

☐ To slow down the traffic

☐ To test the suspension

RES s7 **HC r153**

10.5 What shape is the arrowed sign?

Mark **one** answer

☐ Circular

☐ Triangular

☐ Rectangular

☐ Square

KYTS p18

Section eleven

Road and traffic signs

In this section, you'll learn about

- what the shapes of road sign can tell you
- what road markings mean
- the sequence and meaning of traffic lights
- motorway warning lights
- the signals used by other drivers and by police officers.

Road and traffic signs

Road and traffic signs give important information to keep you safe on the road, so it's essential that you know what they mean and what you need to do when you see them.

Signs

The shape and colour of a road sign tell you about its meaning.

Circular sign give orders.

Blue circles give an instruction or show which sort of road user can use a route, eg cyclists, pedestrians, trams.

Red rings or circles tell you what you mustn't do.

Triangular signs give warnings

Rectangular signs give information.

Signs with a brown background give tourist information.

KYTS p9, 84, 100–104

The exception to the shape rule is the 'stop' sign: this is octagonal so that it stands out and can be understood even if it's partly covered; for example, by snow.

HC r109 RES s7 KYTS p9

Maximum speed limits are shown inside red circles: you **MUST NOT** go faster than the speed shown. Where no speed limit is shown, the national speed limits (given on page 292) apply. Speed-limit signs may be combined with other signs, such as those indicating a traffic-calmed area.

HC p106 KYTS p20

It's impossible to mention all the signs here. *Know Your Traffic Signs* shows all the signs you're likely to see and *The Official Highway Code* contains important advice, information on current laws in Great Britain, and best practice in road safety. It's important that you get to know these to make sure that you don't break the law.

 Test your knowledge of signs using the activity on the Safe Driving for Life website.

safedrivingforlife.info/road-signs-quiz

Road markings

Markings on the road give information, orders or warnings. As a general rule, the more paint there is, the more important the message.

HC r127–131 RES s7 KYTS p62–64

There are three types of road markings.

Along the middle of the road

Short broken white lines mark the centre of the road.

Longer broken white lines are hazard warning lines: only overtake if you can see that the road ahead is clear.

Along the middle of the road

You **MUST NOT** cross or straddle double white lines with a solid white line on your side of the road unless

- you're turning into a junction or an entrance
- you need to pass a stationary vehicle
- you need to overtake a cyclist, horse or road maintenance vehicle if they're moving at 10 mph or less.

White diagonal stripes or chevrons separate lanes of traffic or protect traffic turning right.

Sometimes red tarmac is used within a block of white lines or diagonals. This highlights the area that separates traffic flowing in opposite directions.

HC p114 RES s7 KYTS p62–64

Along the side of the road

A white line shows the edge of the carriageway.

Yellow lines show waiting and stopping restrictions.

White zigzag lines at pedestrian crossings mean no stopping or parking at any time.

HC p115, 116 RES s7 KYTS p39–44, 56, 65, 122

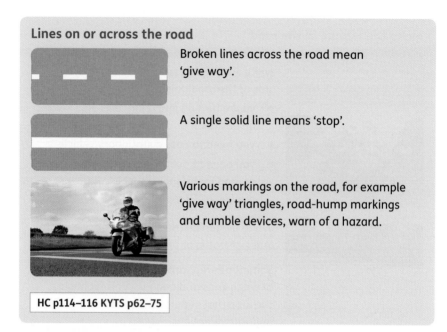

Lines on or across the road

Broken lines across the road mean 'give way'.

A single solid line means 'stop'.

Various markings on the road, for example 'give way' triangles, road-hump markings and rumble devices, warn of a hazard.

HC p114–116 KYTS p62–75

As with signs, you should look at *Know Your Traffic Signs* and *The Official Highway Code* to learn more about road markings.

You may see reflective studs on motorways and other roads. These are especially useful at night and when visibility is poor, as they help to make the lanes and edges of the road easier to see. Different coloured studs are used on motorways to help drivers and riders identify which lane they're using. See section 9, Motorway riding, for more details.

HC r132

Traffic lights and warning lights

Traffic lights work in a sequence.

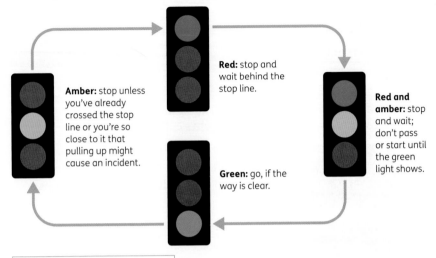

Red: stop and wait behind the stop line.

Amber: stop unless you've already crossed the stop line or you're so close to it that pulling up might cause an incident.

Red and amber: stop and wait; don't pass or start until the green light shows.

Green: go, if the way is clear.

> **HC p102 RES s7 KYTS p119–120**

On some traffic lights there's a green filter arrow. This means you can go in the direction of the arrow, even if the main light isn't showing green.

If a set of traffic lights is out of order, ride very carefully: nobody has priority. There may be a sign telling you that the lights aren't working.

> **RES s7**

Red flashing lights are used at level crossings and other locations, such as lifting bridges and outside some fire stations. You **MUST** stop when these show.

> **HC r293, p102 KYTS p13, 26–29, 120**

327

At roadworks, traffic can be controlled by

- a police officer
- traffic lights
- a 'stop/go' board.

HC r288 KYTS p136

On motorways, signals on the overhead gantries or at the roadside may also have flashing lights.

Amber warns you of a hazard (eg lane closures, to leave at the next exit, fog) or a temporary maximum speed advised for the conditions.

If red lights flash on a signal and a red X is showing, you **MUST NOT** drive in the lane shown as closed beyond the signal.

If red lights flash on a signal in the central reservation or on the side of the road and the lane closed sign is showing, you **MUST NOT** go beyond the signal in any lane. If red lights flash at the start of a slip road, you **MUST NOT** enter the slip road or try and join the motorway at that junction.

HC r255–258, p102 KYTS p89–91

Signals given by drivers and the police

Road users normally signal where they're intending to turn by using their indicators. Make sure that you cancel your indicators after you've turned, to avoid confusing other road users. Be aware that another driver may have left their indicator on by mistake.

If you're emerging from a junction and a driver coming along the main road from the right is close to you and indicating left, wait until the vehicle starts to turn before you emerge.

HC r103–104 RES s5

You may need to use an arm signal to strengthen or clarify the message given by your indicators, such as when you're signalling to turn right in busy traffic.

However, don't keep signalling with your arm while you're turning left or right, because you'll have less control over the steering.

If you're slowing down and stopping just after a junction, wait to signal until you're passing the junction, or just after it.

You can use the horn to warn others that you're there. You **MUST NOT** use it between 11.30 pm and 7.00 am when riding in a built-up area, except when another road user puts you in danger. You **MUST NOT** use your horn when stationary unless another vehicle is likely to cause a danger.

The only reason you should flash your headlights is to warn other road users that you're there.

HC r110–112 RES s6

Tip

If you're riding on a motorway or unrestricted dual carriageway, you can briefly use your hazard warning lights to warn drivers behind you when there's an obstruction ahead.

HC r116 RES s5, 11

Police or traffic officers may signal to you if they're directing traffic. Make sure that you know all the official arm signals they might use, in case you need to react to them.

HC p103–105

A police or traffic officer following you in a patrol vehicle may flash their headlights, indicate left and point to the left to direct you to stop. Pull up on the left as soon as it's safe to do so.

HC r106

Remember, you **MUST** obey any signals given by police or traffic officers, traffic wardens and signs used by school crossing patrols.

HC r105–108, p104–105

Road lanes

Contraflow lanes are lanes that flow in the opposite direction to most of the traffic. Bus and cycle contraflow lanes may be found in one-way streets. They'll be signed and marked on the road. Don't try to ride against the flow of traffic in these lanes.

HC r140–141, 143 RES s7

You may also see contraflow lanes at roadworks. When you see the signs

- reduce your speed and comply with any temporary speed limits
- choose an appropriate lane in good time
- keep the correct distance from the vehicle in front.

RES s11 KYTS p128–133

The centre and right-hand lanes of a three-lane motorway are overtaking lanes. Always move back to a lane on your left after overtaking, to allow other vehicles to overtake. On a free-flowing motorway or dual carriageway, you mustn't overtake other vehicles on their left.

HC r264, 268 RES s11

Meeting the standards

You must be able to

respond correctly to all
- permanent traffic signals, signs and road markings
- temporary traffic signals, signs and road markings.

You must know and understand

the meaning of all mandatory traffic signs and how to respond to them

the meaning of all warning signs and how to respond to them

the meaning of all road markings and how to respond to them.

Notes

You can use this page to make your own notes or diagrams about the key points you need to remember.

Think about

- When are you allowed to cross double white lines along the centre of the road?
- What must you never do on zigzag lines?
- What shape is the 'stop' sign?
- What should you do at an amber traffic light?
- When might you need to use arm signals?

Your notes

_____

_____

_____

_____

_____

_____

_____

_____

 # Things to discuss and practise with your trainer

These are just a few examples of what you could discuss and practise with your trainer. Read more about road and traffic signs to come up with your own ideas.

Discuss with your trainer

- which is the only octagonal road sign and why it's unique
- what these shapes of sign tell you
  - round
  - triangular
  - rectangular
- what signs are relevant to solo motorcycles and what they mean.

Practise with your trainer

- identifying signs, from _The Official Highway Code_ and _Know Your Traffic Signs_
- riding through a busy town centre and identifying all the warning signs that you see. Discuss these after your lesson
- riding to a level crossing and identifying the signs and signals that you find there.

How should you give an arm signal to turn left?

☐   ☐

☐   ☐

Arm signals can be effective during daylight, especially when you're wearing bright clothing. Practise giving arm signals when you're learning. You need to be able to keep full control of your motorcycle with one hand off the handlebars.

You're giving an arm signal, ready to turn left. Why should you return your hand to the handlebars while you turn?

Consider giving an arm signal if it will help other road users; for example, in bright sunshine, when your indicators may be difficult to see. Don't maintain an arm signal when turning, but return your hand to the handlebars to help you steer through the turn.

☐   Because you might hit a pedestrian on the corner

☐   To help you keep control of the steering

☐   Because you'll need to hold the clutch lever

☐   To stop other motorists thinking that you're stopping on the corner

11.3 — Mark one answer — RES s12, HC p109, KYTS p12

What does this sign mean?

Side winds can suddenly blow you off course. Keep your speed down when it's very windy, especially on exposed roads.

☐ Side winds
☐ Airport
☐ Slippery road
☐ Service area

11.4 — Mark one answer — RES s7, HC p106, KYTS p17

Which of these signs are you allowed to ride past on a solo motorcycle?

Most regulatory signs are circular. A red circle tells you what you mustn't do.

11.5 — Mark one answer — RES s6, HC r103, p103

Which of these signals should you give when slowing or stopping your motorcycle?

Arm signals can be given to reinforce your flashing indicators, especially if the indicator signal could cause confusion; for example, if you intend to pull up close to a side road.

Why should you make sure that you cancel your motorcycle's indicators after you've turned at a junction?

☐ To avoid flattening the battery

☐ To avoid misleading other road users

☐ To avoid dazzling other road users

☐ To avoid damage to the indicator relay

Always check that you've cancelled your indicators after turning. Failing to cancel your indicators could lead to a serious or even fatal collision. Other road users might pull out in front of you if they think you're going to turn off before you reach them.

Your indicators are difficult to see due to bright sunshine. What could you do to let other road users know your intentions?

☐ Give an arm signal

☐ Sound your horn

☐ Flash your headlights

☐ Keep both hands on the handlebars

Arm signals can be used to confirm your intentions when you aren't sure that your indicators can be seen by other road users. Use the signals shown in The Highway Code and return your hand to the handlebars before you turn.

You're riding on a motorway. What should you do if there's a slow-moving vehicle ahead with this sign displayed?

If this vehicle is in your lane, you'll have to move to the left. Use your mirrors and signal if necessary. When it's safe, move into the lane on your left. You should always look well ahead so that you can spot such hazards early, giving yourself time to react safely.

☐ Pass on the right

☐ Pass on the left

☐ Leave at the next exit

☐ Drive no further

11.9   Mark one answer   RES s7, HC p106, KYTS p9, 16

How can you identify traffic signs that give orders?

☐ They're rectangular with a yellow border

☐ They're triangular with a blue border

☐ They're square with a brown border

☐ They're circular with a red border

There are three basic types of traffic sign: those that warn, those that inform and those that give orders. Generally, triangular signs warn, rectangular signs give information or directions and circular signs give orders. An exception is the eight-sided 'stop' sign.

11.10   Mark one answer   RES s7, HC p106, KYTS p9, 16

What shape are traffic signs giving orders?

Road signs in the shape of a circle give orders. Those with a red circle are mostly prohibitive. The 'stop' sign is octagonal to give it greater prominence. Signs giving orders must always be obeyed.

11.11   Mark one answer   RES s7, HC p106, KYTS p9, 16

Which type of sign tells you what you must not do?

Signs in the shape of a circle give orders. A sign with a red circle means that you aren't allowed to do something. Study Know Your Traffic Signs to ensure that you understand what the different traffic signs mean.

What does this sign mean?

☐ Maximum speed limit with traffic calming

☐ Minimum speed limit with traffic calming

☐ '20 cars only' parking zone

☐ Only 20 cars allowed at any one time

If you're in a place where there are likely to be pedestrians (for example, outside a school, near a park, in a residential area or in a shopping area), you should be cautious and keep your speed down.

Many local authorities have taken steps to slow traffic down by creating traffic-calming measures such as road humps. They're there for a reason; slow down.

What does this sign mean?

☐ New speed limit 20 mph

☐ No vehicles over 30 tonnes

☐ Minimum speed limit 30 mph

☐ End of 20 mph zone

Where you see this sign, the 20 mph restriction ends and a 30 mph restriction starts. Check all around for possible hazards and only increase your speed if it's safe to do so.

11.14   Mark one answer   RES s7, HC p106, KYTS p17

What does this sign mean?

A sign will indicate which types of vehicles are prohibited from certain roads. Make sure that you know which signs apply to the vehicle you're using.

☐ No overtaking

☐ No motor vehicles

☐ Clearway (no stopping)

☐ Cars and motorcycles only

11.15   Mark one answer   RES s7, HC p106, KYTS p17

What does this sign mean?

'No entry' signs are used in places such as one-way streets to prevent vehicles driving against the traffic. To ignore one would be dangerous, both for yourself and for other road users, as well as being against the law.

☐ No parking

☐ No road markings

☐ No through road

☐ No entry

What does this sign mean?

The 'no right turn' sign may be used to warn road users that there's a 'no entry' prohibition on a road to the right ahead.

- ☐ Bend to the right
- ☐ Road on the right closed
- ☐ No traffic from the right
- ☐ No right turn

Which sign means 'no entry'?

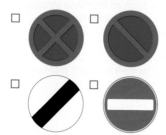

Look for and obey traffic signs. Disobeying or not seeing a sign could be dangerous. It may also be an offence for which you could be prosecuted.

What does this sign mean?

Avoid blocking tram routes. Trams are fixed on their route and can't manoeuvre around other vehicles or pedestrians. Modern trams travel quickly and are quiet, so you might not hear them approaching.

- ☐ Route for trams only
- ☐ Route for buses only
- ☐ Parking for buses only
- ☐ Parking for trams only

11.19   Mark one answer   RES s7, HC p106, KYTS p23

Which type of vehicle does this sign apply to?

The triangular shapes above and below the dimensions indicate a height restriction that applies to the road ahead.

- ☐ Wide vehicles
- ☐ Long vehicles
- ☐ High vehicles
- ☐ Heavy vehicles

11.20   Mark one answer   RES s7, HC p106, KYTS p17

Which sign means no motor vehicles allowed?

☐   ☐

☐   ☐

This sign is used to enable pedestrians to walk free from traffic. It's often found in shopping areas.

Mark one answer   RES s7, HC p106, KYTS p18

What does this sign mean?

Road signs that prohibit overtaking are placed in locations where passing the vehicle in front is dangerous. If you see this sign, don't attempt to overtake. The sign is there for a reason; you must obey it.

☐ You have priority
☐ No motor vehicles
☐ Two-way traffic
☐ No overtaking

Mark one answer   RES s7, HC p107, KYTS p54

What does this sign mean?

There'll be a plate or additional sign to tell you when the restrictions apply.

☐ Waiting restrictions apply
☐ Waiting permitted
☐ National speed limit applies
☐ Clearway (no stopping)

11.23

Mark one answer

RES s7, HC p112, KYTS p54

What does this sign mean?

Even though you've left the restricted area, make sure that you park where you won't endanger other road users or cause an obstruction.

- ☐ End of restricted speed area
- ☐ End of restricted parking area
- ☐ End of clearway
- ☐ End of cycle route

11.24

Mark one answer

RES s7, HC p107, KYTS p55

Which sign means 'no stopping'?

Stopping where this clearway restriction applies is likely to cause congestion. Allow the traffic to flow by obeying the signs.

11.25

Mark one answer

RES s7, HC p107, KYTS p55

What does this sign mean?

This is the sign for a clearway. Clearways are stretches of road where you aren't allowed to stop unless it's an emergency. Stopping where these restrictions apply may be dangerous and is likely to cause an obstruction. Restrictions might apply for several miles and this may be indicated on the sign.

- ☐ National speed limit applies
- ☐ Waiting restrictions apply
- ☐ No stopping
- ☐ No entry

What does this sign mean?

If you intend to stop and rest, this sign allows you time to reduce speed and pull over safely.

- ☐ Distance to parking place ahead
- ☐ Distance to public telephone ahead
- ☐ Distance to public house ahead
- ☐ Distance to passing place ahead

What does this sign mean?

In order to keep roads free from parked cars, there are some areas where you're allowed to park on the verge. Only do this where you see the sign. Parking on verges or footways anywhere else could lead to a fine.

- ☐ Vehicles may not park on the verge or footway
- ☐ Vehicles may park on the left-hand side of the road only
- ☐ Vehicles may park fully on the verge or footway
- ☐ Vehicles may park on the right-hand side of the road only

11.28   **Mark one answer**   RES s7, HC p106, KYTS p18

What does this traffic sign mean?

Priority signs are normally shown where the road is narrow and there isn't enough room for two vehicles to pass. Examples are narrow bridges, roadworks and where there's a width restriction.

Make sure you know who has priority; don't force your way through. Show courtesy and consideration to other road users.

☐ No overtaking allowed

☐ Give priority to oncoming traffic

☐ Two-way traffic

☐ One-way traffic only

11.29   **Mark one answer**   RES s7, HC p113, KYTS p73

What's the meaning of this traffic sign?

Don't force your way through. Show courtesy and consideration to other road users. Although you have priority, make sure oncoming traffic is going to give way before you continue.

☐ End of two-way road

☐ Give priority to vehicles coming towards you

☐ You have priority over vehicles coming towards you

☐ Bus lane ahead

What shape is a 'stop' sign?

To make it easy to recognise, the 'stop' sign is the only sign of this shape. You must stop and take effective observation before proceeding.

In winter, road signs can become covered by snow. What does this sign mean?

The 'stop' sign is the only road sign that's octagonal. This is so that it can be recognised and obeyed even if it's obscured (for example, by snow).

- ☐ Crossroads
- ☐ Give way
- ☐ Stop
- ☐ Turn right

11.32   Mark one answer   RES s7, HC p107, KYTS p21

What does this sign mean?

This sign is shown where slow-moving vehicles would impede the flow of traffic; for example, in tunnels. However, if you need to slow down or even stop to avoid an incident or potential collision, you should do so.

☐ Service area 30 miles ahead
☐ Maximum speed 30 mph
☐ Minimum speed 30 mph
☐ Lay-by 30 miles ahead

11.33   Mark one answer   RES s7, HC p107, KYTS p19

What does this sign mean?

These signs are often seen in one-way streets that have more than one lane. When you see this sign, use the route that's the most convenient and doesn't require a late change of direction.

☐ Give way to oncoming vehicles
☐ Approaching traffic passes you on both sides
☐ Turn off at the next available junction
☐ Pass either side to get to the same destination

What does this sign mean?

Take extra care when you encounter trams. Look out for road markings and signs that alert you to them. Modern trams are very quiet and you may not hear them approaching.

☐ Route for trams
☐ Give way to trams
☐ Route for buses
☐ Give way to buses

What messages are given by circular traffic signs that have a blue background?

Signs with blue circles generally give mandatory instruction. These are often found in urban areas and include signs for mini-roundabouts and directional arrows.

☐ They give temporary directions during a diversion
☐ They give directions to car parks
☐ They give motorway information
☐ They give mandatory instructions

11.36   Mark one answer   RES s7, HC p107, KYTS p33, 35

Where would you see a contraflow bus lane?

The traffic permitted to use a contraflow lane travels in the opposite direction to traffic in the other lanes on the road.

- ☐ On a dual carriageway
- ☐ On a roundabout
- ☐ On an urban motorway
- ☐ On a one-way street

11.37   Mark one answer   RES s7, HC p107, KYTS p33

What does this sign mean?

There will also be markings on the road surface to indicate the bus lane. You mustn't use this lane for parking or overtaking.

- ☐ Bus station on the right
- ☐ Contraflow bus lane
- ☐ With-flow bus lane
- ☐ Give way to buses

11.38   Mark one answer   RES s7, KYTS p84

What does a sign with a brown background show?

Signs with a brown background give directions to places of interest. They're often seen on a motorway, directing you along the easiest route to the attraction.

- ☐ Tourist directions
- ☐ Primary roads
- ☐ Motorway routes
- ☐ Minor roads

Mark one answer RES s7, KYTS p100

What does this sign mean?

These signs indicate places of interest and are designed to guide you by the easiest route. They're particularly useful when you're unfamiliar with the area.

☐ Tourist attraction
☐ Beware of trains
☐ Level crossing
☐ Beware of trams

Mark one answer RES s7, HC p108, KYTS p10

What's the purpose of triangular shaped signs?

Triangular signs warns you of hazards ahead. Make sure you look at each sign that you pass on the road, so that you don't miss any vital instructions or information.

☐ To give warnings
☐ To give information
☐ To give orders
☐ To give directions

11.41

Mark one answer

RES s7, HC p108, KYTS p10

What does this sign mean?

This type of sign warns you of hazards ahead. Make sure you look at each sign and road marking that you pass, so that you don't miss any vital instructions or information. This sign shows there's a T-junction with priority over vehicles from the right.

☐ Turn left ahead
☐ T-junction
☐ No through road
☐ Give way

11.42

Mark one answer

RES s7, HC p109, KYTS p13

What does this sign mean?

It will take up to 10 times longer to stop when it's icy. Where there's a risk of icy conditions, you need to be aware of this and take extra care. If you think the road may be icy, don't brake or steer harshly, as your tyres could lose their grip on the road.

☐ Multi-exit roundabout
☐ Risk of ice
☐ Six roads converge
☐ Place of historical interest

What does this sign mean?

The priority through the junction is shown by the broader line. You need to be aware of the hazard posed by traffic crossing or pulling out onto a major road.

☐ Crossroads
☐ Level crossing with gate
☐ Level crossing without gate
☐ Ahead only

What does this sign mean?

As you approach a roundabout, look well ahead and check all signs. Decide which exit you wish to take and move into the correct position as you approach the roundabout, signalling as required.

☐ Ring road
☐ Mini-roundabout
☐ No vehicles
☐ Roundabout

11.45   Mark one answer   RES s7, HC p108–109, KYTS p10–14

What information would be shown in a triangular road sign?

Warning signs are there to make you aware of potential hazards on the road ahead. Take note of the signs so you're prepared and can take whatever action is necessary.

☐ Road narrows
☐ Ahead only
☐ Keep left
☐ Minimum speed

11.46   Mark one answer   RES s7, HC p109, KYTS p36

What does this sign mean?

Where there's a cycle route ahead, a sign will show a bicycle in a red warning triangle. Watch out for children on bicycles and cyclists rejoining the main road.

☐ Cyclists must dismount
☐ Cycles aren't allowed
☐ Cycle route ahead
☐ Cycle in single file

Which sign means that pedestrians may be walking along the road?

☐   ☐

☐   ☐

When you pass pedestrians in the road, leave plenty of room. You might have to use the right-hand side of the road, so look well ahead, as well as in your mirrors, before pulling out. Take great care if a bend in the road obscures your view ahead.

Which sign means there's a double bend ahead?

☐   ☐

☐

Triangular signs give you a warning of hazards ahead. They're there to give you time to prepare for the hazard; for example, by adjusting your speed.

What does this sign mean?

Obey the 'give way' signs. Trams are unable to steer around you if you misjudge when it's safe to enter the junction.

☐ Wait at the barriers
☐ Wait at the crossroads
☐ Give way to trams
☐ Give way to farm vehicles

11.50   Mark one answer   RES s7, HC p109, KYTS p72

What does this sign mean?

☐ Hump bridge
☐ Humps in the road
☐ Entrance to tunnel
☐ Soft verges

These humps have been put in place to slow the traffic down. They're usually found in residential areas. Slow down to an appropriate speed.

11.51   Mark one answer   RES s7, HC p108, KYTS p11

Which sign means the end of a dual carriageway?

☐   ☐

☐   ☐

If you're overtaking, make sure you move back safely into the left-hand lane before you reach the end of the dual carriageway.

11.52   Mark one answer   RES s7, HC p108, KYTS p11

What does this sign mean?

☐ End of dual carriageway
☐ Tall bridge
☐ Road narrows
☐ End of narrow bridge

Don't wait until the last moment before moving into the left-hand lane. Plan ahead and don't rely on other traffic letting you in.

What does this sign mean?

A warning sign with a picture of a windsock indicates that there may be strong side winds. This sign is often found on exposed roads.

☐ Side winds
☐ Road noise
☐ Airport
☐ Adverse camber

What does this traffic sign mean?

This sign is there to alert you to the likelihood of danger ahead. It may be accompanied by a plate indicating the type of hazard. Be ready to reduce your speed and take avoiding action.

☐ Slippery road ahead
☐ Tyres liable to punctures ahead
☐ Danger ahead
☐ Service area ahead

11.55   Mark one answer   RES s7, HC p109, KYTS p13-14

You're about to overtake. What should you do when you see this sign?

Hidden dip

☐ Overtake the other driver as quickly as possible

☐ Move to the right to get a better view

☐ Switch your headlights on before overtaking

☐ Hold back until you can see clearly ahead

You won't be able to see any hazards that might be hidden in the dip. As well as oncoming traffic, the dip may conceal

- cyclists
- horse riders
- parked vehicles
- pedestrians

in the road.

11.56   Mark one answer   RES s7, HC p108, KYTS p26

What does this sign mean?

☐ Level crossing with gate or barrier

☐ Gated road ahead

☐ Level crossing without gate or barrier

☐ Cattle grid ahead

Some crossings have gates but no attendant or signals. You should stop, look both ways, listen and make sure that no train is approaching. If there's a telephone, contact the signal operator to make sure it's safe to cross.

What does this sign mean?

This sign tells you to beware of trams. If you don't usually drive in a town where there are trams, remember to look out for them at junctions and look for tram rails, signs and signals.

☐ No trams ahead
☐ Oncoming trams
☐ Trams crossing ahead
☐ Trams only

What does this sign mean?

This sign gives you an early warning that the road ahead will slope downhill. Prepare to alter your speed and gear. Looking at the sign from left to right will show you whether the road slopes uphill or downhill.

☐ Adverse camber
☐ Steep hill downwards
☐ Uneven road
☐ Steep hill upwards

11.59

Mark one answer   RES s7, HC p109, KYTS p12

What does this sign mean?

This sign is found where a shallow stream crosses the road. Heavy rainfall could increase the flow of water. If the water looks too deep or the stream has spread over a large distance, stop and find another route.

- ☐ Uneven road surface
- ☐ Bridge over the road
- ☐ Road ahead ends
- ☐ Water across the road

11.60

Mark one answer   RES s7, KYTS p114

What does this sign mean?

This sign shows you that you can't get through to another route by turning left at the junction ahead.

- ☐ Turn left for parking area
- ☐ No through road on the left
- ☐ No entry for traffic turning left
- ☐ Turn left for ferry terminal

What does this sign mean?

You won't be able to find a through route to another road. Use this road only for access.

☐ T-junction
☐ No through road
☐ Telephone box ahead
☐ Toilet ahead

Which is the sign for a ring road?

Ring roads are designed to relieve congestion in towns and city centres.

☐   ☐

☐   ☐

What does this sign mean?

Yellow-and-black temporary signs may be used to inform you about roadworks or lane restrictions. Look well ahead. If you have to change lanes, do so in good time.

☐ The right-hand lane ahead is narrow
☐ Right-hand lane for buses only
☐ Right-hand lane for turning right
☐ The right-hand lane is closed

11.64

Mark one answer   RES s7, HC p113, KYTS p130

What does this sign mean?

☐ Change to the left-hand lane

☐ Leave at the next exit

☐ Contraflow system

☐ One-way street

If you use the right-hand lane in a contraflow system, you'll be travelling with no permanent barrier between you and the oncoming traffic. Observe speed limits and keep a good distance from the vehicle ahead.

11.65

Mark one answer   RES s7, 11, HC r139

What does this sign mean?

☐ Leave motorway at next exit

☐ Lane for heavy and slow vehicles

☐ All lorries use the hard shoulder

☐ Rest area for lorries

Where there's a long, steep, uphill gradient on a motorway, a crawler lane may be provided. This helps the traffic to flow by diverting the slower heavy vehicles into a dedicated lane on the left.

11.66

Mark one answer   RES s7, HC p102, KYTS p119

What does a red traffic light mean?

☐ You should stop unless turning left

☐ Stop, if you're able to brake safely

☐ You must stop and wait behind the stop line

☐ Proceed with care

Whatever light is showing, you should know which light is going to appear next and be able to take appropriate action. For example, when amber is showing on its own, you'll know that red will appear next. This should give you ample time to anticipate and respond safely.

11.67

At traffic lights, what does it mean when the amber light shows on its own?

☐ Prepare to go

☐ Go if the way is clear

☐ Go if no pedestrians are crossing

☐ Stop at the stop line

When the amber light is showing on its own, the red light will follow next. The amber light means stop, unless you've already crossed the stop line or you're so close to it that stopping may cause a collision.

11.68

You're at a junction controlled by traffic lights. When should you wait at a green light?

☐ When pedestrians are waiting to cross

☐ When your exit from the junction is blocked

☐ When you think the lights may be about to change

☐ When you intend to turn right

As you approach the traffic lights, look into the road you wish to take. Only proceed if your exit road is clear. If the road is blocked, hold back, even if you have to wait for the next green signal.

11.69

You're in the left-hand lane at traffic lights, waiting to turn left. Which signal means you must wait?

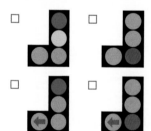

At some junctions, there may be separate signals for different lanes. These are called 'filter' lights. They're designed to help traffic flow at major junctions. Make sure that you're in the correct lane and proceed if the way is clear and the green light shows for your lane.

11.70 — Mark one answer — RES s7, HC p108, KYTS p139

What does this sign mean?

You might see this sign where traffic lights are out of order. Proceed with caution, as nobody has priority at the junction.

☐ Traffic lights out of order
☐ Amber signal out of order
☐ Temporary traffic lights ahead
☐ New traffic lights ahead

11.71 — Mark one answer — RES s7

Who has priority when traffic lights are out of order?

☐ Traffic going straight on
☐ Traffic turning right
☐ Nobody
☐ Traffic turning left

When traffic lights are out of order, you should treat the junction as an unmarked crossroads. Be cautious, as you may need to give way or stop. Look for traffic attempting to cross the junction, unaware that it doesn't have priority.

11.72 — Mark one answer — RES s7, HC p102, KYTS p13, 26, 120

Where would you find these flashing red light signals?

These signals are found at level crossings, swing or lifting bridges, some airfields and emergency access sites. The flashing red lights mean stop whether or not the way seems to be clear.

☐ Pelican crossings
☐ Motorway exits
☐ Zebra crossings
☐ Level crossings

Mark one answer RES s8, HC r191, KYTS p122

What do these zigzag white lines mean?

The approach to, and exit from, a pedestrian crossing is marked with zigzag lines. You mustn't park on them or overtake the leading vehicle when approaching the crossing. Parking here would block the view for pedestrians and approaching traffic.

☐ No parking at any time
☐ Parking allowed only for a short time
☐ Slow down to 20 mph
☐ Sounding horns isn't allowed

Mark one answer RES s7, HC r129, p114, KYTS p64

When may you cross a double solid white line in the middle of the road?

You may cross the solid white line to pass a stationary vehicle or to pass a pedal cycle, horse or road maintenance vehicle if it's travelling at 10 mph or less. You may also cross the solid white line to enter a side road or access a property.

☐ To pass traffic that's queuing back at a junction
☐ To pass a car signalling to turn left ahead
☐ To pass a road maintenance vehicle travelling at 10 mph or less
☐ To pass a vehicle that's towing a trailer

11.75 Mark one answer RES s7, HC r127, p114, KYTS p62

What does this road marking mean?

A single broken line along the centre of the road, with long markings and short gaps, is a hazard warning line. Don't cross it unless you can see that the road is clear well ahead.

☐ Don't cross the line
☐ No stopping allowed
☐ You're approaching a hazard
☐ No overtaking allowed

11.76 Mark one answer RES s7, KYTS p73

Where would you see this road marking?

Because the road has a dark colour, changes in level aren't easily seen. White triangles painted on the road surface give you an indication of where there are road humps.

☐ At traffic lights
☐ On road humps
☐ Near a level crossing
☐ At a box junction

11.77 Mark one answer RES s7, HC r127, p114, KYTS p62

Which diagram shows a hazard warning line?

☐   ☐

☐   ☐

You need to know the difference between the normal centre line and a hazard warning line. If there's a hazard ahead, the markings are longer and the gaps shorter. This gives you advance warning of an unspecified hazard.

Why does this junction have a 'stop' sign and a stop line on the road?

Where emerging traffic has a very restricted view of the main road, you may find a 'stop' sign and a solid white stop line. You must stop at the line and then check carefully before you emerge.

- ☐ Speed on the major road is derestricted
- ☐ It's a busy junction
- ☐ Visibility along the major road is restricted
- ☐ The junction is on a downhill gradient

What does this line across the road at the entrance to a roundabout mean?

Slow down as you approach the roundabout and check for traffic from the right. If you need to stop and give way, stay behind the broken line until it's safe to emerge onto the roundabout.

- ☐ Give way to traffic from the right
- ☐ Traffic from the left has right of way
- ☐ You have right of way
- ☐ Stop at the line

11.80   Mark one answer   RES s7, HC r106

How will a police officer in a patrol vehicle signal for you to stop?

☐ Flash the headlights, indicate left and point to the left

☐ Overtake and give a slowing down arm signal

☐ Use the siren, overtake, cut in front and stop

☐ Pull alongside you, use the siren and wave you to stop

You must obey signals given by the police. If a police officer in a patrol vehicle wants you to pull over, they'll indicate this without causing danger to you or other traffic.

11.81   Mark one answer   HC p104

You're approaching a junction where the traffic lights aren't working. What should you do when a police officer gives this signal?

When a police officer or traffic warden is directing traffic, you must obey them. They'll use the arm signals shown in The Highway Code. Learn what these signals mean and obey them.

☐ Turn left only

☐ Turn right only

☐ Continue ahead only

☐ Stop at the stop line

What does this arm signal mean?

There might be an occasion where another driver uses an arm signal. This may be because the vehicle's indicators are obscured by other traffic. In order for such signals to be effective, all drivers should know their meaning. Be aware that the 'left turn' signal might look similar to the 'slowing down' signal.

☐ The driver is slowing down

☐ The driver intends to turn right

☐ The driver wishes to overtake

☐ The driver intends to turn left

What does this motorway sign mean?

On the motorway, signs sometimes show temporary warnings due to traffic or weather conditions. They may be used to indicate

☐ Change to the lane on your left

☐ Leave the motorway at the next exit

☐ Change to the opposite carriageway

☐ Pull up on the hard shoulder

- lane closures
- temporary speed limits
- weather warnings.

What does this motorway sign mean?

Look out for signs above your lane or on the central reservation. These will give you important information or warnings about the road ahead. To allow for the high speed of motorway traffic, these signs may light up some distance from any hazard. Don't ignore the signs just because the road looks clear to you.

☐ Temporary minimum speed 50 mph

☐ No services for 50 miles

☐ Obstruction 50 metres (164 feet) ahead

☐ Temporary maximum speed 50 mph

| 11.85 | Mark one answer | RES s11, HC p102, KYTS p90 |

What does this sign mean?

☐ Through traffic to use left lane
☐ Right-hand lane T-junction only
☐ Right-hand lane closed ahead
☐ 11 tonne weight limit

You should change lanes as directed by the sign. Here, the right-hand lane is closed but the left-hand and centre lanes are available. Merging in turn is recommended when it's safe and traffic is going slowly; for example, at roadworks or a road traffic incident. When vehicles are travelling at speed, this isn't advisable and you should move into the appropriate lane in good time.

| 11.86 | Mark one answer | RES s11, HC p110, KYTS p79 |

What does '25' mean on this motorway sign?

☐ The distance to the nearest town
☐ The route number of the road
☐ The number of the next junction
☐ The speed limit on the slip road

Before you set out on your journey, use a road map to plan your route. When you see an advance warning of your junction, make sure you get into the correct lane in plenty of time. Last-minute harsh braking and cutting across lanes at speed is extremely hazardous.

| 11.87 | Mark one answer | RES s11 |

How should the right-hand lane of a three-lane motorway be used?

☐ As a high-speed lane
☐ As an overtaking lane
☐ As a right-turn lane
☐ As an acceleration lane

You should stay in the left-hand lane of a motorway unless you're overtaking another vehicle. The right-hand lane of a motorway is an overtaking lane; it isn't the 'fast lane'. After overtaking, move back to the left when it's safe to do so.

369

Where can you find reflective amber studs on a motorway?

☐ Separating the slip road from the motorway

☐ On the left-hand edge of the road

☐ On the right-hand edge of the road

☐ Separating the lanes

At night or in poor visibility, reflective studs on the road help you to judge your position on the carriageway.

Where would you find green reflective studs on a motorway?

☐ Separating driving lanes

☐ Between the hard shoulder and the carriageway

☐ At slip-road entrances and exits

☐ Between the carriageway and the central reservation

Knowing the colours of the reflective studs on the road will help you judge your position, especially at night, in foggy conditions or when visibility is poor.

What should you do when you see this sign as you travel along a motorway?

You'll see this sign if the motorway is closed ahead. Pull into the left-hand lane as soon as it's safe to do so. Don't wait until the last moment before you move across, because the lane may be busy and you'll have to rely on another driver making room for you.

☐ Leave the motorway at the next exit

☐ Turn left immediately

☐ Change lane

☐ Move onto the hard shoulder

11.91
Mark one answer   RES s11, HC p112, KYTS p89

What does this sign mean?

□ No motor vehicles

□ End of motorway

□ No through road

□ End of bus lane

When you leave the motorway, make sure that you check your speedometer. You may be going faster than you realise. Slow down and look for speed-limit signs.

11.92
Mark one answer   RES s7, HC p106, KYTS p20

Which sign means that the national speed limit applies?

You should know the speed limit for the road on which you're travelling and for your vehicle. The different speed limits are shown in The Highway Code.

11.93
Mark one answer   HC p40

What's the national speed limit on a single carriageway road?

□ 50 mph

□ 60 mph

□ 40 mph

□ 70 mph

If you're travelling on a dual carriageway that becomes a single carriageway road, reduce your speed gradually so that you aren't exceeding the limit as you enter. There might not be a sign to remind you of the limit, so make sure you know the speed limits for different types of road and vehicle.

What does this sign mean?

Temporary restrictions on motorways are shown on signs that have flashing amber lights. At the end of the restriction, you'll see this sign without any flashing lights.

☐ End of motorway
☐ End of restriction
☐ Lane ends ahead
☐ Free recovery ends

What does this sign indicate?

When a diversion route has been put in place, drivers are advised to follow a symbol, which may be a black triangle, square, circle or diamond shape on a yellow background.

☐ A diversion route
☐ A picnic area
☐ A pedestrian zone
☐ A cycle route

11.96   **Mark one answer**   **RES s7, HC p113, KYTS p138**

What does this traffic sign mean?

The sign gives you an early warning of a speed restriction. If you're travelling at a higher speed, slow down in good time. You could come across queuing traffic due to roadworks or a temporary obstruction.

☐ Compulsory maximum speed limit

☐ Advisory maximum speed limit

☐ Compulsory minimum speed limit

☐ Advised separation distance

11.97   **Mark one answer**   **RES s7, HC p108, KYTS p139**

What should you do when you see this sign at a crossroads?

When traffic lights are out of order, treat the junction as an unmarked crossroads. Be very careful and be prepared to stop; no-one has priority.

☐ Maintain the same speed

☐ Carry on with great care

☐ Find another route

☐ Telephone the police

Mark one answer RES s7, KYTS p17

What does this sign mean?

You must comply with all traffic signs and be especially aware of those signs that apply specifically to the type of vehicle you're using.

☐ Motorcycles only

☐ No cars

☐ Cars only

☐ No motorcycles

11.99 **Mark one answer** RES s7, HC p113, KYTS p135

You're on a motorway. A lorry has stopped in the right-hand lane. What should you do when you see this sign on the lorry?

Sometimes work is carried out on the motorway without closing the lanes. When this happens, signs are mounted on the back of lorries to warn other road users of the roadworks ahead.

☐ Move into the right-hand lane

☐ Stop behind the flashing lights

☐ Pass the lorry on the left

☐ Leave the motorway at the next exit

11.100 **Mark one answer** RES s7, HC p102, KYTS p91

You're on a motorway. What should you do if there's a red cross showing on the signs above your lane only?

☐ Continue in that lane and look for further information

☐ Don't continue in that lane

☐ Pull onto the hard shoulder

☐ Stop and wait for an instruction to proceed

A red cross above your lane shows that your lane is closed. You should move into another lane as soon as you can do so safely.

11.101 — Mark one answer — RES s6, HC r112

When may you sound your vehicle's horn?

☐ To give you right of way

☐ To attract a friend's attention

☐ To warn others of your presence

☐ To make slower drivers move over

Never sound your vehicle's horn aggressively. You mustn't sound it in a built-up area between 11.30 pm and 7.00 am, or when you're stationary, unless another road user poses a danger. Don't scare animals by sounding your horn.

11.102 — Mark one answer — RES s6, HC r112

Your vehicle is stationary. When may you use its horn?

☐ When another road user poses a danger

☐ When the road is blocked by queuing traffic

☐ When it's used only briefly

☐ When signalling that you've just arrived

When your vehicle is stationary, only sound the horn if you think there's a risk of danger from another road user. Don't use it just to attract someone's attention. This causes unnecessary noise and could be misleading.

11.103 — Mark one answer — RES s7, HC p107, KYTS p55

What does this sign mean?

URBAN CLEARWAY
Monday to Friday

am	pm
8.00 - 9.30	4.30 - 6.30

☐ You can park on the days and times shown

☐ No parking on the days and times shown

☐ No parking at all from Monday to Friday

☐ End of the urban clearway restrictions

Urban clearways are provided to keep traffic flowing at busy times. You may stop only briefly to set down or pick up passengers. Times of operation will vary from place to place, so always check the signs.

375

What does this sign mean?

You should be careful in these locations, as the road surface is likely to be wet and slippery. There may be a steep drop to the water, and there may not be a barrier along the edge of the road.

- ☐ Quayside or river bank
- ☐ Steep hill downwards
- ☐ Uneven road surface
- ☐ Road liable to flooding

Which sign means you have priority over oncoming vehicles?

☐   ☐

☐   ☐

Even though you have priority, be prepared to give way if other drivers don't. This will help to avoid congestion, confrontation or even a collision.

What do the long white lines along the centre of the road mean?

The centre of the road is usually marked by a broken white line, with lines that are shorter than the gaps. When the lines become longer than the gaps, this is a hazard warning line. Look well ahead for these, especially when you're planning to overtake or turn off.

- ☐ Bus lane
- ☐ Hazard warning
- ☐ Give way
- ☐ Lane marking

11.107
Mark one answer   RES s7, HC r130, p114 KYTS p64

What's the reason for the hatched area along the centre of this road?

Areas of 'hatched markings' such as these separate traffic streams that could be a danger to each other. They're often seen on bends or where the road becomes narrow. If the area is bordered by a solid white line, you mustn't enter it except in an emergency.

☐ It separates traffic flowing in opposite directions

☐ It marks an area to be used by overtaking motorcyclists

☐ It's a temporary marking to warn of the roadworks

☐ It separates the two sides of the dual carriageway

11.108
Mark one answer   RES s6, HC r110

Other drivers may sometimes flash their headlights at you. What's the official meaning of this signal?

☐ There's a radar speed trap ahead

☐ They're giving way to you

☐ They're warning you of their presence

☐ There's a fault with your vehicle

If other drivers flash their headlights, this isn't a signal to show priority. The flashing of headlights has the same meaning as sounding the horn: it's a warning of their presence.

11.109
Mark one answer
RES s7, HC p102, KYTS p31

What does this signal mean?

The white light shows that trams must stop. The green light shows that other vehicles can go if the way is clear. Trams are being introduced into more cities, so you're likely to come across them and you should learn which signs apply to them.

- ☐ Cars must stop
- ☐ Trams must stop
- ☐ Both trams and cars must stop
- ☐ Both trams and cars can continue

11.110
Mark one answer
KYTS p69

Where would you find these road markings?

These markings show the direction in which the traffic should go at a mini-roundabout.

- ☐ At a railway crossing
- ☐ At a mini-roundabout
- ☐ On a motorway
- ☐ On a pedestrian crossing

11.111
Mark one answer
RES s8, HC r106

A police car is following you. What should you do if the police officer flashes the headlights and points to the left?

You must pull up on the left as soon as it's safe to do so and switch off your engine.

- ☐ Turn left at the next junction
- ☐ Pull up on the left
- ☐ Stop immediately
- ☐ Move over to the left

11.112 Mark one answer
RES s7, HC p102, KYTS p119

You see this amber traffic light ahead. Which light, or lights, will come on next?

☐ Red alone

☐ Red and amber together

☐ Green and amber together

☐ Green alone

At junctions controlled by traffic lights, you must stop behind the white line until the lights change to green. A red light, an amber light, and red and amber lights showing together all mean stop.

You may proceed when the light is green unless your exit road is blocked or pedestrians are crossing in front of you.

If you're approaching traffic lights that are visible from a distance and the light has been green for some time, be ready to slow down and stop, because the lights are likely to change.

11.113 Mark one answer
RES s11, HC p102, KYTS p90

What does it mean if you see this signal on the motorway?

☐ Leave the motorway at the next exit

☐ All vehicles use the hard shoulder

☐ Sharp bend to the left ahead

☐ Stop: all lanes ahead closed

You'll see this sign if there has been an incident ahead and the motorway is closed. You must obey the sign. Make sure that you prepare to leave in good time.

Don't cause drivers to take avoiding action by cutting in at the last moment.

What must you do when you see this sign?

'Stop' signs are situated at junctions where visibility is restricted or where there's heavy traffic. They must be obeyed: you must stop. Look carefully before moving off.

☐ Stop only if traffic is approaching
☐ Stop even if the road is clear
☐ Stop only if children are waiting to cross
☐ Stop only if a red light is showing

Which shape is used for a 'give way' sign?

Other warning signs are the same shape and colour, but the 'give way' triangle points downwards. When you see this sign, you must give way to traffic on the road that you're about to enter.

What does this sign mean?

When you see this sign, look out for any direction signs and judge whether you need to signal your intentions. Do this in good time so that other road users approaching the roundabout know what you're planning to do.

☐ Buses turning
☐ Ring road
☐ Mini-roundabout
☐ Keep right

| 11.117 | Mark one answer | RES s7, HC p108, KYTS p11 |

What does this sign mean?

Be prepared for traffic approaching from junctions on either side of you. Try to avoid unnecessary changing of lanes just before the junction.

☐ Two-way traffic straight ahead
☐ Two-way traffic crosses a one-way road
☐ Two-way traffic over a bridge
☐ Two-way traffic crosses a two-way road

| 11.118 | Mark one answer | RES s7, HC p108, KYTS p11 |

What does this sign mean?

This sign may be at the end of a dual carriageway or a one-way street. It's there to warn you of oncoming traffic.

☐ Two-way traffic crosses a one-way road
☐ Traffic approaching you has priority
☐ Two-way traffic straight ahead
☐ Motorway contraflow system ahead

What does this sign mean?

☐ Hump bridge
☐ Traffic-calming hump
☐ Low bridge
☐ Uneven road

You'll need to slow down. At hump bridges, your view ahead will be restricted and the road will often be narrow. If the bridge is very steep, sound your horn to warn others of your approach. Going over the bridge too fast is highly dangerous to other road users and could even cause your wheels to leave the road, with a resulting loss of control.

Which sign informs you that you're coming to a 'no through road'?

☐ ☐

☐ ☐

This sign is found at the entrance to a road that can only be used for access.

What does this sign mean?

☐ Direction to park-and-ride car park
☐ No parking for buses or coaches
☐ Direction to bus and coach park
☐ Parking area for cars and coaches

To ease the congestion in town centres, some cities and towns provide park-and-ride schemes. These allow you to park in a designated area and ride by bus into the centre.

Park-and-ride schemes are usually cheaper and easier than car parking in the town centre.

11.122 — Mark one answer — RES s7, HC p102, KYTS p119

What should you do when you're approaching traffic lights that have red and amber showing together?

☐ Pass the lights if the road is clear

☐ Take care because there's a fault with the lights

☐ Wait for the green light

☐ Stop because the lights are changing to red

Be aware that other traffic might still be clearing the junction as you approach. A green light means you may go on, but only if the way is clear.

11.123 — Mark one answer — RES s7, HC r293, p102

You've stopped at a railway level crossing. What should you do if the red lights continue to flash after a train has gone by?

☐ Phone the signal operator

☐ Alert drivers behind you

☐ Wait

☐ Proceed with caution

You must always obey red flashing stop lights. If a train passes but the lights continue to flash, another train will be passing soon. Cross only when the lights go off and the barriers open.

11.124 — Mark one answer — RES s16, KYTS p116

You're in a tunnel and you see this sign. What does it mean?

☐ Direction to an emergency pedestrian exit

☐ Beware of pedestrians: no footpath ahead

☐ No access for pedestrians

☐ Beware of pedestrians crossing ahead

If you have to leave your vehicle and get out of a tunnel by an emergency exit, do so as quickly as you can. Follow the signs directing you to the nearest exit point. If there are several people using the exit, don't panic but try to leave in a calm and orderly manner.

Which sign shows that you're entering a one-way system?

If the road has two lanes, you can use either lane and overtake on either side. Use the lane that's more convenient for your destination unless signs or road markings indicate otherwise.

What does this sign mean?

- ☐ With-flow bus and cycle lane
- ☐ Contraflow bus and cycle lane
- ☐ No buses and cycles allowed
- ☐ No waiting for buses and cycles

Buses and cycles can travel in this lane. In this example, they'll flow in the same direction as other traffic. If it's busy, they may be passing you on the left, so watch out for them. Times on the sign will show the lane's hours of operation; if no times are shown, or there's no sign at all, this means the lane is in operation 24 hours a day. In some areas, other vehicles, such as taxis and motorcycles, are allowed to use bus lanes. The sign will show if this is the case.

Which of these signs warns you of a zebra crossing?

Look well ahead and check the pavements and surrounding areas for pedestrians. Look for anyone walking towards the crossing. Check your mirrors for traffic behind, in case you have to slow down or stop.

11.128   Mark one answer   RES s7, HC p109, KYTS p13

What does this sign mean?

- ☐ School crossing patrol
- ☐ No pedestrians allowed
- ☐ Pedestrian zone - no vehicles
- ☐ Zebra crossing ahead

Look well ahead and be ready to stop for any pedestrians crossing, or about to cross, the road. Also check the pavements for anyone who looks like they might step or run into the road.

11.129   Mark one answer   RES s7, HC p108, KYTS p11

Which sign means there will be two-way traffic crossing your route ahead?

☐ ☐

☐ ☐

This sign is found in or at the end of a one-way system. It warns you that traffic will be crossing your path from both directions.

11.130   Mark one answer   RES s6, HC r103, p103

Which arm signal tells you that the car you're following is going to pull up?

☐ ☐

☐ ☐

There may be occasions when drivers need to give an arm signal to confirm their intentions. This could include in bright sunshine, at a complex road layout, when stopping at a pedestrian crossing or when turning right just after passing a parked vehicle. You should understand what each arm signal means. If you give arm signals, make them clear, correct and decisive.

Which sign means turn left ahead?

□ □

□ □

Blue circles tell you what you must do and this sign gives a clear instruction to turn left ahead. You should be looking out for signs at all times and know what they mean.

What should you be aware of if you've just passed this sign?

In a one-way system, traffic may pass you on either side. Always be aware of all traffic signs and understand their meaning. Look well ahead and react to them in good time.

☐ This is a single-track road

☐ You can't stop on this road

☐ Only one lane is in use

☐ All traffic is going one way

11.133   Mark one answer   RES s7, HC p102, KYTS p119

You're approaching traffic lights and the red light is showing. What signal will show next?

☐ Red and amber

☐ Green alone

☐ Amber alone

☐ Green and amber

If you know which light is going to show next, you can plan your approach accordingly. This can help prevent excessive braking or hesitation at the junction.

11.134   Mark one answer   RES s7, HC p108, KYTS p12

What does this sign mean?

When approaching a tunnel, switch on your dipped headlights. Be aware that your eyes might need to adjust to the sudden darkness. You may need to reduce your speed.

☐ Low bridge ahead

☐ Tunnel ahead

☐ Ancient monument ahead

☐ Traffic danger spot ahead

Case study practice – 11 Road and traffic signs

You're riding in the town centre. As you approach the first junction, you see a staggered junction sign.

At the second junction there's a 'no entry' sign, while at the third is a one-way traffic sign.

At a large junction there are traffic lights with filter arrows for traffic going left.

Beyond the junction, there are bus lanes on either side of the road.

There are no signs showing times of operation.

11.1 What describes the first junction?
Mark **one** answer

☐ Where the joining side roads are both narrow one-way streets

☐ Where the joining side roads are exactly opposite each other

☐ Where the joining side roads are reserved for pedestrians only

☐ Where the joining side roads are slightly offset from each other

RES s9 **HC p108**

11.2 What type of sign is at the second junction?
Mark **one** answer

☐ Advisory

☐ Warning

☐ Regulatory

☐ Information

HC p106 KYTS p16

11.3 What does the third sign look like?

Mark **one** answer

☐ White with red arrow

☐ Blue with white arrow

☐ Red with green arrow

☐ White with black arrow

HC p107 KYTS p19

11.4 What colour are the filter arrows?

Mark **one** answer

☐ White

☐ Amber

☐ Green

☐ Blue

RES s7 **HC p102**

11.5 When are the bus lanes in operation?

Mark **one** answer

☐ All the time

☐ During rush hour

☐ At the weekend

☐ They're not in operation

HC r141

Section twelve

Essential documents

In this section, you'll learn about

- the documents you need when owning and keeping a motorcycle
- the driving licence
- buying insurance
- the MOT test.

Essential documents

Before you can ride as a learner on a public road, you **MUST** have

- successfully completed a compulsory basic training (CBT) course, given by a DVSA-approved training body
- checked that the vehicle tax has been paid on the motorcycle you're riding
- a valid provisional driving licence
- valid insurance cover
- L plates (D plates in Wales) correctly displayed at the front and rear of the motorcycle
- a valid MOT certificate, if it's required for the motorcycle you're using.

You won't be able to tax your motorcycle unless you have

- a valid MOT certificate (if your motorcycle requires one)
- appropriate, current insurance cover.

HC p120–123 RES s2

As a learner, you **MUST NOT** carry a **pillion passenger**, pull a trailer or ride your motorcycle on a motorway. You can do these things once you've passed your practical tests, provided your motorcycle has an engine capacity

- over 125 cc if you wish to tow a trailer
- of at least 50 cc if you wish to ride on the motorway.

HC r85, p120 RES s2

pillion passenger
a passenger who sits on the rear seat of a motorcycle, behind the rider

Registering and owning a motorcycle

The vehicle registration certificate (V5C) contains details of

- the vehicle, including make, model, engine size and year of registration
- the registered keeper.

If you're the registered keeper, you **MUST** tell the Driver and Vehicle Licensing Agency (DVLA) when you change

- your motorcycle
- your name
- your permanent address.

If you buy a second-hand motorcycle, tell DVLA immediately that the keeper of the motorcycle has changed.

 Find out more about the V5C at this website.

www.gov.uk

Vehicle tax **MUST** be paid on all motor vehicles used or kept on public roads (unless the vehicle is exempt – see **www.gov.uk** for more details).

HC p122 RES s2

If you're not going to use your motorcycle on public roads, you won't have to pay vehicle tax as long as you tell DVLA in advance. This is called a Statutory Off-Road Notification (SORN) and lasts until you tax, sell or scrap your vehicle.

RES s2

Your motorcycle licence

Before riding on a public road, a learner **MUST** have a valid provisional driving licence and a CBT completion certificate. The CBT certificate is valid for two years. If you don't pass a practical test within that time, you'll have to retake CBT.

HC p118–119 RES s2

You **MUST** tell the licensing authority if

- your health is likely to affect your riding
- your eyesight doesn't meet the required standard.

HC r90 RES s1

Eyesight: to be able to ride you **MUST** be able to read in good daylight, with glasses or contact lenses if you wear them, a vehicle number plate from 20 metres (about 66 feet).

For two years after you pass your first practical test (car or motorcycle), there's a probation period. This means that if you get six or more penalty points within this two-year probation period, you'll lose your licence. You'll then have to

- reapply for a provisional licence
- take your CBT, theory and practical tests again.

Any points on your provisional licence will be transferred to your new licence when you pass your test.

HC p127, 134

Insurance

You **MUST** have at least third-party insurance cover before riding on public roads. This covers

- injury to another person
- damage to someone else's property
- damage to other vehicles.

Riding without insurance is a criminal offence. It can lead to an unlimited fine, and possibly disqualification.

HC p121–122 RES s2

You'll need to show your insurance certificate when you're taxing your motorcycle or if a police officer asks you for it. Your insurer may give you a temporary cover note until you receive your insurance certificate.

Remember, if your vehicle is unused or off the road it **MUST** have either a SORN or valid insurance. If you have neither, and ignore any subsequent reminders sent to you as the registered keeper, you risk

- a fixed-penalty fine of £100
- court prosecution and a fine of up to £1000
- having the vehicle clamped, seized and destroyed.

RES s2

Tip

If a police officer asks to see your documents and you don't have them with you, you can produce them at a police station within seven days.

HC p122 RES s16

Your insurance policy may have an excess of, for example, £100. This means you'll have to pay the first £100 of any claim for damage to your vehicle. The cost of your insurance is generally lower if you're over 25 years old.

Before you ride anyone else's motorcycle, make sure that it's insured for your use.

HC p121–122 RES s2

MOT test

The MOT test makes sure your motorcycle meets road safety and environmental standards. Motorcycles **MUST** first have an MOT test when they're three years old (four in Northern Ireland). MOT certificates are valid for one year.

HC p121 RES s2

If your motorcycle has a sidecar, the MOT costs slightly more. Motorcycle trailers don't need an MOT, but they do need to be kept in good order.

Unless your motorcycle is exempt from MOT testing (see **www.gov.uk** for rules exempting vehicles from MOT testing), the only time when you can ride your motorcycle without an MOT certificate is when you're riding to or from an appointment at an MOT centre or to have MOT repairs carried out.

If your motorcycle needs an MOT certificate and you don't have one

- you won't be able to renew your vehicle tax
- you could be prosecuted
- your insurance may be invalid.

HC p121 RES s2

For more information about MOT tests, see this website.

www.gov.uk

Meeting the standards

You must be able to

make sure that your driving licence is valid for the category of machine that you're riding

make sure that the machine is registered and the vehicle tax has been paid

make sure that you have valid insurance for your use of the machine

make sure that the machine has a current MOT certificate (if necessary).

You must know and understand

that you must have a valid driving licence for the machine you ride. You must also comply with any restrictions on your licence

that the machine must be registered with DVLA

that you must tell DVLA/DVA if you
- change your name
- change your address
- have or develop a medical condition that will affect your ability to ride

the MOT requirements for vehicles being used on the road.

Notes

You can use this page to make your own notes or diagrams about the key points you need to remember.

Think about

- What documents do you need when taxing your motorcycle?
- You must tell DVLA/DVA when certain details change: what are they?
- What's a SORN?
- What's the minimum level of insurance you must have before riding on public roads?
- What does an MOT test cover?

Your notes

_____

_____

_____

_____

_____

_____

_____

_____

_____

_____

_____

_____

_____

_____

_____

_____

_____

 ## Things to discuss and practise with your trainer

These are just a few examples of what you could discuss and practise with your trainer. Read more about essential documents to come up with your own ideas.

Discuss with your trainer

- what the New Drivers Act means to someone whose first full licence is a motorcycle licence
- what the letters 'SORN' stand for and what this means to the keeper of a vehicle
- different types of insurance for your motorcycle and what they cover.

Practise with your trainer

It's difficult to practise your knowledge and understanding of documents. Just remember that the safer and more responsibly you ride, the less likely you are to

- cause high wear and tear to your motorcycle
- accumulate penalty points
- be involved in an incident and damage your motorcycle.

This means that

- your motorcycle will be more likely to be roadworthy and pass its MOT test
- you'll be able to find cheaper insurance
- you won't lose your licence under the New Drivers Act and beyond.

12.1   Mark one answer   RES s2, HC p122

What information is found on a vehicle registration document?

- ☐ The make and model
- ☐ The service history
- ☐ The ignition-key security number
- ☐ The original purchase price

Every vehicle should have a registration document showing the registered keeper. It's your legal responsibility to make sure all the information is correct. This includes make, model and engine size. If you buy a new vehicle, the dealer will register it with DVLA, who will send the registration document to you.

12.2   NI EXEMPT   Mark one answer   RES s2, HC p118–119

Who can carry out compulsory basic training (CBT)?

- ☐ Any approved driving instructor (ADI)
- ☐ Any road safety officer
- ☐ Any Driver and Vehicle Standards Agency (DVSA)-approved training body
- ☐ Any motorcycle main dealer

CBT courses can only be given by training bodies that are approved by DVSA. The standard of training is monitored by DVSA examiners. The course is designed to teach riders basic skills before they start riding on the road.

12.3   Mark one answer   RES s2

What should you check before riding anyone else's motorcycle?

- ☐ That the owner has third-party insurance cover
- ☐ That your own motorcycle has insurance cover
- ☐ That the motorcycle is insured for your use
- ☐ That the owner has the insurance documents with them

If you borrow a motorcycle, you must make sure that you're insured to ride it. It's better to find this out for yourself, rather than taking somebody else's word for it.

12.4   NI EXEMPT   Mark one answer   RES s2, HC p121

How long after first registration must a motorcycle have its first MOT test?

- ☐ One year
- ☐ Three years
- ☐ Five years
- ☐ Seven years

Any motorcycle you ride must be roadworthy and in good condition. If it's over three years old, it must pass an MOT test to remain in use on the road (unless it's exempt from the MOT test – see GOV.UK).

12.5 — Mark one answer — RES s2, HC p122

What information can be found on a motorcycle's registration document?

- ☐ The registered keeper's name
- ☐ The type of insurance cover required
- ☐ The service history
- ☐ The date of the MOT

Every vehicle on the road has a registration document. This records any change of ownership and gives specific information relating to the vehicle and owner. This includes the date of first registration, the registration number, the make and colour of the vehicle, and the registered keeper's name.

12.6 — Mark one answer — RES s2, HC p120, 122

You own a motorcycle licensed in the UK. When do you have a duty to contact the Driver and Vehicle Licensing Agency (DVLA)?

- ☐ When you go abroad on holiday
- ☐ When your job involves riding abroad
- ☐ When your permanent address changes
- ☐ When you change your job status

DVLA need to keep their records up to date. They'll send you a reminder when you need to tax your vehicle. To do this, they need your current address. Every vehicle in the country is registered so that its history can be traced.

12.7 — Mark one answer — RES s2, HC p121

What does third-party insurance cover?

- ☐ Damage to your motorcycle
- ☐ All damage and injury
- ☐ Injury to yourself
- ☐ Injury to others

Third-party insurance is usually cheaper than comprehensive insurance. It covers injuries to other people and damage to their property, but it doesn't cover any damage to your own motorcycle or property. Nor does it provide cover if your motorcycle is stolen.

12.8 — Mark one answer — RES s2, HC p121

What's the legal minimum insurance cover you must have to ride on public roads?

- ☐ Third-party, fire and theft
- ☐ Comprehensive
- ☐ Third-party only
- ☐ Personal injury cover

The minimum insurance cover required by law is third-party only. This covers the other people and vehicles involved in a collision, but not you or your vehicle. Also, basic third-party insurance won't cover you for theft or fire damage. Make sure you read your policy carefully and understand what it covers.

12.9   Mark one answer   RES s2

What information will you find on your motorcycle registration document?

☐ The service history

☐ The year of first registration

☐ The purchase price

☐ The tyre sizes

A motorcycle registration document contains a number of details that are unique to a particular vehicle. You must notify DVLA of any changes to, for example, the registered keeper or registration number. You must also tell them about any modifications made to the motorcycle.

12.10   Mark one answer   RES s2, HC p121

What's the purpose of an MOT test?

☐ To make sure your motorcycle is roadworthy

☐ To certify how many miles per gallon it does

☐ To prove you own the motorcycle

☐ To allow you to park in restricted areas

It's your responsibility to make sure that any motorcycle you ride is in a roadworthy condition. Any faults that develop should be corrected promptly. If your motorcycle fails an MOT test, it shouldn't be used on the road unless you're taking it to have the faults repaired or for a previously arranged retest.

12.11   NI EXEMPT   Mark one answer   RES s2, HC p118

What do you need before you can take a practical motorcycle test?

☐ A valid full moped licence

☐ A valid full car licence

☐ A valid compulsory basic training (CBT) certificate

☐ 12 months' riding experience

The purpose of a CBT course is to teach you basic theory and practical skills before you ride on the road, on your own, for the first time. CBT courses can only be given by approved training bodies (ATBs).

12.12   Mark one answer   RES s2, HC r90, 92, p122

When must you notify the licensing authority?

☐ When your insurance is due for renewal

☐ When you have a medical condition that affects your riding

☐ When you intend to take your motorcycle abroad on holiday

☐ When you wish to renew your motorcycle's MOT certificate

The licensing authorities hold the records of all vehicles, drivers and riders in Great Britain and Northern Ireland. They need to keep their records up to date and you must notify them if any aspect of your health affects your ability to ride your motorcycle.

12.13   Mark one answer   RES s2, HC p127, 134

You've just passed your practical motorcycle test. This is your first full licence. What will you have to do if you accumulate six or more penalty points within the next two years?

☐ Retake only your theory test
☐ Reapply for your full licence immediately
☐ Retake only your practical test
☐ Reapply for your provisional licence

If the number of points on your licence reaches six or more during your first two years of holding a full licence, your licence will be revoked. This includes offences you committed before you passed your test. You may ride only as a learner until you pass both the theory and practical tests again.

12.14   Mark one answer   RES s2, HC r85, 253, p123

What does a provisional motorcycle licence restrict you from doing?

☐ Exceeding 30 mph
☐ Riding on a dual carriageway
☐ Riding after dark
☐ Carrying a pillion passenger

Provisional entitlement means that restrictions apply to your use of motorcycles. For example, you may not ride on a motorway or carry a passenger. The requirements are there to protect you and other road users. Make sure you're aware of all the restrictions that apply before you ride your motorcycle on the road.

12.15   Mark one answer   RES s2, HC p118–120

What's the maximum engine size a full category A1 motorcycle licence will allow you to ride?

☐ 125 cc
☐ 250 cc
☐ 350 cc
☐ 425 cc

When you pass your test on a motorcycle between 120 cc and 125 cc, you'll be issued with a full light motorcycle licence of category A1. You'll then be allowed to ride any motorcycle up to 125 cc and with a power output not exceeding 11 kW (14.6 bhp).

12.16   NI EXEMPT   Mark one answer   RES s14, HC r85

When may a motorcyclist carry a pillion passenger?

☐ When the rider has successfully completed compulsory basic training (CBT).
☐ When the rider holds a full licence for the category of motorcycle they're riding
☐ When no sidecar is fitted to the machine
☐ When the rider has a full car licence and is over 21

Before carrying a passenger on a motorcycle, the rider must hold a full licence for the category of motorcycle being ridden. They must also ensure that a proper passenger seat and footrests are fitted.

12.17 NI EXEMPT — Mark one answer — RES s2, HC p118

How long is a compulsory basic training (CBT) certificate valid?

☐ One year
☐ Two years
☐ Three years
☐ Four years

All new learner motorcycle and moped riders must complete a CBT course before riding on the road. This can only be given by an approved training body (ATB). If you don't pass your practical test within two years, you'll need to successfully complete CBT again, before you continue riding on the road.

12.18 — Mark one answer — RES s2, HC r85

What do you need before you can give someone a lift on your motorcycle?

☐ A motorcycle with an engine larger than 125 cc
☐ Three years' motorcycle riding experience
☐ A motorcycle with extended mirror stalks
☐ A full motorcycle licence

By law, you can only carry a pillion passenger after you've gained a full motorcycle licence for the class of motorcycle you're using. It makes no difference if the passenger holds a full licence. As a learner, you're also prohibited from towing a trailer or riding on motorways.

12.19 — Mark one answer — RES s2

What does it mean if your motorcycle insurance policy has an excess of £100?

☐ The insurance company will pay the first £100 of any claim
☐ You'll be paid £100 if you don't have a crash
☐ Your motorcycle is insured for a value of £100 if it's stolen
☐ You'll have to pay the first £100 of any claim

This is a method used by insurance companies to keep annual premiums down. Generally, the higher the excess you choose to pay, the lower the annual premium you'll be charged.

12.20 — Mark one answer — RES s2, HC p121

For how long is an MOT certificate normally valid?

☐ Three years after the date it was issued
☐ 10,000 miles
☐ One year after the date it was issued
☐ 30,000 miles

Some garages will remind you that your vehicle is due for its annual MOT test, but not all do. To ensure continuous cover, you may take your vehicle for its MOT up to one month before its existing MOT certificate expires. The expiry date on the new certificate will be 12 months after the expiry date on the old certificate.

12.21 — Mark one answer — RES s2, HC p121–122

What's a cover note?

☐ A document issued before you receive your driving licence

☐ A document issued before you receive your insurance certificate

☐ A document issued before you receive your registration document

☐ A document issued before you receive your MOT certificate

Sometimes an insurance company will issue a temporary insurance certificate called a cover note. It gives you the same insurance cover as your certificate but lasts for a limited period, usually one month.

12.22 — Mark one answer — HC p127, 134

You've just passed your first practical driving test. What will you have to do if you get six penalty points on your licence in the next two years?

☐ Retake only your theory test

☐ Retake your theory and practical tests

☐ Retake only your practical test

☐ Reapply for your full licence immediately

If you accumulate six or more penalty points within two years of gaining your first full licence, it will be revoked. The six or more points include any gained due to offences you committed before passing your test. If this happens, you may only drive as a learner until you pass both the theory and practical tests again.

12.23 — Mark one answer — RES s2, HC p122

For how long is a Statutory Off-Road Notification (SORN) valid?

☐ Until the vehicle is taxed, sold or scrapped

☐ Until the vehicle is insured and MOT'd

☐ Until the vehicle is repaired or modified

☐ Until the vehicle is used on the road

A SORN allows you to keep a vehicle off-road and untaxed. SORN will end when the vehicle is taxed, sold or scrapped.

12.24 — Mark one answer — RES s2, HC p122

What's a Statutory Off-Road Notification (SORN)?

☐ A notification to tell DVSA that a vehicle doesn't have a current MOT

☐ Information kept by the police about the owner of a vehicle

☐ A notification to tell DVLA that a vehicle isn't being used on the road

☐ Information held by insurance companies to check a vehicle is insured

If you want to keep a vehicle untaxed and off the public road, you must make a SORN. It's an offence not to do so. Your SORN is valid until your vehicle is taxed, sold or scrapped.

12.25   NI EXEMPT   Mark one answer   RES s2, HC p126

What's the maximum fine for driving or riding without insurance?

☐ Unlimited

☐ £500

☐ £1000

☐ £5000

Driving or riding without insurance is a serious offence. As well as an unlimited fine, you may be disqualified or incur penalty points.

12.26   Mark one answer   RES s2, HC p122

Who's legally responsible for ensuring that a vehicle registration certificate (V5C) is updated?

☐ The registered vehicle keeper

☐ The vehicle manufacturer

☐ Your insurance company

☐ The licensing authority

It's your legal responsibility to keep the details on your vehicle registration certificate (V5C) up to date. You should tell the licensing authority about any changes. These include your name, address or vehicle details. If you don't do this, you may have problems when you try to sell your vehicle.

12.27   Mark one answer   RES s2, HC p122

Your insurer will issue you with an insurance certificate. When must you produce this document for inspection?

☐ When making a SORN

☐ When buying or selling a vehicle

☐ When a police officer asks you for it

☐ When your vehicle is having an MOT test

You must produce a valid insurance certificate when requested by a police officer. If you can't do this immediately, you may be asked to take it to a police station. Other documents you may be asked to produce are your driving licence and the vehicle's MOT certificate.

12.28   Mark one answer   RES s2

When must your vehicle have valid insurance cover?

☐ Before you can make a SORN

☐ Before you can sell the vehicle

☐ Before you can scrap the vehicle

☐ Before you can tax the vehicle

Your vehicle must have valid insurance cover before you can tax it. If required, it will also need to have a valid MOT certificate. You can tax your vehicle online, by phone or at certain post offices.

12.29 — Mark one answer — RES s2, HC p120-122

What do you need before you can legally use a motor vehicle on the road?

☐ An appropriate driving licence
☐ Breakdown cover
☐ Proof of your identity
☐ A vehicle handbook

Using a motor vehicle on the road illegally carries a heavy fine and can lead to penalty points on your driving licence. You must

- hold a valid driving licence for the class of vehicle you're using
- be insured to drive the vehicle.

If required, the vehicle must have a current MOT test certificate and be taxed for use on the road.

12.30 — Mark one answer — RES s2

What must you have when you apply to renew your vehicle tax?

☐ Valid insurance
☐ The vehicle's chassis number
☐ The handbook
☐ A valid driving licence

You can renew your vehicle tax online, at post offices and by phone using the DVLA vehicle tax service. When applying, make sure you have all the relevant valid documents, including a valid MOT test certificate where applicable.

12.31 — Mark one answer — RES s2, HC p122

A police officer asks to see your documents. You don't have them with you. How many days do you have to produce them at a police station?

☐ 5 days
☐ 7 days
☐ 14 days
☐ 21 days

You don't have to carry your vehicle's documents wherever you go. If a police officer asks to see them and you don't have them with you, you may be asked to produce them at a police station within 7 days.

12.32 — Mark one answer — RES s2, HC p122

When should you update your vehicle registration certificate?

☐ When you pass your driving test
☐ When you move house
☐ When your vehicle needs an MOT
☐ When you have a collision

As the registered keeper of a vehicle, it's up to you to inform DVLA of any changes in your details; for example, your name or address. You do this by completing and sending off the relevant section of the registration certificate.

Case study practice – 12 Essential documents

You buy a second-hand motorcycle, which you want to ride immediately.

There are three days left on its MOT certificate.

You take your new motorcycle for its MOT test, which it fails as it needs some repair work.

For the repairs, you ride it to a garage a few miles away from the MOT centre.

A week later, you have the motorcycle retested. It successfully passes the second MOT.

You have the most basic type of insurance cover available.

12.1 What must you do before you can legally ride your motorcycle on the road?

Mark **one** answer

☐ Tax it and display a disc from the post office

☐ Tax it using the new keeper supplement

☐ Tax it with the V5C registration certificate

☐ Tax it using the last-chance warning letter

RES s2

12.2 When did the motorcycle pass its last MOT?

Mark **one** answer

- ☐ Almost six months ago
- ☐ Almost twelve months ago
- ☐ Almost two years ago
- ☐ Almost three years ago

RES s2 HC p121

12.3 Why could you ride your motorcycle to the garage?

Mark **one** answer

- ☐ It's allowed during daylight hours, but not at night
- ☐ It's allowed, but only until the vehicle tax expires
- ☐ It's allowed in order to get the motorcycle to a repairer
- ☐ It's allowed for a period of seven days after failure

HC p121

12.4 What's your type of insurance called?

Mark **one** answer

- ☐ Third policy
- ☐ Third practice
- ☐ Third party
- ☐ Third procedure

RES s2 HC p121–122

12.5 What does your insurance cover?

Mark **one** answer

- ☐ Damage to your vehicle
- ☐ Damage to other vehicles
- ☐ Injury to yourself
- ☐ All damage and injury

HC p121–122

Section thirteen

Incidents, accidents and emergencies

In this section, you'll learn about

- what to do if your motorcycle breaks down
- how to ride safely in a tunnel, and what to do if you have an emergency
- what to do if you're the first to arrive at an incident
- first aid and how to help casualties at an incident
- reporting an incident to the police.

Incidents, accidents and emergencies

If you're involved in an incident on the road, such as your motorcycle breaking down or arriving first at the scene of a crash, knowing what to do can prevent a more serious situation from developing.

Tip

It's useful to carry a first aid kit, a warning triangle and a fire extinguisher for use in an emergency. This equipment could help to prevent or lessen an injury. You may be able to tackle a small fire if you have a fire extinguisher, but don't take any risks.

Breakdowns

Knowing what to do if your motorcycle breaks down will help keep you safe, and avoid creating problems for other road users, such as traffic jams.

If a warning light shows on the instrument panel of your motorcycle, you may have a problem that affects the safety of the vehicle. If necessary, stop as soon as you can do so safely and check the problem.

HC p128

If a tyre bursts or you get a puncture while you're riding

- hold the handlebars firmly
- gently roll to a stop at the side of the road.

Tip

If you smell petrol while you're riding, stop and investigate as soon as you can do so safely. Don't ignore it.

409

If an emergency happens while you're on a motorway, try to get onto the hard shoulder and call for help from an emergency telephone. Marker posts show you the way to the nearest phone. An operator will answer and ask you

- the number on the phone, which will tell the services where you are
- details of yourself and your motorcycle
- whether you belong to a motoring organisation.

HC r270, 275 RES s16

 Driver location signs can help you give the emergency services precise information about where you are. See this link for more details.

direct.gov.uk/prod_consum_dg/groups/dg_digitalassets/@dg/ @en/documents/digitalasset/dg_185820.pdf

If you break down on a level crossing, get yourself, any passenger and your motorcycle off the crossing area immediately. If you can't move your motorcycle, phone the signal operator and follow any instructions given to you.

If you're waiting at a level crossing and the red light signal continues to flash after a train has gone by, you **MUST** wait, as another train may be coming.

HC r293, 299 RES s7 KYTS p27

 Tip
If your motorcycle catches fire while you're riding, pull up as quickly and safely as possible. Get yourself and any passenger away from the motorcycle and then call the fire service.

HC p130 RES s11

 Watch the Think! 'Van of Elvises' video to find out what to do if you break down on a motorway.

youtube.com/thinkuk

Warning others of a breakdown or incident

Use your hazard warning lights

- if you need to suddenly slow down or stop on a motorway or unrestricted dual carriageway because of an incident or hazard ahead; as soon as the traffic behind you has reacted to your hazard lights, you should turn them off
- when your vehicle has broken down and is temporarily obstructing traffic.

HC r116, 274

If you have a warning triangle, place it at least 45 metres (147 feet) behind your motorcycle. This will warn other road users that you've broken down. Never place a warning triangle on a motorway: there's too much danger from passing traffic.

HC r274 RES s16

Tip
If you're riding on a motorway and you see something fall from another vehicle, or if anything falls from your motorcycle, stop at the next emergency telephone and report the hazard to the police. Don't try to retrieve it yourself.

RES s16

Safety in tunnels

You need to take extra care when riding in a tunnel because

- when you enter the tunnel, visibility is suddenly reduced
- the confined space can make incidents difficult to deal with.

Before riding through a tunnel, remove your sunglasses or sun visor if you're using them and make sure your dipped headlights are on. It's particularly important to keep a safe distance from the vehicle in front when riding in a tunnel, even if it's congested.

Look out for signs that warn of incidents or congestion.

If your motorcycle is involved in an incident or breaks down in a tunnel

- switch off the engine
- put your hazard warning lights on
- go and call for help immediately from the nearest emergency telephone point.

RES s8

Stopping at an incident

If you're the first to arrive at the scene of an incident or crash, stop and warn other traffic. Switch on your hazard warning lights. Don't put yourself at risk.

- Make sure that the emergency services are called as soon as possible.
- Ensure that the engines of any vehicles at the scene are switched off.
- Move uninjured people away from the scene.

HC r283 RES s16

A vehicle carrying dangerous goods will display an orange label or a hazard warning plate on the back. If a vehicle carrying something hazardous is involved in an incident, report what the label says when you call the emergency services. The different plates are shown in *The Official Highway Code.*

HC p117 RES s16

Helping others and giving first aid

Even if you don't know any first aid, you can help any injured people by

- calling the emergency services on 999 or 112
- keeping them warm and comfortable
- keeping them calm by talking to them reassuringly
- making sure they're not left alone.

HC p131–132 RES s16

Don't move an injured person if the area is safe. Only move them if they're in obvious danger, and then with extreme care. If a motorcyclist is involved, never remove their helmet unless it's essential in order to keep them alive, because removing the helmet could cause more serious injury. Always get medical help and never offer a casualty any food or drink, or a cigarette to calm them down.

HC p131–133 RES s16

If the casualty is unconscious, check that they can breathe normally. If they can, place them in the recovery position until medical help arrives. Keep checking them and make sure their airway remains clear.

If you need to provide emergency care, follow the **DR ABC** code.

Danger

Check that it's safe to approach.

Response

Try to get a response by gently shaking the casualty's shoulders and asking loudly 'Are you all right?' If they respond, check for injuries.

Airway

If there's no response, open the casualty's airway by placing your fingers under their chin and lifting it forward.

Breathing

Check that the casualty is breathing normally. Look for chest movements, look and listen for breathing, and feel for breath on your cheek.

If there are no signs of breathing, start CPR. Interlock your fingers, place them in the centre of the casualty's chest and press down hard and fast – around 5–6 centimetres and about twice a second. You may only need one hand for a child and shouldn't press down as far. For infants, use two fingers in the middle of the chest and press down about a third of the chest depth. Don't stop until the casualty starts breathing again or a medical professional takes over.

Circulation

If the casualty is responsive and breathing, check for signs of bleeding. Protect yourself from exposure to blood and check for anything that may be in the wound, such as glass. Don't remove anything that's stuck in the wound. Taking care not to press on the object, build up padding on either side of the object. If nothing is embedded, apply firm pressure over the wound to stem the flow of blood. As soon as practical, fasten a pad to the wound with a bandage or length of cloth. Use the cleanest material available.

People at the scene may be suffering from shock: signs include a rapid pulse, sweating and pale grey skin.

To help someone suffering from shock

- reassure them confidently
- keep them warm
- make them as comfortable as you can
- avoid moving them unless it's necessary
- make sure they're not left alone.

If someone is suffering from burns

- douse the burns thoroughly with cool water for at least 20 minutes
- don't remove anything sticking to the burn.

Reporting an incident

You **MUST** stop and give your name and address if you're involved in an incident. If there's damage to another vehicle, property or animal, report it to the owner. If you don't do this at the time, you **MUST** report the incident to the police as soon as is reasonably practicable, and in any case within 24 hours (immediately in Northern Ireland).

If another person is injured and you don't produce your insurance certificate at the time of the incident, you **MUST** report the incident to the police as soon as is reasonably practicable, and in any case within 24 hours (immediately in Northern Ireland).

HC r286, 287 RES s16

If another vehicle is involved, find out

- who owns the vehicle
- the make and registration number of the vehicle
- the other driver's name, address and telephone number and details of their insurance.

Following an incident (or at any other time), the police may ask you for

- your insurance certificate
- the MOT certificate for the motorcycle you're riding
- your driving licence.

HC r286, p122

Meeting the standards

At the scene of an incident, you must be able to

stop and park your machine in a safe place, if necessary

make sure that warning is given to other road users

give help to others if you can

where possible, record information about what you saw or the scene that you found. It may be helpful to take photographs and draw sketch plans.

You must know and understand

how to keep control of the machine, where possible, if it breaks down

how and when to use hazard warning lights

what the law says about stopping if you're involved in an incident that causes damage or injury to

- any other person
- another vehicle
- an animal
- someone's property

This includes what to do about

- stopping
- providing your details
- giving statements
- producing documents

how to contact the emergency services and how important it is to give them accurate information.

417

Notes

You can use this page to make your own notes or diagrams about the key points you need to remember.

Think about

- What should you do if your motorcycle breaks down on the motorway?
- How can you warn other road users if you've broken down on the road?
- If you're the first person to arrive at the scene of a crash, what should you do?
- If a motorcyclist is involved in the crash, should you remove their helmet?
- What does DR ABC stand for?
- If you're involved in an incident with another vehicle, what must you do?

Your notes

_____

_____

_____

_____

_____

_____

_____

_____

_____

_____

_____

_____

_____

_____

_____

 ## Things to discuss and practise with your trainer

These are just a few examples of what you could discuss and practise with your trainer. Read more about incidents, accidents and emergencies to come up with your own ideas.

Discuss with your trainer

- what it means if you see a driver displaying a 'help' pennant
- when you may and may not use your hazard warning lights
- what you should do if you arrive at the scene of a crash and find
  - an injured motorcyclist wearing a helmet
  - someone bleeding badly with nothing embedded in their wound
  - someone with a burn
  - someone who isn't breathing normally.

Practise with your trainer

Hopefully, you won't have the opportunity to practise what to do in the event of an incident or emergency during your lesson. Instead, practise with your trainer

- learning the rules relating to
  - breakdowns on all roads, including motorways
  - obstructions
  - incidents, warning signs and flashing lights
  - passing and being involved in a crash
  - incidents involving dangerous goods
  - which documents you'll need to produce if you're involved in a crash
  - incidents in tunnels.

13.1   Mark one answer   RES s11, HC r275

Your motorcycle has broken down on a motorway. How will you know the direction of the nearest emergency telephone?

☐ By walking with the flow of traffic

☐ By following an arrow on a marker post

☐ By walking against the flow of traffic

☐ By remembering where the last phone was

If you break down on a motorway, pull onto the hard shoulder and stop as far over to the left as you can. Switch on your hazard warning lights (if fitted) and go to the nearest emergency telephone. Marker posts spaced every 100 metres will show you where the nearest telephone is.

13.2   Mark one answer   RES s5

When should you use the engine cut-out switch?

☐ To stop the engine in an emergency

☐ To stop the engine after a short journey

☐ To save wear on the ignition switch

☐ To start the engine if you lose the key

Most motorcycles are fitted with an engine cut-out switch. This is designed to stop the engine in an emergency and so reduce the risk of electrical sparks starting a fire.

13.3   Mark one answer   HC r116

You're riding on a motorway. What does it mean if the car in front switches on its hazard warning lights?

☐ The driver is going to take the next exit

☐ There's danger ahead

☐ There's a police car ahead

☐ The driver is trying to change lanes

Drivers and riders may switch on their hazard warning lights to warn following traffic of an obstruction or danger ahead. This only applies on motorways and dual carriageways that are subject to the national speed limit. The hazard warning lights should be turned off again when it's clear the warning has been seen.

13.4   Mark one answer   RES s16, HC r116, 274

What should you do if your motorcycle breaks down while you're riding through a tunnel?

☐ Switch on hazard warning lights

☐ Remain on your motorcycle

☐ Wait for the police to find you

☐ Rely on CCTV cameras seeing you

If your motorcycle breaks down in a tunnel, it could present a danger to other traffic. First switch on your hazard warning lights and then call for help from an emergency telephone point. Don't rely on being found by the police or being seen by a CCTV camera.

13.5   Mark one answer   RES s11, HC r116

You're on a motorway. When can you use hazard warning lights?

☐ When a vehicle is following too closely

☐ When you slow down quickly because of danger ahead

☐ When you're being towed by another vehicle

☐ When you're riding on the hard shoulder

Briefly using your hazard warning lights will warn the traffic behind you that there's a hazard ahead. Turn them off again when following drivers have seen and responded to your signal.

13.6   Mark one answer   RES s11, HC r280

What should you do if luggage falls from your motorcycle while you're riding on a motorway?

☐ Stop at the next emergency telephone and report the hazard

☐ Stop on the motorway and put on hazard warning lights while you pick it up

☐ Walk back up the motorway to pick it up

☐ Pull up on the hard shoulder and wave traffic down

If any of your luggage falls onto the road, pull onto the hard shoulder near an emergency telephone and call for assistance. Don't stop on the carriageway or attempt to retrieve anything.

13.7   Mark one answer   RES s16, HC r286–287

What information should you find out if you're involved in a collision where someone is injured?

☐ Whether the driver owns the other vehicle involved

☐ Whether the other driver is licensed to drive

☐ The occupation of the other driver

☐ The other driver's vehicle insurance details

If you're involved in a collision where someone is injured, your first priority is to warn other traffic and call the emergency services. Make sure you have all the information you need before you leave the scene – such as the other driver's name, phone number and insurance details. Don't ride your motorcycle if it's unroadworthy.

13.8   Mark one answer   RES s16, HC r116

When are you allowed to use hazard warning lights?

☐ When stopped and temporarily obstructing traffic

☐ When travelling during darkness without headlights

☐ When parked on double yellow lines to visit a shop

☐ When travelling slowly because you're lost

You mustn't use hazard warning lights while moving, except to warn traffic behind when you slow suddenly on a motorway or unrestricted dual carriageway.

Never use hazard warning lights to excuse dangerous or illegal parking.

Mark one answer RES s8, HC r126

What should you do if you have to stop while you're going through a congested tunnel?

☐ Pull up very close to the vehicle in front to save space

☐ Ignore any message signs, as they're never up to date

☐ Keep a safe distance from the vehicle in front

☐ Make a U-turn and find another route

It's important to keep a safe distance from the vehicle in front at all times. This still applies in congested tunnels, even if you're moving very slowly or have stopped. If the vehicle in front breaks down, you may need room to manoeuvre past it.

13.10 **Mark one answer** RES s16, HC p133

You arrive at the scene of a crash where someone is bleeding heavily from a wound in their arm. Nothing is embedded in the wound. What could you do to help?

☐ Walk them around and keep them talking

☐ Dab the wound

☐ Get them a drink

☐ Apply pressure over the wound

If possible, lay the casualty down. Protect yourself from exposure to blood and, when you're sure there's nothing in the wound, apply firm pressure using clean material.

13.11 **Mark one answer** RES s16, HC p132

You're at an incident. What could you do to help an unconscious casualty?

☐ Take photographs of the scene

☐ Check that they're breathing normally

☐ Move them to somewhere more comfortable

☐ Splash their face with cool water

If a casualty is unconscious, you need to check that they're breathing normally. Look for chest movements, look and listen for breathing, and feel for breath on your cheek.

13.12 **Mark one answer** RES s16, HC p132

A casualty isn't breathing normally and needs CPR. At what rate should you press down and release on the centre of their chest?

☐ 10 times per minute

☐ 120 times per minute

☐ 60 times per minute

☐ 240 times per minute

If a casualty isn't breathing normally, cardiopulmonary resuscitation (CPR) may be needed to maintain circulation. Place two hands on the centre of the chest and press down hard and fast – around 5–6 centimetres and about twice a second.

13.13 — Mark one answer — RES s16

Following a collision, a person has been injured. What would be a warning sign for shock?

- [ ] Flushed complexion
- [ ] Warm dry skin
- [ ] Slow pulse
- [ ] Rapid shallow breathing

The effects of shock may not be immediately obvious. Warning signs to look for include

- a rapid pulse
- sweating
- pale grey skin
- rapid shallow breathing.

13.14 — Mark one answer — RES s16, HC p132

An injured person has been placed in the recovery position. They're unconscious but breathing normally. What else should be done?

- [ ] Press firmly between their shoulders
- [ ] Place their arms by their side
- [ ] Give them a hot sweet drink
- [ ] Check their airway remains open

After a casualty has been placed in the recovery position, make sure their airway remains open and monitor their condition until medical help arrives. Where possible, don't move a casualty unless there's further danger.

13.15 — Mark one answer — RES s16, HC p132

An injured motorcyclist is lying unconscious in the road. The traffic has stopped and there's no further danger. What could you do to help?

- [ ] Remove their safety helmet
- [ ] Seek medical assistance
- [ ] Move the person off the road
- [ ] Remove their leather jacket

If someone has been injured, the sooner proper medical attention is given the better. Ask someone to phone for help or do it yourself. An injured person should only be moved if they're in further danger. An injured motorcyclist's helmet shouldn't be removed unless it's essential.

13.16 — Mark one answer — RES s11, HC r280

What should you do if you see a large box fall from a lorry onto the motorway?

- [ ] Go to the next emergency telephone and report the hazard
- [ ] Catch up with the lorry and try to get the driver's attention
- [ ] Stop close to the box until the police arrive
- [ ] Pull over to the hard shoulder, then remove the box

Lorry drivers can be unaware of objects falling from their vehicles. If you see something fall onto a motorway, look to see if the driver pulls over. If they don't stop, don't attempt to retrieve the object yourself. Pull onto the hard shoulder near an emergency telephone and report the hazard.

13.17　Mark one answer　RES s8

You're going through a long tunnel. What will warn you of congestion or an incident ahead?

☐ Hazard warning lines

☐ Other drivers flashing their lights

☐ Variable message signs

☐ Areas with hatch markings

Follow the instructions given by the signs or by tunnel officials. In congested tunnels, a minor incident can soon turn into a major one, with serious or even fatal results.

13.18　Mark one answer　RES s16, HC p132

An adult casualty isn't breathing. To maintain circulation, CPR should be given. What's the correct depth to press down on their chest?

☐ 1 to 2 centimetres

☐ 5 to 6 centimetres

☐ 10 to 15 centimetres

☐ 15 to 20 centimetres

An adult casualty isn't breathing normally. To maintain circulation, place two hands on the centre of the chest. Then press down hard and fast – around 5–6 centimetres and about twice a second.

13.19　Mark one answer　RES s16, HC p131–132

You're the first person to arrive at an incident where people are badly injured. You've switched on your hazard warning lights and checked all engines are stopped. What else should you do?

☐ Make sure that an ambulance has been called

☐ Stop other cars and ask the drivers for help

☐ Try and get people who are injured to drink something

☐ Move the people who are injured clear of their vehicles

If you're the first to arrive at a crash scene, the first concerns are the risk of further collision and fire. Ensuring that vehicle engines are switched off will reduce the risk of fire. Use hazard warning lights so that other traffic knows there's a need for caution. Make sure the emergency services are contacted; don't assume it's already been done.

13.20 — Mark one answer — RES s16, HC p132

You arrive at the scene of a motorcycle crash. The rider is injured. When should their helmet be removed?

☐ Only when it's essential
☐ Always straight away
☐ Only when the motorcyclist asks
☐ Always, unless they're in shock

Don't remove a motorcyclist's helmet unless it's essential. Remember they may be suffering from shock. Don't give them anything to eat or drink, but do reassure them confidently.

13.21 — Mark one answer — RES s16, HC p132

You arrive at an incident. There's no danger from fire or further collisions and the emergency services have been called. What's your first priority when attending to an unconscious motorcyclist?

☐ Check whether they're breathing normally
☐ Check whether they're bleeding
☐ Check whether they have any broken bones
☐ Check whether they have any bruising

At the scene of an incident, always be aware of danger from further collisions or fire. The first priority when dealing with an unconscious person is to ensure they can breathe. This may involve clearing their airway if you can see an obstruction or if they're having difficulty breathing.

13.22 — Mark one answer — RES s16, HC p132

At an incident, someone is unconscious and you want to help. What would be the first thing to check?

☐ Whether their vehicle is insured
☐ Whether they have any allergies
☐ Whether they're comfortable
☐ Whether their airway is open

Remember this procedure by saying DR ABC. This stands for Danger, Response, Airway, Breathing, Circulation. Give whatever first aid you can and stay with the injured person until a medical professional takes over.

13.23 — Mark one answer — RES s16, HC p131–132

What could you do to help injured people at an incident?

☐ Keep them warm and comfortable
☐ Give them something to eat
☐ Keep them on the move by walking them around
☐ Give them a warm drink

There are a number of things you can do to help, even without expert training. Be aware of further danger from other traffic and fire; make sure the area is safe. People may be in shock. Don't give them anything to eat or drink. Keep them warm and comfortable and reassure them. Don't move injured people unless there's a risk of further danger.

There's been a collision. How can you help a driver who's suffering from shock?

☐ Give them a drink

☐ Reassure them confidently

☐ Ask who caused the incident

☐ Offer them a cigarette

A casualty suffering from shock may have injuries that aren't immediately obvious. Call the emergency services, then stay with the person in shock, offering reassurance until the experts arrive.

You arrive at the scene of a motorcycle crash. No other vehicle is involved. The rider is unconscious and lying in the middle of the road. What's the first thing you should do at the scene?

☐ Move the rider out of the road

☐ Warn other traffic

☐ Clear the road of debris

☐ Give the rider reassurance

The motorcyclist is in an extremely vulnerable position, exposed to further danger from traffic. Approaching vehicles need advance warning in order to slow down and safely take avoiding action or stop. Don't put yourself or anyone else at risk. Use the hazard warning lights on your vehicle to alert other road users to the danger.

At an incident, how could you help a small child who isn't breathing?

☐ Find their parents and explain what's happening

☐ Open their airway and begin CPR

☐ Put them in the recovery position and slap their back

☐ Talk to them confidently until an ambulance arrives

If a young child has stopped breathing, first check that their airway is open and then begin CPR. With a young child, you may only need to use one hand and you shouldn't press down as far as you would with an adult. Continue the procedure until the child is breathing again or until a medical professional takes over.

At an incident, a casualty isn't breathing. What should you do while helping them to start breathing again?

☐ Put their arms across their chest

☐ Shake them firmly

☐ Roll them onto their side

☐ Open their airway

It's important to ensure that the airway is open before you start CPR. To open the casualty's airway, place your fingers under their chin and lift it forward.

13.28   Mark one answer   RES s16, HC p133

At an incident, someone is suffering from severe burns. How could you help them?

☐ Apply lotions to the injury

☐ Burst any blisters

☐ Remove anything sticking to the burns

☐ Douse the burns with clean, cool water

Your priority is to cool the burns with clean, cool water. Its coolness will help take the heat out of the burns and relieve the pain. Keep the wound doused for at least 20 minutes. If blisters appear, don't attempt to burst them, as this could lead to infection.

13.29   Mark one answer   RES s16, HC p133

You arrive at an incident. A pedestrian is bleeding heavily from a leg wound. The leg isn't broken and there's nothing in the wound. How could you help?

☐ Dab the wound to stop the bleeding

☐ Keep the casualty's legs flat on the ground

☐ Give them a warm drink

☐ Apply firm pressure over the wound

You should protect yourself from exposure to blood, and then apply firm pressure over the wound to stem the flow of blood. As soon as practical, fasten a pad to the wound with a bandage or length of cloth. Use the cleanest material available.

13.30   Mark one answer   RES s16, HC p131–132

At an incident, a casualty is unconscious but breathing. When should you move them?

☐ When an ambulance is on its way

☐ When bystanders tell you to move them

☐ When there's a risk of further danger

☐ When bystanders offer to help you

Don't move a casualty unless there's further danger; for example, from other traffic or fire. They may have unseen or internal injuries. Moving them unnecessarily could cause further injury. Don't remove a motorcyclist's helmet unless it's essential.

13.31   Mark one answer   RES s16, HC p131–132

At an incident, it's important to look after any casualties. What should you do with them when the area is safe?

☐ Move them away from the vehicles

☐ Ask them how it happened

☐ Give them something to eat

☐ Keep them where they are

When the area is safe and there's no danger from other traffic or fire, it's better not to move casualties. Moving them may cause further injury.

Which sign shows that a tanker is carrying dangerous goods?

☐ ☐

☐ ☐

Tankers will display a hazard warning plate on the side and rear of the vehicle. Details of hazard warning symbols are given in The Highway Code. If a tanker is involved in a collision, you may need to report the tanker's hazard labelling to the emergency services.

Which document may the police ask you to produce after you've been involved in a collision?

☐ Your vehicle registration document
☐ Your driving licence
☐ Your theory test certificate
☐ Your vehicle service record

You must stop if you've been involved in a collision that results in injury or damage. The police may ask to see your driving licence and insurance details at the time or later at a police station.

After a collision, someone is unconscious in their vehicle. When should you call the emergency services?

☐ Only as a last resort
☐ As soon as possible
☐ After you've woken them up
☐ After checking for broken bones

It's important to make sure that the emergency services arrive as soon as possible. When a person is unconscious, they could have serious injuries that aren't immediately obvious.

A collision has just happened. An injured person is lying in a busy road. What's the first thing you should do?

☐ Treat the person for shock
☐ Warn other traffic
☐ Place them in the recovery position
☐ Make sure the injured person is kept warm

The most immediate danger is further collisions and fire. You could warn other traffic by switching on hazard warning lights, displaying an advance warning triangle or sign (but not on a motorway), or by any other means that doesn't put you or others at risk.

13.36 — Mark one answer — RES s16, HC p132

At an incident, how could you help a casualty who has stopped breathing?

☐ Keep their head tilted forwards as far as possible

☐ Follow the DR ABC code

☐ Raise their legs to help with circulation

☐ Try to give them something to drink

The DR ABC code has been devised by medical experts to give the best outcome until the emergency services arrive and take care of casualties.

13.37 — Mark one answer — RES s16, HC p132

You're at the scene of an incident. How could you help someone who's suffering from shock?

☐ Reassure them confidently

☐ Offer them a cigarette

☐ Give them a warm drink

☐ Offer them some food

If someone is suffering from shock, try to keep them warm and as comfortable as you can. Don't give them anything to eat or drink but reassure them confidently and try not to leave them alone.

13.38 — Mark one answer — RES s16, HC p132

There's been a collision. A motorcyclist is lying injured and unconscious. Why should you only remove their helmet if it's essential?

☐ They might not want you to remove it

☐ Removing it could make any injuries worse

☐ Removing it could let them get cold

☐ You could scratch the helmet as you remove it

When someone is injured, any movement that isn't absolutely necessary should be avoided, since it could make the injuries worse. Unless it's essential to remove a motorcyclist's helmet, it's generally safer to leave it in place.

Case study practice – 13 Incidents, accidents and emergencies

You witness an incident involving a car and a motorcycle. The car driver isn't obviously injured but their skin has turned a grey colour, they're sweating and their breathing is rapid and shallow.

The motorcyclist is lying against the kerb with his helmet still on. He's conscious but very dazed, bruised and shocked.

You leave your own motorcycle standing on the road with the hazard warning lights on.

You call the emergency services and stay with both people involved in the incident until the services arrive.

You give your contact details to a police officer.

13.1 What condition is the car driver most likely to be suffering from?

Mark **one** answer

☐ Hunger

☐ Travel sickness

☐ Headache

☐ Shock

HC p132

13.2 Why should the helmet stay on for the time being?

Mark **one** answer

☐ Someone might steal the helmet if they take it off

☐ The helmet may get lost on the way to hospital

☐ Because removing it could cause further injuries

☐ The helmet will keep their head from getting cold

HC r283, p132

13.3 Why would you leave your motorcycle positioned in that way?

Mark **one** answer

☐ To warn following traffic of the hazard

☐ To ensure that the battery stays fully charged

☐ To highlight the incident for the emergency services

☐ To help you locate your motorcycle again later

RES s16 **HC r283**

13.4 How should you deal with the motorcyclist?

Mark **one** answer

☐ Offer them food

☐ Give them a drink

☐ Keep them warm

☐ Leave them alone

RES s16 **HC p132**

13.5 Why would you provide your details?

Mark **one** answer

☐ You were in a hurry to leave

☐ You witnessed the incident

☐ You wanted to be involved

☐ You left your licence at home

RES s16

Section fourteen

 # Motorcycle loading

In this section, you'll learn about

- how to carry loads safely
- using a sidecar
- carrying a pillion passenger safely
- towing a trailer.

Motorcycle loading

Loading your motorcycle carefully will help to ensure that you can travel safely, whether your load is a passenger, a trailer or simply an overnight bag.

Keeping your motorcycle stable

You need to make sure that your motorcycle isn't overloaded. Overloading can seriously affect the motorcycle's handling, especially the steering and braking.

> **HC r98 RES s14**

You **MUST** securely fasten any load you're carrying before you start riding: it's an offence to travel with an insecure load.

A heavy or bulky load can make your motorcycle less stable.

When carrying a passenger or a heavy load on a motorcycle, you may need to adjust

- the tyre pressures
- the headlight aim
- the suspension.

RES s14

Tip

You should inflate your tyres to a higher pressure than normal

- when you're carrying a heavy load or pillion passenger
- if you're riding for a long distance on a dual carriageway or motorway at the speed limit for these roads.

Your motorcycle handbook should tell you the correct pressure for different circumstances.

RES s14, 15

Sidecars

Before fitting a sidecar, you need to make sure that your motorcycle is suitable for use with a sidecar. The sidecar must be aligned correctly, otherwise your motorcycle will be difficult to control and is likely to be dangerous to ride.

When you ride for the first time with a sidecar fitted, keep your speed down and be careful when riding round bends and corners and at junctions. A motorcycle with a sidecar handles very differently from a solo motorcycle.

Remember that your stopping distance may also increase due to the extra weight of the sidecar.

RES s14

Pillion passengers

A pillion passenger **MUST** wear a helmet that's correctly fastened. (This does not apply to a follower of the Sikh religion while wearing a turban.) They **MUST** sit astride the machine, facing forwards, on a proper passenger seat. Your motorcycle should have passenger footrests too.

You **MUST NOT** carry a pillion passenger unless

- you've passed a practical motorcycle test
- you have a full motorcycle licence for the category of motorcycle being ridden.

HC r83, 85 RES s14

Your pillion passenger needs to understand that they should lean with you when you lean the motorcycle over to steer around bends. If it's the first time the passenger has ridden, explain what to do and how to hold onto either your waist or the passenger grab rail.

Children should only be carried as pillion passengers when they can reach the handholds and footrests. They **MUST** also wear a helmet that's the right size and securely fastened, and sit properly on the pillion seat, facing forwards.

The extra weight of a passenger may change the way the motorcycle handles, so give yourself time to get used to it. The additional weight may also increase your stopping distance, so keep well back when following other traffic.

When you're riding with a passenger, think about their comfort and try to ride smoothly, avoiding harsh acceleration or braking.

Your passenger's clothing should be

- warm
- waterproof
- bright or reflective.

Passengers who wear protective motorcyclist clothing will gain protection from

- the weather
- the road surface, if they fall off the motorcycle.

Don't let your passenger wear a trailing scarf or belt, as this could become tangled in the rear wheel or drive chain and cause a serious incident.

RES s14

Towing a trailer

To tow a trailer, you must have a full motorcycle licence and your motorcycle must have an engine capacity of more than 125 cc. A motorcycle trailer must be no wider than 1 metre (3 feet 3 inches). Remember that your stopping distance may increase due to the extra weight of the trailer.

If the trailer starts to swerve or snake as you're riding along

- ease off the throttle
- reduce your speed gradually to regain control.

There's a lower national speed limit for all vehicles towing trailers.

| On a dual carriageway or motorway | Maximum speed 60 mph (96 km/h)

A vehicle towing a trailer on a motorway that has more than two lanes **MUST NOT** be driven in the right-hand lane. |
| On a single carriageway | Maximum speed 50 mph (80 km/h) |

HC r98, p40 RES s14

 Find out more about towing a trailer at this website.

www.gov.uk

Meeting the standards

You must be able to

make sure that a pillion passenger is seated legally, correctly and securely

make sure that loads are secure and distributed correctly, depending on the machine

allow for the effect that any extra load may have on how the machine handles.

You must know and understand

what to tell a passenger about how to behave when being carried on the machine

how to adjust the machine to allow for extra weight. For example, you may need to put more air in the tyres

how to change your riding to allow for extra weight; for example
- earlier braking
- use of lower gears.

Notes

You can use this page to make your own notes or diagrams about the key points you need to remember.

Think about

- What sorts of load might you carry on your motorcycle that could affect its stability?
- When might you need to increase the tyre pressures?
- What would you need to tell a first-time pillion passenger about before you began riding?
- If you wanted to tow a trailer, what speed limits would you have to observe?

Your notes

Things to discuss and practise with your trainer

These are just a few examples of what you could discuss and practise with your trainer. Read more about motorcycle loading to come up with your own ideas.

Discuss with your trainer

- the effects that carrying a heavy load, such as panniers or a top box, might have on your riding
- the rules and advice for carrying a pillion passenger
    - your licence requirement
    - how a passenger should sit and behave on your motorcycle
    - what they should wear
    - the riding technique that you should use when carrying a passenger
- the techniques that you'll need to use and rules to follow when
    - riding with a sidecar
    - pulling a trailer.

Practise with your trainer

- the checks that you'll need to make when carrying a load
    - your tyre pressure
    - the preload on your shock absorbers
    - the angle of your headlights.

What should you do if a trailer you're towing swerves or snakes?

☐ Ease off the throttle and reduce your speed

☐ Let go of the handlebars and let it correct itself

☐ Brake hard and hold the brake on

☐ Accelerate until it stabilises itself

Don't be tempted to use harsh braking to stop swerving or snaking, as this could make things worse. You should reduce your speed gradually by easing off the throttle.

What should you be aware of when you ride a sidecar outfit for the first time?

☐ You need time to get used to it

☐ You'll be able to stop in a shorter distance

☐ You need to accelerate around bends

☐ You can approach corners without braking

A motorcycle with a sidecar, or a trike, will feel very different to ride than a solo motorcycle. It requires a specific technique, especially when cornering, with different methods used for right and left turns. Keep your speed down until you get used to the outfit, especially when negotiating bends and junctions.

What may you need to adjust when you're carrying a heavy load on your motorcycle?

☐ The footrests

☐ The gear lever

☐ The seat height

☐ The tyre pressure

Carrying extra weight, such as luggage or a pillion passenger, can affect the feel and handling of your motorcycle. If possible, some items may need to be adjusted to help overcome this. These adjustments include the aim of the headlights, the suspension settings, the tyre pressures and the mirrors.

14.4   NI EXEMPT   Mark one answer   RES s2

What are the minimum test vehicle requirements for a motorcycle used to obtain a full category 'A' licence?

☐ Solo, with a maximum power of at least 25 kW (33 bhp)

☐ Solo, with a maximum power of at least 11 kW (14.6 bhp)

☐ Fitted with a sidecar, and with a maximum power of at least 35 kW (46.6 bhp)

☐ Solo, with a maximum power of at least 40 kW (53.6 bhp)

To obtain the full category 'A' on your driving licence, the motorcycle you use for your practical test must be a solo machine with a cylinder capacity of at least 595 cc and a power output of at least 40 kW (53.6 bhp).

14.5   Mark one answer   RES s14

What must you do when you're carrying a load on your motorcycle's luggage rack?

☐ Make sure the load is securely fastened

☐ Make sure the load is unevenly balanced

☐ Make sure the load is highly visible

☐ Make sure the load is covered with plastic sheeting

If you carry a load on your motorcycle you must make sure it's securely fastened. It's an offence to travel with an insecure load as it could fall into the path of following vehicles and cause danger.

14.6   Mark one answer   RES s14, HC r83

What does a person need to do when they ride as a pillion passenger?

☐ Have a provisional motorcycle licence

☐ Be lighter than the rider

☐ Wear a motorcycle helmet

☐ Give signals for the rider

Pillion passengers must wear a correctly fastened motorcycle helmet. They must also sit astride the motorcycle, on a proper passenger seat, and use the fitted passenger footrests.

14.7   Mark one answer   RES s14

What should a pillion passenger do while they're being carried on a motorcycle?

☐ Give the rider directions

☐ Lean with the rider when going around bends

☐ Take rear observation for the rider

☐ Give arm signals for the rider

When you ride with a pillion passenger, your motorcycle may feel unbalanced and its acceleration and braking distance may also be affected. Make sure your passenger knows they must lean with you while cornering. If they don't, they could cause the motorcycle to become unstable and difficult to control.

What should your pillion passenger do while you're riding around a bend?

☐ Give arm signals for you

☐ Check behind for other vehicles

☐ Lean with you

☐ Lean to one side to see ahead

A pillion passenger shouldn't give signals or look around for you – that's your responsibility as the rider. If your passenger has never been on a motorcycle before, make sure they know that they need to lean with you when going around bends.

What might need to be adjusted if you carry a pillion passenger?

☐ Indicators

☐ Exhaust

☐ Fairing

☐ Headlights

Your headlights must be properly adjusted to avoid dazzling other road users. You might need to do this when carrying a pillion passenger, because the extra weight can cause the headlight beam to aim higher than normal. You may also need to adjust the tyre pressures and the suspension.

What's the speed limit on a single carriageway road for a motorcycle towing a trailer?

☐ 50 mph

☐ 40 mph

☐ 60 mph

☐ 70 mph

When you tow a trailer, remember that you must obey the reduced speed limits of 50 mph on a single carriageway and 60 mph on a dual carriageway or motorway. Make sure that the trailer is hitched correctly and that any load in the trailer is secure. You should also bear in mind that your stopping distance may increase.

14.11
Mark one answer

How will a heavy load in your top box affect your motorcycle?

Carrying a heavy load in your top box could make your motorcycle unstable, because the weight is high up and at the very back of the machine.

- ☐ It will improve stability
- ☐ It will reduce stability
- ☐ It will reduce tyre wear
- ☐ It will improve braking

14.12
Mark one answer

Who's responsible for making sure that a motorcycle is correctly loaded?

- ☐ The rider of the motorcycle
- ☐ The owner of the items being carried
- ☐ The licensing authority
- ☐ The owner of the motorcycle

Correct loading is the responsibility of the rider. Overloading a motorcycle can seriously affect the control and handling. It could result in a crash, with serious or even fatal consequences.

14.13
Mark one answer

What should you do before fitting a sidecar to a motorcycle?

- ☐ Have the wheels balanced
- ☐ Have the engine tuned
- ☐ Pass the extended motorcycle test
- ☐ Check that the motorcycle is suitable

If you want to fit a sidecar to your motorcycle, check that the motorcycle is suitable and can cope with the extra load. Make sure that the sidecar is securely fixed and properly aligned. If your motorcycle was registered on or after 1 August 1981, the sidecar must be fitted on the left-hand side of the motorcycle.

You're using throwover saddlebags. Why is it important to make sure they're evenly loaded?

☐ Uneven loads can make the engine overheat

☐ Uneven loads can make the motorcycle uncomfortable

☐ Uneven loads can make the motorcycle unstable

☐ Uneven loads can make the battery overcharge

Panniers or saddlebags should be loaded so that you carry about the same weight in each bag. Uneven loading could make the motorcycle unstable, especially when cornering.

What could be affected if you fit a bulky tank bag to your motorcycle?

☐ Your ability to steer

☐ Your ability to accelerate

☐ Your view ahead

☐ Your insurance premium

If your tank bag is too bulky, it could get in the way of your arms or restrict the movement of the handlebars.

What must you have if you want to carry a pillion passenger on your motorcycle?

☐ A full car licence

☐ A full motorcycle licence

☐ Comprehensive insurance

☐ Breakdown insurance

Before you can carry a pillion passenger, the law requires you to have a full licence for the category of motorcycle you're using.

What might you need to adjust when you carry a heavy load on your motorcycle?

☐ The seat height

☐ The rear brake

☐ The steering-head bearings

☐ The tyre pressures

Take care if you're carrying a heavy load on your motorcycle. Try to carry the weight as low down as possible – ideally in panniers, with the weight evenly spread on each side. You may need to adjust your tyre pressures, your headlight aim and your rear shock-absorber preload setting.

14.18 — Mark one answer — RES s14

You're carrying a pillion passenger on your motorcycle. What should you do when you're following other traffic?

☐ Keep to your normal following distance

☐ Get your passenger to keep checking behind

☐ Keep further back than you normally would

☐ Get your passenger to signal for you

The extra weight of a passenger may increase your stopping distance. Allow for this when following another vehicle by increasing the separation distance.

14.19 — Mark one answer — RES s14

When can you carry a child as a pillion passenger?

☐ When they're over 14 years old

☐ When they're over 16 years old

☐ When they can reach the floor from the seat

☐ When they can reach the handholds and footrests

Any passenger you carry – no matter how old they are – must be able to reach the footrests and handholds properly to remain safe on your machine. Also make sure they're wearing protective weatherproof clothing and a properly fitting helmet.

14.20 — Mark one answer — RES s14

What should you check when you fit a sidecar to your motorcycle?

☐ That the sidecar has a registration plate

☐ That the sidecar is correctly aligned

☐ That the sidecar has a waterproof cover

☐ That the sidecar has a spare wheel

If the sidecar isn't correctly aligned with the mounting points, the outfit will be difficult to control and could be dangerous. Riding with a sidecar attached requires a different technique from riding a solo motorcycle. You should keep your speed down while learning this skill.

14.21 — Mark one answer — RES s14

How will riding a motorcycle and sidecar differ from riding a solo motorcycle?

☐ It will allow you to corner more quickly

☐ It will allow you to brake later for hazards

☐ It will require a different riding technique

☐ It will improve your fuel consumption

You'll need to adapt your riding technique when riding a motorcycle fitted with a sidecar. The extra weight will affect the handling and may increase your overall stopping distance.

You're carrying a pillion passenger on your motorcycle. What should you adjust to allow for the extra weight?

☐ The preload on the front forks

☐ The preload on the rear shock absorber(s)

☐ The balance of the rear wheel

☐ The front and rear wheel alignment

When carrying a passenger or other extra weight, you may need to make adjustments, particularly to the rear shock absorber(s), tyre pressures and headlight alignment. Check your owner's handbook for details.

What's the maximum width allowed for a trailer being towed by a motorcycle?

☐ 0.5 metres (1 foot 8 inches)

☐ 1 metre (3 feet 3 inches)

☐ 1.5 metres (4 feet 11 inches)

☐ 2 metres (6 feet 6 inches)

When you're towing a trailer, you must remember that you may not be able to filter through traffic. Don't forget that the trailer is there, especially when riding round bends and negotiating junctions.

What should you do when you tow a trailer with your motorcycle?

☐ Make sure the motorcycle also has a sidecar

☐ Make sure the trailer weighs more than the motorcycle

☐ Make sure the trailer is fitted with brakes

☐ Make sure the trailer isn't more than 1 metre (3 feet 3 inches) wide

To tow a trailer behind a motorcycle, you must have a full motorcycle licence and a motorcycle with an engine larger than 125 cc. Motorcycle trailers mustn't exceed 1 metre (3 feet 3 inches) in width.

What effect will a sidecar have when it's fitted to your motorcycle?

☐ It will reduce the motorcycle's stability

☐ It will make the steering lighter

☐ It will increase the stopping distance

☐ It will increase the fuel economy

A sidecar will alter the handling considerably. Give yourself time to adjust to the different characteristics and allow a greater stopping distance.

14.26 — Mark one answer — RES s2, 14

How is a learner motorcyclist's licence restricted?

- [ ] They mustn't carry a pillion passenger
- [ ] They mustn't use the right-hand lane on dual carriageways
- [ ] They mustn't carry panniers on their motorcycle
- [ ] They mustn't ride faster than 30 mph

Learner motorcyclists aren't allowed to

- tow a trailer
- carry a pillion passenger
- use the motorway.

In addition, they must display red L plates (D plates in Wales) to the front and rear of the motorcycle.

14.27 — Mark one answer — RES s14, HC p119

When may you tow a trailer behind your motorcycle?

- [ ] When you display a 'long vehicle' sign on the back of the trailer
- [ ] When you have fitted a larger battery to your motorcycle
- [ ] When you hold a full motorcycle licence
- [ ] When your motorcycle has shaft drive

You may not ride a motorcycle towing a trailer if you only hold a provisional motorcycle licence.

When you tow a trailer, you need to be aware that lower speed limits apply and the trailer must be no more than 1 metre wide. The trailer's laden weight should be no more than 150 kg or two-thirds of the kerbside weight of the motorcycle – whichever is less.

14.28 — Mark one answer — RES s14, HC r85

What must your motorcycle have if you're going to carry a pillion passenger?

- [ ] A passenger seat and footrests
- [ ] A passenger communication system
- [ ] A passenger luggage box
- [ ] A passenger grab handle and an adjustable shock absorber

When carrying a pillion passenger, you should explain to them that they must keep their feet on the footrests. Tell them not to give hand signals, lean away from the rider when cornering, fidget or move around. Also check that they aren't wearing anything long or loose that could get caught in the rear wheel or drive chain.

14.29   Mark one answer   RES s14

What items should you carry in a motorcycle top box?

☐ Heavy items

☐ Personal items

☐ Emergency items

☐ Lightweight items

Carrying a heavy weight in a top box can cause handling problems, particularly when riding at speed. If you have heavy items to carry, it's better to carry them in panniers and keep the weight roughly the same on either side.

14.30   Mark one answer   RES s2, HC r85

You hold a provisional motorcycle licence. Are you allowed to carry a pillion passenger?

☐ Only if the passenger holds a full licence

☐ Not at any time

☐ Not unless you're undergoing training

☐ Only if the passenger is under 21

You aren't allowed to carry a pillion passenger until you hold a full motorcycle licence for the category of motorcycle that you're riding. Even when you've passed your test, don't carry a passenger if you aren't confident that you can do so safely. You're responsible for their safety.

14.31 — Mark one answer — RES s14

What may be seriously affected if you overload your motorcycle?

- ☐ The gearbox
- ☐ The weather protection
- ☐ The handling
- ☐ The battery life

Any load will affect the handling of your motorcycle by changing its centre of gravity. When using panniers, spread the weight evenly on each side. Avoid carrying heavy items in a top box, as this could make your steering dangerously light.

14.32 — Mark one answer — HC r124, 265

What restrictions apply if you're towing a trailer on a three-lane motorway?

- ☐ You mustn't exceed 50 mph
- ☐ You mustn't overtake
- ☐ You must have a stabiliser fitted
- ☐ You mustn't use the right-hand lane

The motorway regulations for towing a trailer state that you mustn't

- use the right-hand lane of a three-lane motorway unless directed to do so (for example, at roadworks or due to a lane closure)
- exceed 60 mph.

Case study practice – 14 Motorcycle loading

You and a friend are taking a road trip on your motorcycle.

You carefully connect up and check the loaded trailer. Your friend evenly packs the rigid panniers.

You go to the service station to buy fuel and make final checks.

Your journey takes you onto a three-lane motorway, where you travel at the speed limit when it's safe to do so. You increase the separation distance from the vehicle in front.

You don't use the right-hand lane.

14.1 Why do you check the trailer?

Mark **one** answer

☐ To make sure you haven't forgotten anything

☐ To make sure the paintwork isn't scratched

☐ To make sure the load is secure

☐ To make sure the colour matches the motorcycle

RES s14

14.2 Why would your friend pack the panniers in this way?

Mark **one** answer

- ☐ So that nothing rattles while you're riding
- ☐ Uneven load distribution can affect balance
- ☐ So that you don't forget anything
- ☐ Even loads on each side look tidier

RES s14 **HC r98**

14.3 What's the speed limit for your motorcycle on this trip?

Mark **one** answer

- ☐ 40 mph
- ☐ 50 mph
- ☐ 60 mph
- ☐ 70 mph

RES s14 **HC r124**

14.4 Why would you increase the separation distance?

Mark **one** answer

- ☐ The trailer might become detached from the motorcycle
- ☐ Your friend doesn't like you riding too close to other vehicles
- ☐ The motorway isn't very busy, so there's plenty of room
- ☐ Stopping distance is increased on a fully loaded vehicle

RES s14

14.5 Why would you not use that lane?

Mark **one** answer

- ☐ Your trailer might cause buffeting and wind resistance
- ☐ That lane mustn't be used by vehicles with trailers
- ☐ You're not going in that direction
- ☐ You don't want to travel at a very high speed

HC r265

Section fifteen

 Case study practice

Case study practice

Some of the questions within the test will be presented as a case study.

You'll be presented with a scenario – the case study – which will appear on the left-hand side of the screen. The scenario will be presented in a text format and may be accompanied by a supporting picture or diagram. As you move within the case study, the questions will appear, one by one, on the right-hand side of the screen, and you'll be asked to respond. You can re-read the scenario throughout the case study should you wish to do so.

A case study example is shown below and on the following pages.

In this section, you'll also find five mixed-topic, practice case studies similar to the ones in the actual test. Use these to help you prepare for the real thing.

Answers to all the case studies in this book are in section 16, Answers.

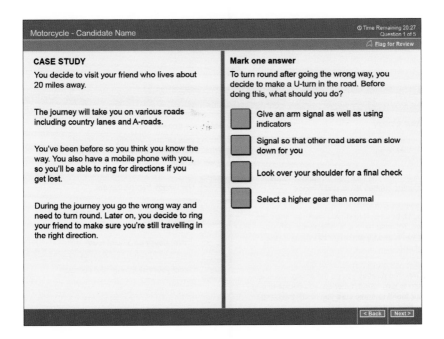

Motorcycle - Candidate Name

⏱ Time Remaining 20:27
Question 1 of 5

△ Flag for Review

CASE STUDY

You decide to visit your friend who lives about 20 miles away.

The journey will take you on various roads including country lanes and A-roads.

You've been before so you think you know the way. You also have a mobile phone with you, so you'll be able to ring for directions if you get lost.

During the journey you go the wrong way and need to turn round. Later on, you decide to ring your friend to make sure you're still travelling in the right direction.

Mark one answer

To turn round after going the wrong way, you decide to make a U-turn in the road. Before doing this, what should you do?

☐ Give an arm signal as well as using indicators

☐ Signal so that other road users can slow down for you

☐ Look over your shoulder for a final check

☐ Select a higher gear than normal

< Back | Next >

CASE STUDY

You decide to visit your friend who lives about 20 miles away.

The journey will take you on various roads including country lanes and A-roads.

You've been before so you think you know the way. You also have a mobile phone with you, so you'll be able to ring for directions if you get lost.

During the journey you go the wrong way and need to turn round. Later on, you decide to ring your friend to make sure you're still travelling in the right direction.

Mark one answer

What should you do as you approach this bridge on your journey?

☐ Move to the right

☐ Slow down

☐ Change gear

☐ Keep to 30 mph

< Back   Next >

CASE STUDY

You decide to visit your friend who lives about 20 miles away.

The journey will take you on various roads including country lanes and A-roads.

You've been before so you think you know the way. You also have a mobile phone with you, so you'll be able to ring for directions if you get lost.

During the journey you go the wrong way and need to turn round. Later on, you decide to ring your friend to make sure you're still travelling in the right direction.

Mark one answer

During your journey, you ring your friend. What's the safest way for you to use your mobile phone?

☐ Use hands-free equipment

☐ Make the call when you've stopped in a suitable place

☐ Travel slowly on a quiet road

☐ Direct your call through the operator

< Back   Next >

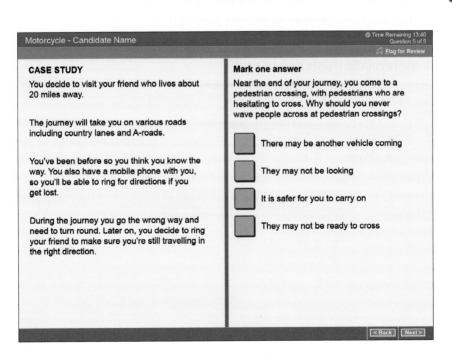

CASE STUDY

You decide to visit your friend who lives about 20 miles away.

The journey will take you on various roads including country lanes and A-roads.

You've been before so you think you know the way. You also have a mobile phone with you, so you'll be able to ring for directions if you get lost.

During the journey you go the wrong way and need to turn round. Later on, you decide to ring your friend to make sure you're still travelling in the right direction.

Mark one answer

You're travelling along a country road. A horse and rider are approaching. What should you do?

☐ Increase your speed

☐ Sound your horn

☐ Flash your headlights

☐ Go slowly past

< Back   Next >

CASE STUDY

You decide to visit your friend who lives about 20 miles away.

The journey will take you on various roads including country lanes and A-roads.

You've been before so you think you know the way. You also have a mobile phone with you, so you'll be able to ring for directions if you get lost.

During the journey you go the wrong way and need to turn round. Later on, you decide to ring your friend to make sure you're still travelling in the right direction.

Mark one answer

Near the end of your journey, you come to a pedestrian crossing, with pedestrians who are hesitating to cross. Why should you never wave people across at pedestrian crossings?

☐ There may be another vehicle coming

☐ They may not be looking

☐ It is safer for you to carry on

☐ They may not be ready to cross

< Back   Next >

Case study practice – A

You're taking your friend to collect their new motorcycle. They're already wearing the recommended helmet and clothing.

You reach a level crossing where the half-barriers are down. A train passes but the barriers stay down and the red lights continue to flash.

Further on, the road surface is cracked. You can see several potholes on your side of the road.

Later, there's a high-occupancy vehicle lane marked on the road and motorcycles are allowed to use it.

At the end of your journey you turn right into the motorcycle dealer's car park.

1 What might your friend be wearing?

Mark **one** answer

☐ Leather clothing, high-visibility waistcoat and white helmet

☐ Jeans, anorak, trainers and a light-coloured helmet

☐ Thick trousers, boots, high-visibility jacket and black helmet

☐ Tracksuit bottoms, high-visibility jacket and a dark helmet

RES s4 **HC r86**

2 What should you do at the level crossing?
Mark **one** answer

- ☐ Ride around the barriers as the lights may be faulty
- ☐ Wait, as another train will be coming
- ☐ Turn round and find an alternative route
- ☐ Immediately phone the signal operator and report a fault

RES s7 **HC r293**

3 What might you need to do on this road surface?
Mark **one** answer

- ☐ Ride in the gutter until you're past the affected area
- ☐ Dismount and quickly wheel the motorcycle past
- ☐ Ride along on the other side of the road for a while
- ☐ Slow down to ride over this patch of road

RES s8

4 How can you tell that you're allowed to ride in this lane?
Mark **one** answer

- ☐ The yellow sign shows a motorcycle
- ☐ The brown sign shows a motorcycle
- ☐ The blue sign shows a motorcycle
- ☐ The green sign shows a motorcycle

RES s7 **HC r142 KYTS p140**

5 What should you do just before turning into the car park?
Mark **one** answer

- ☐ Take a look over your right shoulder
- ☐ Take a look in the left-hand mirror
- ☐ Take a look over your left shoulder
- ☐ Take a look at the road ahead

RES s8

Case study practice – B

You're going away for the weekend with a friend as pillion passenger and carrying your luggage in a trailer.

It's daylight and the weather is dry, but windy.

On the motorway, all three lanes are very busy. You avoid using the right-hand lane.

Later, there's a roundabout. You need to take the second exit, going straight on. There are two lanes on approach but no other road markings.

After the roundabout there are signs telling you that roadworks are being carried out further ahead.

1 What important check should you make before you set out?
Mark **one** answer

☐ Headlight aim

☐ Throttle cable

☐ Wheel alignment

☐ Seat position

RES s15 **HC p98**

2 What problem might you face under these weather conditions?

Mark **one** answer

☐ Being tired and very cold

☐ Being slowed right down

☐ Being overtaken by others

☐ Being blown off course

RES s12 **HC r232–233**

3 Why would you avoid the right-hand lane on the motorway?

Mark **one** answer

☐ Traffic travelling in the right-hand lane moves too fast

☐ You can't see road signs properly from the right-hand lane

☐ Vehicles with a trailer mustn't travel in the right-hand lane

☐ Only cars are allowed to travel in the right-hand lane

RES s11 **HC r265**

4 How should you approach the roundabout?

Mark **one** answer

☐ In the right-hand lane while signalling left

☐ In the left-hand lane without giving a signal

☐ In the left-hand lane while signalling right

☐ In the right-hand lane while signalling right

RES s9 **HC r186**

5 After the roundabout, what should you anticipate seeing?

Mark **one** answer

☐ Police officers

☐ Traffic wardens

☐ Crossing patrols

☐ Road workers

RES s8 **HC r288**

Case study practice – C

> You're going on holiday. You'll be carrying heavy camping equipment in two bags.
>
> The first part of your journey is along a dual carriageway. The national speed limit applies.
>
> Later, you visit a garage, where you check your oil level.
>
> You leave your motorcycle to buy a snack at the shop.
>
> Near your destination, you follow a tractor along a country road.

1   Where should you carry the bags?
Mark **one** answer

☐ In a backpack

☐ In the tank bag

☐ In the panniers

☐ In the top box

RES s14

2   What's the speed limit on the first part of your journey?
Mark **one** answer

☐ 50 mph

☐ 60 mph

☐ 70 mph

☐ 80 mph

RES s7 **HC r124, p40**

3 Why might your check at the garage not be accurate?
Mark **one** answer

☐ Because the engine is warm

☐ Because the fuel is low

☐ Because your hands are cold

☐ Because your motorcycle is fully loaded

RES s15

4 What should you do when you go to buy a snack?
Mark **one** answer

☐ Leave your helmet and gloves on the seat

☐ Lock your motorcycle and remove the key

☐ Make sure you remove your helmet first

☐ Chain your motorcycle to a fuel pump

RES s8 HC p131

5 What should you do on the country road?
Mark **one** answer

☐ Ride closely behind the tractor to keep out of the wind

☐ Sound your horn to allow the tractor driver to hear you

☐ Flash your lights to allow the tractor driver to see you

☐ Drop back slightly so you can see the road ahead

HC r164

Case study practice – D

On a summer day you plan to make an early start on a trip.

Before you leave, you're given some upsetting news over the phone.

It's a hot, sunny day and you think about what you should wear on your journey.

At the beginning of your trip, you're cut up by a driver at a roundabout.

Riding through town, you stop at a red traffic light behind a cyclist at an advanced stop line.

Later, you witness a crash between a car and another motorcycle.

1   What should you do after your phone call?
Mark **one** answer

☐ Make as early a start as you can

☐ Calm yourself down before you set off

☐ Start your journey but ride slowly

☐ Set off quickly to make up lost time

RES s1

2   What helmet should you wear on a day like today?

Mark **one** answer

☐ A brightly coloured helmet

☐ A dark full-face helmet

☐ A dark open-face helmet

☐ A lightweight cycling helmet

RES s4 **HC r86**

3   What should you do at the roundabout?

Mark **one** answer

☐ Catch up with the driver and complain

☐ Sound your horn twice at the driver

☐ Flash your headlights at the driver

☐ Keep calm and continue riding

RES s9 **HC r147**

4   What should you do when the traffic lights change to green?

Mark **one** answer

☐ Ride off quickly ahead of the cyclist

☐ Allow the cyclist plenty of room

☐ Follow closely behind the cyclist

☐ Ride around the cyclist to get in front

RES s10 **HC r178, 212**

5   What should you do at the crash scene?

Mark **one** answer

☐ Warn other road users of the danger

☐ Move the driver out of their vehicle

☐ Remove the motorcyclist's helmet

☐ Give the people involved a drink

RES s16 **HC r283**

Case study practice – E

You're shopping for new clothing to wear while riding your motorcycle.

You're about to go on a camping holiday for two weeks.

Three days before you leave, you realise that your MOT certificate will expire while you're away.

On the day you leave, it's raining heavily.

You ride along a busy 'A' road, using the throttle rapidly and braking heavily.

You reach the scene of a crash between a cyclist and a car. The cyclist is unconscious but breathing and lying in the road.

1 What should you buy when out shopping?
Mark **one** answer

☐ Clothing that matches your motorcycle

☐ Clothing that's tight fitting

☐ Clothing that's loose and light

☐ Clothing that keeps you warm and dry

RES s4

2 What should you do before your holiday?

Mark **one** answer

☐ Get your motorcycle through its MOT test

☐ Renew your vehicle tax immediately

☐ Tell your insurance company you're going away

☐ Tell DVLA you'll be away for two weeks

RES s2 **HC p122**

3 What should you be careful of on the day you leave?

Mark **one** answer

☐ Slippery roads

☐ Sticky tarmac

☐ Dry patches

☐ Level surfaces

RES s12

4 What will be the effect of riding in this way on the 'A' road?

Mark **one** answer

☐ Increased journey time

☐ Economical use of fuel

☐ Uneconomical use of fuel

☐ Decreased journey time

RES s17

5 What should you do for the cyclist?

Mark **one** answer

☐ Drag them to the side of the road

☐ Try to remove their cycle helmet

☐ Place them in the recovery position

☐ Administer CPR

HC p132

Section sixteen

Answers

1. Alertness

1.1	☐ Take a lifesaver glance over your shoulder
1.2	☐ A final rearward glance before changing direction
1.3	☐ Slow down before the bend
1.4	☐ Slow down or stop
1.5	☐ Extend the mirror arms
1.6	☐ Stop in a safe place
1.7	☐ As soon as the other vehicle passes you
1.8	☐ Look over your shoulder just before you move off
1.9	☐ You'll lose concentration
1.10	☐ Slow down and stop if necessary
1.11	☐ Before moving off
1.12	☐ To give you the best view of the road behind
1.13	☐ A rearward glance just before manoeuvring
1.14	☐ Never; you should always look for yourself
1.15	☐ Use your mirrors
1.16	☐ Mirrors don't cover blind spots

1.17	☐ Make a lifesaver check
1.18	☐ Assess the width of the central reservation
1.19	☐ Make sure you know where all the controls and switches are
1.20	☐ Take a lifesaver glance over your left shoulder
1.21	☐ Before moving into the left-hand lane
1.22	☐ Concentrate on what's happening ahead
1.23	☐ Look over your shoulder for a final check
1.24	☐ Slow down
1.25	☐ Approaching a dip in the road
1.26	☐ Overtaking traffic should move back to the left
1.27	☐ Leave it until you have stopped in a safe place
1.28	☐ To make you aware of your speed
1.29	☐ Be ready to stop
1.30	☐ Use the mirrors

1.31	☐ You'll give the driver a chance to see you in their mirrors
1.32	☐ To assess how your actions will affect the traffic behind
1.33	☐ Stop and then move forward slowly and carefully for a clear view

1. Case study practice

1.1	To help you to be seen by others
1.2	Because your mirrors have blind spots
1.3	Getting cold and losing concentration
1.4	It would obstruct your view of the road
1.5	Stop your motorcycle and wait patiently

2. Attitude

2.1	☐ Slow down and prepare to stop	2.11	☐ Four seconds
2.2	☐ Well back, so that you can see past the vehicle	2.12	☐ Slow down
		2.13	☐ Bomb disposal
2.3	☐ Slow down and be ready to stop	2.14	☐ Pull over as soon as it's safe to do so
2.4	☐ Pull in when you can to let faster vehicles behind you overtake	2.15	☐ Doctor's car
		2.16	☐ Tram drivers
2.5	☐ Drivers at junctions ahead to see you approaching	2.17	☐ Cycles
		2.18	☐ To alert others to your presence
2.6	☐ Because they're inexperienced	2.19	☐ In the right-hand lane
2.7	☐ Give way to pedestrians already on the crossing	2.20	☐ To help other road users know what you intend to do
2.8	☐ Another vehicle may be coming	2.21	☐ Toucan
2.9	☐ Your view of the road ahead will be restricted	2.22	☐ Allow the vehicle to overtake
2.10	☐ Your view ahead will be reduced	2.23	☐ When letting them know that you're there

2.24	☐ Slow down and look both ways
2.25	☐ When checking your gap from the vehicle in front
2.26	☐ Steady amber
2.27	☐ Slow down, gradually increasing the gap between you and the vehicle in front

2. Case study practice

2.1 60 mph
2.2 Carefully, while increasing the distance from any vehicle in front
2.3 Slowly, leaving plenty of room
2.4 To allow you to see past the large vehicle
2.5 A doctor driving to an emergency

3. Safety and your motorcycle

3.1	☐ The rear wheel could lock
3.2	☐ To keep the motorcycle roadworthy
3.3	☐ Slower-than-normal, until the shiny surface is worn off
3.4	☐ It will be easier for other road users to see you
3.5	☐ Wear protective clothing
3.6	☐ It helps other road users to see you
3.7	☐ To be seen better at night
3.8	☐ Replace it
3.9	☐ 1 mm
3.10	☐ A brightly coloured helmet
3.11	☐ Stop as soon as possible and try to find the cause
3.12	☐ That they're correctly inflated

3.13	☐ The chain could lock the rear wheel
3.14	☐ Slow gently to a stop
3.15	☐ It will have lower exhaust emissions
3.16	☐ Soapy water
3.17	☐ Stop as soon as it's safe and wipe it
3.18	☐ Boots
3.19	☐ To prevent the strap flapping in the wind
3.20	☐ Exhaust emissions
3.21	☐ The wheel alignment
3.22	☐ Between 1 and 2 times
3.23	☐ The rear wheel alignment
3.24	☐ Worn steering-head bearings
3.25	☐ The motorcycle will be difficult to control

3.26	☐ Your suspension will be ineffective
3.27	☐ Incorrect rear wheel alignment
3.28	☐ Replace the tyre before riding the motorcycle
3.29	☐ By checking the vehicle handbook
3.30	☐ Keep the cable oiled
3.31	☐ Increased tyre wear
3.32	☐ Because it gives the best protection from the weather
3.33	☐ Use the steering lock
3.34	☐ Chain it to an immovable object
3.35	☐ Leave it in a low gear
3.36	☐ To stop the engine in an emergency
3.37	☐ Maintain a reduced speed throughout
3.38	☐ Before a long journey
3.39	☐ Take it to a local-authority site
3.40	☐ Check out any strong smell of petrol
3.41	☐ Wearing a brightly coloured helmet
3.42	☐ If the helmet isn't fastened correctly
3.43	☐ When carrying a heavy load
3.44	☐ The number plate

3.45	☐ When you want to stop the engine in an emergency
3.46	☐ The rear wheel alignment
3.47	☐ It may be damaged
3.48	☐ A large bulge in the sidewall
3.49	☐ By lubricating and adjusting them regularly
3.50	☐ Reduced risk of it breaking down
3.51	☐ A locked rear wheel
3.52	☐ When visibility is seriously reduced
3.53	☐ When carrying a pillion passenger
3.54	☐ Oil leaks
3.55	☐ Not on any occasion
3.56	☐ Use the engine cut-out switch
3.57	☐ Wear reflective clothing
3.58	☐ The vehicle's stopping distance would increase
3.59	☐ Between 11.30 pm and 7.00 am in a built-up area
3.60	☐ It's powered by electricity
3.61	☐ To help the traffic flow
3.62	☐ To reduce traffic speed
3.63	☐ To reduce harmful exhaust gases
3.64	☐ When tyres are cold
3.65	☐ When its tyres are under-inflated

3.66	☐ Take it to a local-authority disposal site
3.67	☐ Harsh braking and accelerating
3.68	☐ Distilled water
3.69	☐ When the speed limit exceeds 30 mph
3.70	☐ Keep engine revs low
3.71	☐ A faulty braking system
3.72	☐ Just above the cell plates
3.73	☐ Use a route planner on the internet
3.74	☐ You'll have an easier journey
3.75	☐ Your journey will have fewer delays
3.76	☐ Your original route may be blocked

3.77	☐ Allow plenty of time for the trip
3.78	☐ Increased fuel consumption
3.79	☐ Brake-fluid level

3. Case study practice

3.1 Getting cold

3.2 It makes you easier to see

3.3 It helps to improve your safety

3.4 To give you an unobstructed view behind

3.5 1 mm across three-quarters of the tread breadth and all around

4. Safety margins

4.1	☐ When you're riding with a passenger
4.2	☐ Use both brakes
4.3	☐ Ease off the throttle
4.4	☐ Consider whether your journey is essential
4.5	☐ They help other road users to see you
4.6	☐ When visibility is 100 metres (328 feet) or less
4.7	☐ When visibility is poor

4.8	☐ They'll make it harder to see unlit objects
4.9	☐ The brakes
4.10	☐ Ride slowly, in a low gear
4.11	☐ Dipped-beam headlights
4.12	☐ Keep your visor or goggles clear
4.13	☐ The painted lines may be slippery
4.14	☐ Wear reflective clothing

4.15	☐ Wear suitable clothing
4.16	☐ Wear reflective clothing
4.17	☐ When it's raining
4.18	☐ Loose gravel
4.19	☐ Traffic could be turning here
4.20	☐ Heavy braking
4.21	☐ Ease off the throttle smoothly
4.22	☐ Ride slowly, braking lightly
4.23	☐ Switch on your dipped headlights
4.24	☐ The time gap when following another vehicle in good conditions
4.25	☐ The painted area
4.26	☐ When you overtake a large vehicle
4.27	☐ Waiting buses may have dripped oil onto the road
4.28	☐ 38 metres (125 feet)
4.29	☐ Ten times
4.30	☐ Passing pedal cyclists

4.31	☐ To improve your view of the road
4.32	☐ Go slowly while gently applying the brakes
4.33	☐ The tyre grip
4.34	☐ On an open stretch of road
4.35	☐ Drop back to regain a safe distance
4.36	☐ Increase your distance from the vehicle in front
4.37	☐ Keep a safe distance from the vehicle in front
4.38	☐ Choose an appropriate lane in good time

4. Case study practice

4.1	Tyre pressures and headlight aim
4.2	It would be difficult to hold a steady course
4.3	They would try to avoid cracks and holes
4.4	More slowly
4.5	Check over your right shoulder for overtaking vehicles

5. Hazard awareness

5.1	☐ Your concentration will be impaired
5.2	☐
5.3	☐ Find a way of getting home without riding
5.4	☐ Poor judgement
5.5	☐ At all times when riding
5.6	☐ Your judgement of speed will be worse
5.7	☐ Tinted
5.8	☐ When you're riding on a motorway, to warn traffic behind of a hazard ahead
5.9	☐ To help prevent hearing damage
5.10	☐ Stick to non-alcoholic drinks
5.11	☐ Your insurance may become invalid
5.12	☐ To check for overtaking vehicles
5.13	☐ Ask your doctor
5.14	☐ When your motorcycle has broken down and is causing an obstruction
5.15	☐ A soft road surface
5.16	☐ On a large goods vehicle
5.17	☐ The cyclist crossing the road
5.18	☐ The parked car (arrowed A)
5.19	☐ Slow down and get ready to stop
5.20	☐ Doors opening on parked cars
5.21	☐ The road will bend sharply to the left
5.22	☐ Slow down and allow the cyclist to turn
5.23	☐ The view is restricted
5.24	☐ Buses
5.25	☐ Lorry
5.26	☐ Stop behind the line, then edge forward to see clearly
5.27	☐ Ignore the error and stay calm
5.28	☐ They'll take longer to react to hazards
5.29	☐ Yes, regular stops help concentration
5.30	☐ Stop before the barrier
5.31	☐ Be prepared to stop for any traffic
5.32	☐ Wait for the pedestrian in the road to cross
5.33	☐ Only consider overtaking when you're past the junction

5.34	☐ Be prepared to give way to large vehicles in the middle of the road
5.35	☐ They give a wider field of vision
5.36	☐ Approach with care and overtake on the left of the lorry
5.37	☐ Stay behind and don't overtake
5.38	☐ The bus may move out into the road
5.39	☐ A school bus
5.40	☐ Children running out between vehicles
5.41	☐ The cyclist may swerve into the road
5.42	☐ Stop and take a break
5.43	☐ At a reduced speed
5.44	☐ Because of the level crossing
5.45	☐ To help you select the correct lane in good time

5.46	☐ Traffic in both directions can use the middle lane to overtake
5.47	☐ A tractor
5.48	☐ Stop
5.49	☐ People may cross the road in front of it
5.50	☐ Approaching a junction
5.51	☐ Your ability to judge speed will be reduced

5. Case study practice

5.1 They would be smaller
5.2 Drink soft drinks the whole time
5.3 By making you less visible to others
5.4 Four seconds
5.5 Amber

6. Vulnerable road users

6.1	☐ So your view ahead isn't obstructed
6.2	☐ Give them plenty of room
6.3	☐ Slow down and be ready to stop
6.4	☐ Keep calm and be patient

6.5	☐ Slow down gradually to increase the gap in front of you
6.6	☐ Be prepared to stop
6.7	☐ The rider may be blown across in front of you
6.8	☐ Allow the person to finish crossing

6.9	☐ At junctions
6.10	☐ To check for any overtaking traffic
6.11	☐ Revving your engine
6.12	☐ They lack experience and judgement
6.13	☐ They lack of experience
6.14	☐ You must not wait or park your motorcycle here
6.15	☐
6.16	☐ Give way to them
6.17	☐ Pedestrians
6.18	☐ They may be overtaking on your right
6.19	☐ Cyclists can use it
6.20	☐ By displaying a 'stop' sign
6.21	☐ On the rear of a school bus or coach
6.22	☐ A route for pedestrians and cyclists
6.23	☐ They're deaf and blind
6.24	☐ Be patient and allow them to cross in their own time
6.25	☐ Be careful; they may misjudge your speed
6.26	☐ Give the cyclist plenty of room
6.27	☐ Bicycle

6.28	☐ They're harder to see
6.29	☐ Motorcycles can easily be hidden behind obstructions
6.30	☐ So that the rider can be seen more easily
6.31	☐ To make them more visible
6.32	☐ To check for traffic in their blind area
6.33	☐ Motorcyclist
6.34	☐ Give them plenty of room
6.35	☐ Wait patiently while they cross
6.36	☐ Reduce speed until you're clear of the area
6.37	☐ To allow children to see and be seen when they're crossing the road
6.38	☐ On a school bus
6.39	☐ Any direction
6.40	☐ Stay behind until the moped has passed the junction
6.41	☐ Stay well back
6.42	☐ Be patient and prepare for them to react more slowly
6.43	☐ Be patient, as you expect them to make mistakes
6.44	☐ Pedestrians
6.45	☐ Hold back until the cyclist has passed the junction

475

6.46	☐ In any direction
6.47	☐ Flashing amber beacon
6.48	☐ The vehicle is slow moving
6.49	☐ With-flow cycle lane
6.50	☐ Slow down and be ready to stop
6.51	☐ To ensure children can see and be seen when they're crossing the road
6.52	☐ Watch out for pedestrians walking in the road
6.53	☐ Allow extra room in case they swerve to avoid potholes
6.54	☐ Cycle route ahead
6.55	☐ Allow them space to turn
6.56	☐ Prepare to slow down and stop
6.57	☐ The pedestrian is deaf
6.58	☐ Cyclists and pedestrians

6.59	☐ To allow cyclists to position in front of other traffic
6.60	☐ The cyclist might be unsettled if you pass too near them
6.61	☐ Go very slowly
6.62	☐ You're approaching an organised walk
6.63	☐ By taking further training

6. Case study practice

6.1   Stop the motorcycle and wait until the animals have crossed

6.2   Stop and give way to the pedestrians crossing

6.3   Give way to the pedestrians crossing

6.4   Binmen

6.5   Amber

7. Other types of vehicle

7.1	☐ Keep well back
7.2	☐ Trams can't steer to avoid you
7.3	☐
7.4	☐ Anything overtaking the lorry will be hidden from view
7.5	☐ Stay well back and give it room
7.6	☐ Wait behind the long vehicle
7.7	☐ Keep well back
7.8	☐ To get the best view of the road ahead
7.9	☐ Look for pedestrians
7.10	☐ Drop back until you can see better
7.11	☐ Drop back further

7.12	☐ Allow it to pull away, if it's safe to do so
7.13	☐ Keep well back so that you get a good view of the road ahead
7.14	☐ Cars
7.15	☐ Slow down and be prepared to wait
7.16	☐ Wait for the vehicle to finish turning
7.17	☐ It will take longer to overtake a large vehicle

7. Case study practice

7.1 By using dipped headlights
7.2 Allow it to pull out if it's safe to do so
7.3 The lines could be very slippery
7.4 Diamond
7.5 Pull a little over to the right

8. Road conditions and motorcycle handling

8.1	☐ Check that the neutral lamp shows when the ignition is switched on	8.19	☐ The condition of the tyres
8.2	☐ Slow down and be ready to stop	8.20	☐ When your motorcycle is broken down on the hard shoulder
8.3	☐ Anticipate the actions of others	8.21	☐ Leave parking lights on
8.4	☐ Braking too hard	8.22	☐ Close the throttle and roll to a stop
8.5	☐ Ride slowly in as high a gear as possible	8.23	☐ By a rainbow-coloured pattern on the road surface
8.6	☐ At all times	8.24	☐ Tar banding
8.7	☐ Check that your lights are working	8.25	☐ Apply the front brake just before the rear brake
8.8	☐ On firm, level ground	8.26	☐ Painted road markings can be slippery when they're wet
8.9	☐ Keep your speed down		
8.10	☐ In the centre of your lane	8.27	☐ The steel rails can be slippery
8.11	☐ From the left and apply the front brake	8.28	☐ Release and reapply the brakes
8.12	☐ It will reduce your control of the motorcycle	8.29	☐ Fuel spilt on the road
8.13	☐ Slow down	8.30	☐ Wheelspin when accelerating
8.14	☐ It can become unusually slippery	8.31	☐ Release both brakes together
8.15	☐ Cornering too fast	8.32	☐ Apply both brakes smoothly
8.16	☐ Apply the front brake just before the rear brake	8.33	☐ Place both feet on the ground
8.17	☐ You'll upset your balance	8.34	☐ It will be slippery
8.18	☐ When the motorcycle is upright and moving in a straight line	8.35	☐ When you're cornering

8.36	☐ When you're in a one-way street
8.37	☐ It will be doubled
8.38	☐ Beware of bends in the road ahead
8.39	☐ When oncoming traffic prevents you turning right
8.40	☐ **Humps for ½ mile**
8.41	☐ To slow traffic down
8.42	☐ Red
8.43	☐ Alert you to a hazard
8.44	☐ Leave plenty of time for your journey
8.45	☐ Make sure you don't dazzle other road users
8.46	☐ Slow down and stay behind

8.47	☐ To make you aware of your speed
8.48	☐ Stop at a passing place
8.49	☐ To prevent the motorcycle sliding on the metal drain covers
8.50	☐ Your brakes will be wet
8.51	☐ It's more difficult to see what's ahead

8. Case study practice

8.1 The extra weight can affect your balance

8.2 Lean with you when going round bends

8.3 Headlights

8.4 Edge forward slowly until you can see clearly

8.5 You'll need more room in which to stop safely

9. Motorway riding

9.1	☐ Only in an emergency
9.2	☐ In the left-hand lane
9.3	☐ Adjust your speed to match the speed of the traffic on the motorway
9.4	☐ 50 cc
9.5	☐ The left-hand lane
9.6	☐ 70 mph
9.7	☐ Continuous high speeds increase the risk of your motorcycle breaking down

9.8	☐ Match your speed to traffic in the left-hand lane and filter into a safe gap
9.9	☐ 70 mph
9.10	☐ Any vehicle that isn't overtaking
9.11	☐ Vehicles towing a trailer
9.12	☐ It allows easy location by the emergency services
9.13	☐ Gain speed on the hard shoulder before moving out onto the carriageway

9.14	☐ On a steep gradient
9.15	☐ They're countdown markers to the next exit
9.16	☐ Between the central reservation and the carriageway
9.17	☐ White
9.18	☐ Green
9.19	☐ In the direction shown on the marker posts
9.20	☐ To allow you to fit safely into the traffic flow in the left-hand lane
9.21	☐ Face the oncoming traffic
9.22	☐ Red
9.23	☐ Left
9.24	☐ Keep a good distance from the vehicle ahead
9.25	☐ In the left-hand lane
9.26	☐ Obey the speed limit
9.27	☐ Powered mobility scooters
9.28	☐ Look much further ahead than you would on other roads
9.29	☐ Stay in the left-hand lane
9.30	☐ When you're overtaking

9.31	☐ When you're stopping in an emergency
9.32	☐ Move to the left and reduce your speed to 50 mph
9.33	☐ When you're signalled to do so by traffic signals
9.34	☐ Adjust your speed or change lane if you can do so safely
9.35	☐ Keep to the left-hand lane unless you're overtaking
9.36	☐ When in queues and traffic to your right is moving more slowly than you are
9.37	☐ In cases of emergency or breakdown
9.38	☐ Stop and direct anyone on a motorway
9.39	☐ You shouldn't travel in this lane
9.40	☐ The hard shoulder can be used as a running lane
9.41	☐ By using variable speed limits
9.42	☐ Variable speed limits
9.43	☐ In an emergency or breakdown

9.44	☐ 70 mph
9.45	☐ Well away from the carriageway
9.46	☐ Stop and wait
9.47	☐ The hard shoulder is for emergency or breakdown use only
9.48	☐ Use all the lanes, including the hard shoulder
9.49	☐ At the nearest service area

9. Case study practice

9.1	Steering and braking
9.2	All traffic should do so unless they're overtaking
9.3	Four seconds
9.4	Temporary maximum speed advised
9.5	300 yards

10. Rules of the road

10.1	☐ To check for cyclists
10.2	☐ Tram lane
10.3	☐ Parking for solo motorcycles
10.4	☐ Use mirrors and shoulder checks
10.5	☐ Wait for a regular parking space to become free
10.6	☐ Pull into a passing place on your left
10.7	☐ So you can see approaching traffic
10.8	☐ Watch for vehicles emerging from side roads
10.9	☐ Wait for the green light
10.10	☐ Headlight deflectors
10.11	☐ 125 cc
10.12	☐ 60 mph

10.13	☐ When signalled to do so by a police officer
10.14	☐ National speed limit applies
10.15	☐ 70 mph
10.16	☐ By street lighting
10.17	☐ 30 mph
10.18	☐ End of minimum speed
10.19	☐ Stay behind it if you're in any doubt
10.20	☐ Long vehicle
10.21	☐ Never
10.22	☐ Waiting restrictions
10.23	☐ When you're in a one-way street
10.24	☐ When you're overtaking or turning right

10.25	☐ Continue in that lane
10.26	☐ On either the right or the left
10.27	☐ Signal left before leaving the roundabout
10.28	☐ Long vehicle
10.29	☐ When your exit road is clear
10.30	☐ When oncoming traffic prevents you from turning right
10.31	☐ A police officer
10.32	☐ Be ready to slow down or stop to let them cross
10.33	☐ Cyclists and pedestrians
10.34	☐ Give way to pedestrians on the crossing
10.35	☐ To pick up or set down passengers
10.36	☐ You'll have a clearer view of any approaching traffic
10.37	☐ Children may run out from between the vehicles
10.38	☐ Give way to oncoming traffic
10.39	☐ When you're turning right or overtaking
10.40	☐ No-one has priority
10.41	☐ 10 metres (32 feet)

10.42	☐ In a designated parking space
10.43	☐ Carry on waiting
10.44	☐ End of controlled parking zone
10.45	☐ Obey the speed limit
10.46	☐ So that you can be easily seen by others
10.47	☐ Wait until the road is clear in both directions
10.48	☐ 60 mph
10.49	☐ Leave parking lights switched on
10.50	☐ Approaching a concealed level crossing
10.51	☐ When signalled to stop by a traffic officer
10.52	☐ Signal left just after you pass the exit before the one you're going to take

10. Case study practice

10.1 Blue and white

10.2 Stop and wait until the green light shows

10.3 Take a look over your right shoulder

10.4 To slow down the traffic

10.5 Circular

11. Road and traffic signs

11.1	☐
11.2	☐ To help you keep control of the steering
11.3	☐ Side winds
11.4	☐
11.5	☐
11.6	☐ To avoid misleading other road users
11.7	☐ Give an arm signal
11.8	☐ Pass on the left
11.9	☐ They're circular with a red border
11.10	☐
11.11	☐
11.12	☐ Maximum speed limit with traffic calming

11.13	☐ End of 20 mph zone
11.14	☐ No motor vehicles
11.15	☐ No entry
11.16	☐ No right turn
11.17	☐
11.18	☐ Route for trams only
11.19	☐ High vehicles
11.20	☐
11.21	☐ No overtaking
11.22	☐ Waiting restrictions apply
11.23	☐ End of restricted parking area
11.24	☐
11.25	☐ No stopping
11.26	☐ Distance to parking place ahead
11.27	☐ Vehicles may park fully on the verge or footway
11.28	☐ Give priority to oncoming traffic

11.29	☐ You have priority over vehicles coming towards you
11.30	☐
11.31	☐ Stop
11.32	☐ Minimum speed 30 mph
11.33	☐ Pass either side to get to the same destination
11.34	☐ Route for trams
11.35	☐ They give mandatory instructions
11.36	☐ On a one-way street
11.37	☐ Contraflow bus lane
11.38	☐ Tourist directions
11.39	☐ Tourist attraction
11.40	☐ To give warnings
11.41	☐ T-junction
11.42	☐ Risk of ice
11.43	☐ Crossroads
11.44	☐ Roundabout
11.45	☐ Road narrows
11.46	☐ Cycle route ahead
11.47	☐

11.48	☐
11.49	☐ Give way to trams
11.50	☐ Humps in the road
11.51	☐
11.52	☐ End of dual carriageway
11.53	☐ Side winds
11.54	☐ Danger ahead
11.55	☐ Hold back until you can see clearly ahead
11.56	☐ Level crossing with gate or barrier
11.57	☐ Trams crossing ahead
11.58	☐ Steep hill downwards
11.59	☐ Water across the road
11.60	☐ No through road on the left
11.61	☐ No through road
11.62	☐
11.63	☐ The right-hand lane is closed
11.64	☐ Contraflow system

11.65	☐ Lane for heavy and slow vehicles	**11.82**	☐ The driver intends to turn left
11.66	☐ You must stop and wait behind the stop line	**11.83**	☐ Change to the lane on your left
11.67	☐ Stop at the stop line	**11.84**	☐ Temporary maximum speed 50 mph
11.68	☐ When your exit from the junction is blocked	**11.85**	☐ Right-hand lane closed ahead
11.69	☐	**11.86**	☐ The number of the next junction
		11.87	☐ As an overtaking lane
11.70	☐ Traffic lights out of order	**11.88**	☐ On the right-hand edge of the road
11.71	☐ Nobody	**11.89**	☐ At slip-road entrances and exits
11.72	☐ Level crossings		
11.73	☐ No parking at any time	**11.90**	☐ Leave the motorway at the next exit
11.74	☐ To pass a road maintenance vehicle travelling at 10 mph or less	**11.91**	☐ End of motorway
		11.92	☐
11.75	☐ You're approaching a hazard		
11.76	☐ On road humps	**11.93**	☐ 60 mph
11.77	☐	**11.94**	☐ End of restriction
		11.95	☐ A diversion route
11.78	☐ Visibility along the major road is restricted	**11.96**	☐ Compulsory maximum speed limit
11.79	☐ Give way to traffic from the right	**11.97**	☐ Carry on with great care
11.80	☐ Flash the headlights, indicate left and point to the left	**11.98**	☐ No motorcycles
		11.99	☐ Pass the lorry on the left
11.81	☐ Stop at the stop line		

11.100	☐ Don't continue in that lane
11.101	☐ To warn others of your presence
11.102	☐ When another road user poses a danger
11.103	☐ No parking on the days and times shown
11.104	☐ Quayside or river bank
11.105	☐
11.106	☐ Hazard warning
11.107	☐ It separates traffic flowing in opposite directions
11.108	☐ They're warning you of their presence
11.109	☐ Trams must stop
11.110	☐ At a mini-roundabout
11.111	☐ Pull up on the left
11.112	☐ Red alone
11.113	☐ Leave the motorway at the next exit
11.114	☐ Stop even if the road is clear
11.115	☐
11.116	☐ Mini-roundabout

11.117	☐ Two-way traffic crosses a one-way road
11.118	☐ Two-way traffic straight ahead
11.119	☐ Hump bridge
11.120	☐
11.121	☐ Direction to park-and-ride car park
11.122	☐ Wait for the green light
11.123	☐ Wait
11.124	☐ Direction to an emergency pedestrian exit
11.125	☐
11.126	☐ With-flow bus and cycle lane
11.127	☐
11.128	☐ Zebra crossing ahead
11.129	☐

11.130	☐
11.131	☐
11.132	☐ All traffic is going one way
11.133	☐ Red and amber
11.134	☐ Tunnel ahead

11. Case study practice

11.1	Where the joining side roads are slightly offset from each other
11.2	Regulatory
11.3	Blue with white arrow
11.4	Green
11.5	All the time

12. Essential documents

12.1	☐ The make and model	12.11	☐ A valid compulsory basic training (CBT) certificate
12.2	☐ Any Driver and Vehicle Standards Agency (DVSA)-approved training body	12.12	☐ When you have a medical condition that affects your riding
12.3	☐ That the motorcycle is insured for your use	12.13	☐ Reapply for your provisional licence
12.4	☐ Three years	12.14	☐ Carrying a pillion passenger
12.5	☐ The registered keeper's name	12.15	☐ 125 cc
12.6	☐ When your permanent address changes	12.16	☐ When the rider holds a full licence for the category of motorcycle they're riding
12.7	☐ Injury to others		
12.8	☐ Third-party only	12.17	☐ Two years
12.9	☐ The year of first registration	12.18	☐ A full motorcycle licence
12.10	☐ To make sure your motorcycle is roadworthy	12.19	☐ You'll have to pay the first £100 of any claim
		12.20	☐ One year after the date it was issued

12.21	☐ A document issued before you receive your insurance certificate
12.22	☐ Retake your theory and practical tests
12.23	☐ Until the vehicle is taxed, sold or scrapped
12.24	☐ A notification to tell DVLA that a vehicle isn't being used on the road
12.25	☐ Unlimited
12.26	☐ The registered vehicle keeper
12.27	☐ When a police officer asks you for it
12.28	☐ Before you can tax the vehicle

12.29	☐ An appropriate driving licence
12.30	☐ Valid insurance
12.31	☐ 7 days
12.32	☐ When you move house

12. Case study practice

12.1 Tax it using the new keeper supplement

12.2 Almost twelve months ago

12.3 It's allowed in order to get the motorcycle to a repairer

12.4 Third party

12.5 Damage to other vehicles

13. Incidents, accidents and emergencies

13.1	☐ By following an arrow on a marker post
13.2	☐ To stop the engine in an emergency
13.3	☐ There's danger ahead
13.4	☐ Switch on hazard warning lights
13.5	☐ When you slow down quickly because of danger ahead
13.6	☐ Stop at the next emergency telephone and report the hazard

13.7	☐ The other driver's vehicle insurance details
13.8	☐ When stopped and temporarily obstructing traffic
13.9	☐ Keep a safe distance from the vehicle in front
13.10	☐ Apply pressure over the wound
13.11	☐ Check that they're breathing normally
13.12	☐ 120 times per minute

13.13	☐ Rapid shallow breathing
13.14	☐ Check their airway remains open
13.15	☐ Seek medical assistance
13.16	☐ Go to the next emergency telephone and report the hazard
13.17	☐ Variable message signs
13.18	☐ 5 to 6 centimetres
13.19	☐ Make sure that an ambulance has been called
13.20	☐ Only when it's essential
13.21	☐ Check whether they're breathing normally
13.22	☐ Whether their airway is open
13.23	☐ Keep them warm and comfortable
13.24	☐ Reassure them confidently
13.25	☐ Warn other traffic
13.26	☐ Open their airway and begin CPR
13.27	☐ Open their airway
13.28	☐ Douse the burns with clean, cool water

13.29	☐ Apply firm pressure over the wound
13.30	☐ When there's a risk of further danger
13.31	☐ Keep them where they are
13.32	☐ 2YE 1089
13.33	☐ Your driving licence
13.34	☐ As soon as possible
13.35	☐ Warn other traffic
13.36	☐ Follow the DR ABC code
13.37	☐ Reassure them confidently
13.38	☐ Removing it could make any injuries worse

13. Case study practice

13.1 Shock
13.2 Because removing it could cause further injuries
13.3 To warn following traffic of the hazard
13.4 Keep them warm
13.5 You witnessed the incident

14. Motorcycle loading

14.1	☐ Ease off the throttle and reduce your speed
14.2	☐ You need time to get used to it
14.3	☐ The tyre pressure
14.4	☐ Solo, with a maximum power of at least 40 kW (53.6 bhp)
14.5	☐ Make sure the load is securely fastened
14.6	☐ Wear a motorcycle helmet
14.7	☐ Lean with the rider when going around bends
14.8	☐ Lean with you
14.9	☐ Headlights
14.10	☐ 50 mph
14.11	☐ It will reduce stability
14.12	☐ The rider of the motorcycle
14.13	☐ Check that the motorcycle is suitable
14.14	☐ Uneven loads can make the motorcycle unstable
14.15	☐ Your ability to steer
14.16	☐ A full motorcycle licence
14.17	☐ The tyre pressures
14.18	☐ Keep further back than you normally would
14.19	☐ When they can reach the handholds and footrests

14.20	☐ That the sidecar is correctly aligned
14.21	☐ It will require a different riding technique
14.22	☐ The preload on the rear shock absorber(s)
14.23	☐ 1 metre (3 feet 3 inches)
14.24	☐ Make sure the trailer isn't more than 1 metre (3 feet 3 inches) wide
14.25	☐ It will increase the stopping distance
14.26	☐ They mustn't carry a pillion passenger
14.27	☐ When you hold a full motorcycle licence
14.28	☐ A passenger seat and footrests
14.29	☐ Lightweight items
14.30	☐ Not at any time
14.31	☐ The handling
14.32	☐ You mustn't use the right-hand lane

14. Case study practice

14.1 To make sure the load is secure

14.2 Uneven load distribution can affect balance

14.3 60 mph

14.4 Stopping distance is increased on a fully loaded vehicle

14.5 That lane mustn't be used by vehicles with trailers

15. Case study practice

Case study on pages 453–455

1 Look over your shoulder for a final check
2 Slow down
3 Make the call when you've stopped in a suitable place
4 Go slowly past
5 There may be another vehicle coming

Case study practice A

1 Leather clothing, high-visibility waistcoat and white helmet
2 Wait, as another train will be coming
3 Slow down to ride over this patch of road
4 The blue sign shows a motorcycle
5 Take a look over your right shoulder

Case study practice B

1 Headlight aim
2 Being blown off course
3 Vehicles with a trailer mustn't travel in the right-hand lane
4 In the left-hand lane without giving a signal
5 Road workers

Case study practice C

1 In the panniers
2 70 mph
3 Because the engine is warm
4 Lock your motorcycle and remove the key
5 Drop back slightly so you can see the road ahead

Case study practice D

1 Calm yourself down before you set off
2 A brightly coloured helmet
3 Keep calm and continue riding
4 Allow the cyclist plenty of room
5 Warn other road users of the danger

Case study practice E

1 Clothing that keeps you warm and dry
2 Get your motorcycle through its MOT test
3 Slippery roads
4 Uneconomical use of fuel
5 Place them in the recovery position